PRAISE

BE THE RE

"A book destined to be a classic, setting the bar high for future studies on Asian American Buddhism."

JONATHAN H. X. LEE, author of *Asian American Religious Cultures*

"In this vivid and nuanced presentation of Asian American voices, Han offers what many of us have been longing for: young voices grappling in deep and caring ways with one of the central issues of our time: how we might build a more inclusive Buddhist community—one big enough to hold our *multiple* identities, whether of race, ethnicity, and culture, or of gender and tradition. This book is both impressive and necessary."

JAN WILLIS, author of *Dreaming Me*

"A challenging, poignant, and powerful detailing of the young Asian American Buddhist experience, *Be the Refuge* beautifully interweaves academic research, personal narrative, and advocacy. A deeply valuable contribution to the discussion of Buddhism's development in the West."

SUMI LOUNDON KIM, author of *Blue Jean Buddha*

"*Be the Refuge* connects the dots linking Dharma, ethnic studies, and the politics of erasure and inclusion. At last, we hear the voices of Asian Americans which, for far too long, have been missing from the conversation about American Buddhism. Han's work is refreshing, lyrical, amusing, honest, and immensely personal, all while challenging underrepresentation, misrepresentation, and the standard typologies of who counts as Buddhist and why."

KARMA LEKSHE TSOMO, author of *Women in Buddhist Traditions*

"*Be the Refuge* not only raises the voices of Asian American Buddhists, but makes space for many other communities who feel unseen, erased, or forgotten in our tradition."

LAMA ROD OWENS, author of *Love and Rage*

"Han makes two vital contributions to the study of American Buddhism: her rich, textured ethnography centers and celebrates the depth and diversity of Asian American Buddhist lives, and her incisive theoretical work undoes essentialist typologies of Buddhism in the U.S. and the racial hierarchies too often undergirding them. Timely and compelling, *Be the Refuge* is essential reading for both religious studies and ethnic studies scholars and Buddhist practitioners and teachers."

ANN GLEIG, author of *American Dharma*

"*Be the Refuge* empowers the emergent generation of Asian American experience to reclaim, restore, and reconnect streams of practice, lineage, and history for all generations of Asian descent—without the narratives of Western bias—thus providing us all paths of healing and growth for all of our futures."

LARRY YANG, author of *Awakening Together*

"This groundbreaking book powerfully reveals the voices of Asian American Buddhists. These personal accounts and Chenxing Han's incisive reflections reveal how important the Asian American Buddhist experience is in understanding American Buddhism. Han's book inspires all Buddhists to both be their own refuge and to respect the valuable ways others become their own refuge."

GIL FRONSDAL, author of *The Buddha before Buddhism*

"This important, insightful book focuses on the experience of Asian American Buddhists and calls us toward a Western Buddhism that offers refuge in a truly inclusive way."

TARA BRACH, author of *Radical Acceptance and Radical Compassion*

"*Be the Refuge* is a call to rescue the soul of Buddhism in the Western world. Throughout this amazing and comprehensive work, Han disrupts the habitual and hegemonic Buddhist discourse with the question, 'Whose Buddhism are we talking about?'"

ZENJU EARTHLYN MANUEL, author of *The Way of Tenderness*

BE THE REFUGE

BE THE REFUGE

RAISING THE VOICES OF ASIAN AMERICAN BUDDHISTS

CHENXING HAN

North Atlantic Books
Berkeley, California

Published by
North Atlantic Books
Berkeley, California

Cover design by Jess Morphew
Book design by Happenstance Type-O-Rama
Dharma wheel image © lga A / Alamy Stock Vector

Printed in the United States of America

Be the Refuge: Raising the Voices of Asian American Buddhists is sponsored and published by the Society for the Study of Native Arts and Sciences (dba North Atlantic Books), an educational nonprofit based in Berkeley, California, that collaborates with partners to develop cross-cultural perspectives, nurture holistic views of art, science, the humanities, and healing, and seed personal and global transformation by publishing work on the relationship of body, spirit, and nature.

North Atlantic Books' publications are available through most bookstores. For further information, visit our website at www.northatlanticbooks.com or call 800-733-3000.

Library of Congress Cataloging-in-Publication Data

Names: Han, Chenxing, 1986- author.
Title: Be the refuge : raising the voices of Asian American Buddhists / Chenxing Han.
Description: Berkeley, California : North Atlantic Books, 2021. | Includes bibliographical references and index. | Summary: "Despite the fact that two thirds of U.S. Buddhists identify as Asian American, mainstream perceptions about what it means to be Buddhist in America often whitewash and invisibilize the diverse, inclusive, and intersectional communities that lie at the heart of American Buddhism. Be the Refuge is both critique and celebration, calling out the erasure of Asian American Buddhists while uplifting the complexity and nuance of their authentic stories and vital, thriving communities. Drawn from in-depth interviews with a pan-ethnic, pan-Buddhist group, Be the Refuge is the first book to center young Asian American Buddhists' own voices. With insights from multi-generational, second-generation, convert, and socially engaged Asian American Buddhists, Be the Refuge includes the stories of trailblazers, bridge-builders, integrators, and refuge-makers who hail from a wide range of cultural and religious backgrounds. Championing nuanced representation over stale stereotypes, Han and the 89 interviewees in Be the Refuge push back against false narratives like the Oriental monk, the superstitious immigrant, and the banana Buddhist--typecasting that collapses the multivocality of Asian American Buddhists into tired, essentialized tropes. Encouraging frank conversations about race, representation, and inclusivity among Buddhists of all backgrounds, Be the Refuge embodies the spirit of interconnection that glows at the heart of American Buddhism"— Provided by publisher.
Identifiers: LCCN 2020016462 (print) | LCCN 2020016463 (ebook) | ISBN 9781623175238 (paperback) | ISBN 9781623175245 (epub)
Subjects: LCSH: Buddhism—United States. | Asian Americans—Religion.
Classification: LCC BQ732 .H36 2021 (print) | LCC BQ732 (ebook) | DDC 294.3089/95073—dc23
LC record available at https://lccn.loc.gov/2020016462
LC ebook record available at https://lccn.loc.gov/2020016463

1 2 3 4 5 6 7 8 9 KPC 26 25 24 23 22 21

This book includes recycled material and material from well-managed forests. North Atlantic Books is committed to the protection of our environment. We print on recycled paper whenever possible and partner with printers who strive to use environmentally responsible practices.

for tt and the bears

CONTENTS

PART 4 REFUGE-MAKERS

ACKNOWLEDGMENTS

I have always marveled that every book's acknowledgments is not a tome unto itself, a symphony whose every note is someone that has graced the author's life with kindness. The debts of gratitude I have accumulated in the making of this book are deep, and I won't come close to accounting them fully here. Forgive me for offering only the barest sketch of a melody in these pages.

The staff at North Atlantic Books embraced this project with open arms just when I thought it might never find a home. Special thanks to Gillian Hamel, who shepherded me through the editorial process with patience and aplomb, answering my endless emails with unfaltering promptness and infusing a sometimes stressful journey with much-appreciated goodwill. Thanks also to Hisae Matsuda for ushering my manuscript toward a wider readership.

I can think of no better birthplace for this project than the Institute of Buddhist Studies in Berkeley, California. What great fortune to be part of this intergenerational, multidenominational, Jodo Shinshu-rooted community, first as a graduate student and now as an alumna. I am grateful to my teachers and friends at IBS for cultivating the grounds in which my curiosity about Asian American Buddhists could flourish—and for grounding me in compassion and wisdom. In particular, Scott Mitchell guided my wisp of an idea into a master's thesis, crucially introduced me to the Angry Asian Buddhist, and championed this project long after he stopped being my thesis advisor.

This book would not exist without the writing, inspiration, and friendship of Aaron J. Lee, the person behind the persona of the Angry Asian Buddhist. Thank you, Aaron, for confounding expectations, speaking truth to power, connecting me to so many Asian American Buddhists, and most of all, for the courage to persevere. You are deeply missed.

This book also would not exist without the eighty-nine interviewees who shared so openly of their experiences and perspectives in service of this project. Thank you all for expanding my understanding of what it means to be an Asian American Buddhist—and for making it much less lonely to be one.

To the many people around the world who have engaged with me on this project—whether by sharing your perspectives, offering heartfelt encouragement, or posing thorny challenges—I bow to each of you.

Deep bows of appreciation to the friends who have made the peregrinations of writing less solitary, especially Wanwan Lu, whose films animate the following chapters; Padma Maitland, whose optimism and *mudita* buoyed the journey; Funie Hsu, who brightened the low points with solidarity and humor (let's fighting love!); Kara-Ann Young-ha Owens, who supported this project something fierce from before the beginning (including reading every page of its first iteration); and Dawn Kwan, for lending a listening ear and being up for an adventure anytime, anywhere.

The deepest of bows to my parents, Angi Ye and Xiaoping Han: For the courage to travel distances I can only imagine. For nourishing me with food and freedom, the greatest forms of love I know. For the magic of seeing my words in print for the first time ("Yesterday I Burned the Newspaper"), there in our Pittsburgh apartment (the third one, I think?) where cockroaches danced on toothbrushes and stolen string hugged 粽子 and two-liter pop bottles birthed sausage snatched mid-cure by thieves who left only paw-prints on the wintery roof as our ceiling rained snowmelt into kitchen pots. How far we have traveled.

This book has also been nurtured by the steadfast support of my in-laws Gail and Bob Walker, who have helped with proofreading and plumbing and everything in between—ferrying books across oceans, sheltering a globe-trotting pair from Bay Area rents, making our Phnom Penh and Bangkok apartments more hospitable for writing—with generosity and good cheer always.

And finally, joyously, with unending love and gratitude: to Trent, my សង្សារ, for believing in this book on all the days I didn't, for reading every word, for weathering the waves and wilds of samsara with me, for being my ballast and sails—for more than words can say.

INTRODUCTION

WONDERING

Amituofo amituofo amituofo

A hundred times we invoke the Buddha of infinite light, the melody a slow river as row by row we stand, approaching the center aisle in twinned tributaries, arriving at the altar in pairs.

Amituofo amituofo amituofo

From my prayer-pressed hands a long-stemmed carnation sprouts, stretching to the ceiling as if yearning to break free to the sun-drenched sky beyond.

Amituofo amituofo amituofo

Bending our waists and lowering our hearts, we bow in front of the enlightened ones, a patient stream of mourners dipping in reverence beneath the compassionate gaze of the buddhas.

Amituofo amituofo amituofo

We release our flowers. My carnation nestles atop a dozen others in peaceful repose, green-tipped feet and marigold-bloom head reaching to opposite ends of the rotunda wall.

Amituofo amituofo amituofo amituofo louder and faster the chanting swells *Amituofo amituofo amituofo* a warm sea of voices *Amituofo amituofo* a sweet familiar melody *Amituofo* choking bitterly in my throat:

A – mi – tuo – fo ...

Silence, save for a few hushed sobs. I blink open eyes sticky with tears.

A mountain of flowers rises in *parinirvana*. In the portrait on the altar, Aaron is beaming.

It's as if he's saying to all of us, as he once wrote to me: "Whenever you may feel your energy flagging, know that somewhere I am quietly yet furiously cheering you on with a big smile."

Looking around the overflowing memorial pavilion, it dawns on me that I have never chanted with so many other young adult Asian Americans before. Grief and gratitude unite us on this bright October day in Southern California.

I see I am not the only one smiling through my tears.

Six years earlier, a different chant echoes in another temple.

> *Na – mo – xiang – yun – gai – pu – sa – mo – he – sa ...*

We arrive just as the melody of the Jeweled Censer Praise glides to a close. The fragrance of incense shimmers in the air as the last note fades.

Ding! A nun in brown robes sounds the brass bell. Another nun launches into an energetic rhythm on the wooden fish.

> *Na mo he la da na duo la ya ye*
> *na mo a li ye*
> *po lu jie di shuo bo la ye*
> *pu ti sa duo po ye ...*

Bare feet planted on carpet worn soft by devotions, I struggle to keep up, my Mandarin-inflected words dissolving into the Cantonese-tinted lilt of the voices around me. In the mouths of the other congregants, the Great Compassion Mantra is smooth as stones in a babbling brook. My mouth, meanwhile, is a fount of marbles.

Most of the temple members, having long ago memorized the liturgy, have no need for the service book that I'm clutching like a flotation device. With nary a romanization in sight, the pages are virtually indecipherable to me. The breathtaking speed and Sanskrit origins of the mantra don't help.

摩訶薩埵婆耶
摩訶迦盧尼迦耶
唵
薩皤囉罰曳
數怛那怛寫

The cover of the liturgy book matches the goldenrod robes of the head monk, who was born in the 1940s in Saigon's Chinatown. Most of the temple members appear to be his age, plus or minus a decade or so. Trent and I are the only twenty-somethings in the room. His messy brown locks and my long black ponytail stand out among the graying crowns of our fellow worshippers. With her shock of snow-white hair, one elderly woman is the spitting image of my *waipo*. I have to remind myself that though my grandma is also from southern China, I have never known her to step foot in a Buddhist temple. As far as I know, Waipo is of a leaf with the rest of my family tree: nonreligious going back several generations.

Perhaps it is this atheistic inheritance that explains my anxiety and self-consciousness in Buddhist settings like this one, where my Asian face blends in but my halting tongue does not. Trent, by contrast, seems perfectly at ease, despite being the only white person in the room. When we met during my junior year, I was just beginning to explore a burgeoning interest in Buddhism. Trent was already well acquainted with the tradition, having spent a good portion of his middle- and high-school years at various sanghas in California (after which he'd spent a year in Cambodia studying Khmer Buddhist chant and ordaining as a novice monk).

Here I am, four years after meeting Trent, still afraid I'll commit some unforgivable faux pas every time I go to a temple. Umpteen visits to Chinese, Khmer, Thai, and Vietnamese sanghas in the Bay Area (not to mention a summer of volunteering with a Buddhist chaplaincy organization in Cambodia) don't seem to have alleviated this anxiety much.

Maybe I will bow incorrectly or burn myself on incense or say something stupid to a monk or, as looks to be the case today, have naked feet while everyone else is wearing socks, or—

Na mo bo qie fa di
bi sha she
ju lu bi liu li
bo la po

Such vigor! The chanting arrests my worry mid-thought. My ears open to the enthusiasm enlivening the room.

My eyes take in the haloed Buddha statue in seated meditation. The gleaming altar bedecked in reds and golds. The offering plates piled high with cairns of fruit. The festive lanterns with their dangling tassels.

It's hard to stay anxious when pressed shoulder-to-shoulder with devotees in a temple so unassuming it is virtually indistinguishable from the other narrow two-story homes on this residential block. Services are held in the living room-turned-worship hall. The downstairs garage has been converted into a dining area that doubles as a space for sutra study. From the street, the only indication of the religious purpose of the building is a hand-painted poster in the center pane of the bay window, barely visible beneath the heart-shaped curlicues of the wrought-iron grill. Read from right to left, the three characters reveal, in graceful calligraphy, the name of the temple.

It's hard to stay anxious in a temple named Compassion.

It's especially hard to stay anxious when you suddenly find yourself showered with candies and coins by grinning monastics, upon which a gleeful chaos ensues, grandmas catching haw flakes midair and grandpas snatching dimes from the floor with no less zeal than the children who have materialized underfoot to grab their share of the bounty.

"Don't spoil your appetite," the Venerable reminds us. "It's time for the new year's feast!"

And this is how we welcomed the year of the dragon on a fine winter morning as the fog slowly lifted over a little beige house in San Francisco.

"Have you heard of *Angry Asian Buddhist*?" The new millennium is a decade old and Trent has been poking around the Buddhist blogosphere.

"Do you mean *Angry Asian Man*?" I ask, thinking of Phil Yu's popular blog on Asian American issues. But no: *Angry Asian Buddhist* is more recently established, in 2009 rather than 2001. The blogger writes under the pseudonyms "Arun" and "arunlikhati."[1]

I browse a few articles, surprised to see a fresh perspective on race, culture, and privilege in the American Buddhist community. It dawns on me that I hardly ever see articles by Asian American authors in *Tricycle* and *BuddhaDharma* and *Shambhala*. Arun calls these magazines the "Big Three." Come to think of it, the glossy covers of the Big Three appear to be on endless rotation between images of white meditators, the Dalai Lama, and Buddha statues.

"It's like Asian American Buddhists don't even exist," I grumble.

Perusing another post, it strikes me that Arun is right—it really *is* hard to find groups specifically geared toward young adult Asian American Buddhists. Young adult Asian American Christians, on the other hand? I can't walk through Sproul Plaza on the nearby Cal campus without being asked to join their fellowships, plural.

Piqued curiosity notwithstanding, the Angry Asian Buddhist soon slips from my mind. I am too preoccupied with the pressing question of *What am I going to do with my life?* to vex myself over the invisibility of Asian American Buddhists.

Like many a millennial, I land in grad school. Unlike most millennials, I opt for a three-year MA program in Buddhist studies and Buddhist chaplaincy.

At the end of my second semester, as I am desperately casting about for a master's thesis topic, Trent shows me a May 2012 interview in *Tricycle*.

Who is the Angry Asian Buddhist? Nearly four years ago a blogger on the group blog Dharma Folk *calling himself arunlikhati published a short blog post called "Angry Asian Buddhist," protesting the white-centric views of American Buddhist media and (some) American Buddhists themselves. Since then, he's become an outspoken critic of the various stereotypes swirling around the American Dharma scene and an advocate of the discussion of race in our sanghas. arunlikhati now primarily blogs at* Angry Asian Buddhist, *a site that has over the years proven to be no stranger to controversy.*[2]

"Do you think we should track this mystery man down?" I joke.

I could never have imagined that three months later, my thesis advisor would introduce me to arunlikhati. Ten months later, we would meet in person for the first time. Two years later, he would cry reading my completed master's thesis. Five years later, I would be the one weeping.

"I was lonely. I needed a boyfriend," quips Sumi Loundon Kim when asked what inspired her anthology *Blue Jean Buddha: Voices of Young Buddhists*.[3] Growing up in predominantly white convert communities, Sumi (who is white) rarely met other sangha members her age. To find them, she reached out to Buddhist parents and Dharma teachers at a meditation retreat center. It was their kids who connected her to a broader network of Buddhist youth around the United States.

Through writing *Blue Jean Buddha,* Sumi discovered a community of Dharma peers. Her follow-up anthology, *The Buddha's Apprentices: More Voices of Young Buddhists,* is dedicated to her husband, Ilmee Hwansoo Kim. His story is among the twenty-eight essays featured in the first volume.

Though I wasn't on the market for a romantic partner, I could definitely empathize with Sumi's loneliness. At majority-Asian temples, the preschool-to-retirement-age bracket was sparsely populated at best. Nor was I meeting many young adults, much less Asian Americans, at the majority-white Zen and insight meditation communities I frequented.

I began to wonder: *Where are all the young adult Asian American Buddhists?*

SEEKING

I found some of them in the pages of *Blue Jean Buddha* and *The Buddha's Apprentices.* Taken collectively, their essays offer a glimpse into the astonishing diversity of cultural backgrounds, spiritual practices, family histories, religious communities, and life journeys that make up Buddhist Asian America.

There are monastics and ministers who immigrated from Asia to America: Hojo Tone, a Jodo Shinshu Buddhist minister's son, was raised in Japan and became a minister in Hawai'i. Sister Kristine left Vietnam at the age of eight and ordained as a nun in America. Ajahn Keerati Chatkaew, a Theravada monk from Thailand, works with at-risk Asian American youth in Stockton, California.

There are young laypeople raised in Buddhist households: Jae-ho Lee, the son of devout Korean Buddhists, reconnected with his faith after two family tragedies. Donna Lovong grew up with exposure to Thai and Lao Buddhism but now practices Zen meditation.

There are Asian Americans from non-Buddhist families: Diane Biray Gregorio is a Theravada and Tibetan Buddhist practitioner with a Filipino Catholic upbringing. Maya Putra practices *vipassana* in Houston and hails from Indonesia.

But finding a group of young adult Asian American Buddhists off the page and in the flesh? Not so straightforward. In their research at Thai, Korean, and Taiwanese American Buddhist temples, sociologists of religion Wendy Cadge, Sharon Suh, and Carolyn Chen almost never saw young adults in attendance.[4] In spring 2008, on the group blog *Dharma Folk,* a certain arunlikhati laments, "The real issue for young Buddhists in the Asian American community is that there are very few Buddhist communities that they can go to without having to suppress part of their identity."[5]

"Back when I was in college, we had always hoped to make a national Buddhist youth conference," writes arunlikhati in another *Dharma Folk* post from that spring.[6] (When I got to know the blogger better, I would understand that "we" referred to his Dharma buddies in Southern California—Asian American and otherwise—who were building forums for young Buddhists like themselves to connect. They created on-campus clubs, temple youth groups, sutra study meetings, meditation gatherings in people's homes, and yes, even group blogs.) With his characteristic blend of sincerity and cheekiness, arunlikhati recalls attending one such conference in Boston that fell short of his expectations. He wished it had been truly national (he was the only person not from the Northeast), better organized (he'd had to spend a night in the library), and that people had stayed in touch afterward (things kind of petered out). Not that he had any regrets about going: one of the highlights was meeting Sumi Loundon Kim (small world indeed).

arunlikhati knew of three other groups that hosted conferences for Buddhist youth: The Young Buddhist Association (YBA) of the Buddhist Churches of America (BCA), Gia Đình Phật Tử Việt Nam (GĐPTVN), and Dharma Realm Buddhist Young Adults (DRBY). He wondered how he (a mixed-race Buddhist whose primary practice was in the Theravada tradition, though I wouldn't learn this until later) would fit in at these conferences, which are sponsored by Mahayana Buddhist organizations with majority Japanese, Vietnamese, and Chinese American members.

As he would write in that April 2008 blog post, and as he told me many times before his untimely death in 2017, Aaron dreamed of creating a conference that would unite young adult Asian Americans from a range of ethnicities, across Buddhist traditions.

You could say the Pew Research Center is partially responsible for the existence of *Angry Asian Buddhist.* In 2008, the nonpartisan think tank released a "U.S. Religious Landscape Survey." In it, they reported that Asian Americans make up only one-third of the American Buddhist population, while white Buddhists make up the majority at 53 percent.[7]

arunlikhati wasn't buying it.

Outlining his rationale in a series of posts, the blogger insisted that there must be at least twice as many Asian American Buddhists as the Pew Forum proclaimed.[8] He humbly dubbed his revised numbers "Dharma Folk's Flawed Estimate (DFFE)."[9]

Aaron's skepticism would prove prescient. In a 2012 survey on the religious life of Asian Americans, Pew Forum researchers realized that methodological limitations of the 2008 study had caused them to significantly underestimate the proportion of Asian American Buddhists.[10] The revised findings? Of the estimated 1.0–1.3 percent of the U.S. adult population who say they are Buddhist, 67–69 percent are Asian American.[11]

In other words, people of Asian heritage make up more than two-thirds of American Buddhists. They are not a minority within American Buddhism—they are its clear majority.

DFFE wasn't so flawed after all.

Unfortunately, the updated statistics aren't always cited, as when a 2015 *Washington Post* article mentions "the mostly white convert communities who make up three-quarters of U.S. Buddhists."[12]

Alas, data are no safeguard from erasure.

As if in counterbalance to the fact that two-thirds of American Buddhists are of Asian descent, the same Pew Forum report paints a portrait of a demographic in decline.

> *Overall, Buddhism had the greatest net loss due to changes in religious affiliation within the Asian American community. One in ten Asian Americans (10 percent) were raised Buddhist and have left the faith, while 2 percent of Asian Americans have become Buddhist after being raised in a different faith (or no faith), resulting in a net loss of eight percentage points due to religious switching.*[13]

Hardly a hopeful situation. And, as I would soon discover, hardly the end of disheartening reads about Asian American Buddhists.

"The single story creates stereotypes, and the problem with stereotypes is not that they are untrue but that they are incomplete. They make one story become the only story."

I sat riveted in front of my computer as Chimamanda Adichie delivered her 2009 TED talk on "The Danger of a Single Story." Six years later I would watch the video again, on a projection screen at a Buddhist college in Taiwan, Chinese subtitles translating the Nigerian American author's words for the benefit of my classmates.

The dominant story of Buddhism in America is that there are "two Buddhisms": the Buddhism of white converts and the Buddhism of Asian immigrants.[14] What differentiates these "two distinct and mutually isolated brands of Buddhism"?[15] We are told, for starters, that "Western"/"white" Buddhists focus on meditation practice in keeping with their "rational" and "modernist" bent, whereas "Asian"/"Asian American" Buddhists prefer the "traditional" and "devotional" rituals of chanting and bowing.

It's not hard to guess which group is more likely to be dismissed as "superstitious" and which group is more likely to be celebrated as "scientific."

Though hardly its intended impact, the "two Buddhisms" story too easily lends itself to less-than-flattering portrayals of Asian American Buddhists.[16] In a 2014 blog post on the "Stereotypology of Asian American Buddhists," the Angry Asian Buddhist weighs in, mincing no words.

> *Buddhist Asian Americans are often surprised to encounter so many stereotypes about us. For all the claims [that] we mostly keep to ourselves in "ethnic enclaves," there seems to be a rather thorough set of stereotypes about people whom most white Buddhists claim to barely know. Worse yet is that these stereotypes are routinely cited as solid facts.*
>
> *The stereotypes are generally about how different we are from "American Buddhists." These might sound familiar: We Buddhist Asian Americans are basically immigrants. We cannot speak English and carry a more supernatural bent. We focus our energies into holidays and spiritual beliefs instead of meditative practices.... Some of us are Oriental monks who bring our exotic teachings to the West. The temples we attend aren't about spreading the Dharma—they're just ethnic social clubs. I could go on.[17]*

Perhaps these stereotypes explain why Asians are American Buddhism's invisible majority, their faces and names largely absent from the Buddhist mediascape. In the words of a friend who doesn't call himself Buddhist though the Japanese American side of his family attends a Jodo Shinshu temple: "It's a lot sexier to be Buddhist if you're white than if you're Asian American."

Race is a touchy subject in American Buddhism, as the Angry Asian Buddhist knew all too well. Some commenters discredited his religious credentials (*real* Buddhists wouldn't harp on such divisive issues). Others dissed his grasp of Buddhist teachings (if you *truly* understood the nondual nature of reality, you wouldn't get so hung up about race). Still others accused him of being racist against white Buddhists (Aaron, being half white, must have been tickled by this).

In a 1994 *Tricycle* special issue on "Dharma, Diversity, & Race," African American writer and activist bell hooks expresses her frustration over white Buddhists who "are so attached to the image of themselves as non-racists that they refuse to see their own racism or the ways in which Buddhist communities may reflect racial hierarchies."[18] hooks criticizes the cultural arrogance that leads to white practitioners claiming ownership and control over what constitutes "authentic" American Buddhism. She pleads: *Will the real Buddhist please stand up?*

For bell hooks and the Angry Asian Buddhist—and for me as well—this question is at once personal and political. As Buddhist studies scholar Jan Nattier reminds us, "Every act of definition is, among other things, a political act: to define is inevitably to frame the Other in one's own terms.... To define is, to put it crudely, an act of conquest, in which the Other's self-definition is subordinated to one's own."[19] The title of Natalie Quli's article "Western Self, Asian Other"[20] makes clear who the "Other" in American Buddhism is.

The more I encountered depictions of the docile Oriental monk, the more I read about Asian immigrant Buddhists whose chanting and devotional practices are deemed too "superstitious" for today's rational "Western" meditator par excellence, the more I saw the "two Buddhisms" model slip from sociological description to racial disparagement, the more I wanted to ask: *Will the real Asian American Buddhists please stand up?*

I was dissatisfied with the Tale of Two Separate (and, apparently, not quite equal) Buddhisms that I kept encountering. Nor was I content to be an American convert Buddhist whose Asian heritage is merely a sidenote—a yellow-on-the-outside, white-on-the-inside "banana Buddhist," to borrow a provocative phrase from the Angry Asian Buddhist.

> *If you choose to think of us as Superstitious Immigrants, you will never accept us as real Americans. If you choose to think of us as Banana Buddhists, you then trivialize the value of our heritage. The best way to uproot these stereotypes is first to stop perpetuating them, to encourage others to stop perpetuating them, and then to actually start spending some more time getting to know Buddhist Asian Americans for who we really are.[21]*

I took Arun's advice to heart. I decided to get to know some Asian American Buddhists.

CONNECTING

I didn't intend to write my master's thesis on young adult Asian American Buddhists.

Yes, I was in my twenties, but I knew grandmas more adept at Facebook than me (what is this "Instagram" you speak of?).

Sure, I was a 1.75-generation Chinese American immigrant, but my exposure to Asian American-identified communities was limited; I'd had a dozen addresses by the age of seventeen, and a peripatetic education as a result: day care in Shanghai, elementary years in inner-city Pittsburgh and a semi-rural suburb of Pennsylvania, junior high and high school in Washington State.

And I was clearly more Buddhist than any other religion, but the combination of (1) having been raised to associate religion with brainwashing cults, along with (2) worrying I was an inauthentic and inexpert Buddhist, in addition to (3) not wanting to be seen as a superstitious immigrant, resulted in (4) a tendency to be less than outspoken about my religious identity.

Given my ambivalence around calling myself a "young adult," an "Asian American," and a "Buddhist," it took me a while to consider combining the three into a single identity label.

You could say I was good at missing the obvious.

I wanted to interview young adult Asian American Buddhists, but would they want to meet with me? To play it safe, I cast as wide a net as possible. I was open to talking to anyone of full or partial Asian heritage, regardless of immigration or citizenship status. Participants didn't have to be native English speakers. They didn't have to be card-carrying Buddhists.[22] I didn't set strict age limits on the definition of "young adult."

Now I just had to figure out how to get the word out. My thesis advisor Scott Mitchell, scholar of Western Buddhism and active contributor to the Buddhist blogosphere, knew just the person I needed to contact.

A day after Dr. Mitchell put us in touch, an email from Aaron Lee appeared in my inbox. My fears that he would spurn my request for help vanished upon reading Aaron's first words to me: "Any project about young Asian American Buddhists sounds amazing, so I will be happy to support in any way I can."[23] He asked only that I keep his identity as the Angry Asian Buddhist secret.[24]

At that point, all I knew from reading Aaron's blog posts was that he was male (and even this had taken a lot of sleuthing to confirm). Other identifying details remained a mystery. Despite his impassioned writing on race in American Buddhism, Aaron's ethnicity was ambiguous. Based on the languages he knew, the schools of Buddhism he was familiar with, and the Buddhist news he posted, I presumed he could be Thai, Cambodian, Vietnamese, Japanese, Burmese, or Bangladeshi. Geographically, he was also hard to pin down; his blog revealed ties to the Bay Area, Southern California, Paris, and rural Illinois. Even his Buddhist affiliation wasn't entirely clear. He mentioned an affinity for Theravada Buddhism, but also wrote about visits to Mahayana communities.

Aaron mercifully put an end to my guessing. He was Chinese—specifically, Toishanese—and Polish-Russian Ashkenazi Jewish. He grew up in the Bay Area and Illinois but was living in Southern California. He had strong connections to multiple forms of Buddhism, so much so that his friends regularly joked that "Aaron knows all Buddhists." (Once, over the course of a New York cab ride, Aaron found out that he knew one of the taxi driver's Bangladeshi Buddhist relatives.)

Right on the heels of his first email, Aaron sent me the names and contact information of dozens of Buddhist individuals and organizations who might be willing to help with my research. "The list is incomplete, but I'll update it as often as I can," he promised.

Inspired by Sumi Loundon Kim's networked and decentralized approach for seeking contributors to her anthologies, I set up a website with a call for participants. Aaron spread the word on his blog. I introduced the project to young adults at various Bay Area Buddhist conferences and events.

The number of interested Asian American Buddhists snowballed. It seems I had touched a nerve.

From December 2012 to September 2013, I interviewed twenty-six young adult Asian American Buddhists: twenty-two in the San Francisco Bay Area and four in Southern California.[25] We met in cafés in Sunnyvale and San Francisco and Long Beach and LA's Koreatown. At a temple in San Mateo and a library in San Jose. On the campuses of the University of California, Berkeley, and the Institute of Buddhist Studies and Stanford University and the University of Southern California. One interview took place on a grassy lawn after we decided the cloudless sky was scolding us for staying indoors on a perfect summer day.

When the interviews were at my apartment, we nibbled chocolate-chip cookies (vegan and gluten-free but delicious, I swear), talking at the kitchen table by the still-warm oven. One interviewee lived just down the street and invited me to her apartment, where I was greeted by a plate of *her* favorite homemade vegan cookies. Another invited me to his family's home in the San Gabriel Valley. I drank endless cups of expertly poured tea as we sat on the carpet next to a gorgeous three-tiered altar, my audio recorder capturing his quiet voice against the backdrop of a chant machine playing *namo guanshi yin pu sa* in melodious loop.

Our conversations covered everything from these young adults' cultural and religious backgrounds to their Buddhist practices, beliefs, and communities to their opinions about how Asian American Buddhists are represented. On average, each interview lasted two and a half hours. Some were four to five hours long.

Many interviewees marveled that they had never before pondered the intersection of their racial and religious identities. They reflected on how their experiences differ from those of older Asian American Buddhists, American Buddhists of non-Asian backgrounds, and Asian Americans of other faiths. They were brimming with questions to ask other young adult Asian American Buddhists.[26]

I'd started the project worried about finding enough people to talk to. Now I had the opposite problem: an ever-growing list of individuals who wanted to connect but couldn't meet in person due to geographic distance or scheduling difficulties.

It seemed a disservice not to honor these requests. I adapted my interview to an email format and was amazed to receive sixty-three responses.[27]

I was even more astonished to realize just how diverse this group of young adult Asian American Buddhists was. Not just in terms of ethnicity and age, but also generation and geography, religious practice and belief, occupation and socioeconomic status.[28]

Without these eighty-nine young adults who gave so generously of their time and wisdom, this book would not exist. They are the ones who taught me that Asian American Buddhists are everywhere, even if we are often invisible to the mainstream. Even if, at times, we are invisible to each other.

Where are all the young adult Asian American Buddhists, and what can we learn from them?

Be the Refuge tells the story of my journey to answer these two questions.

Part 1, "Trailblazers," centers the experiences of multi-generation Jodo Shinshu Buddhists whose Japanese American forebears brought Shin

Buddhism to America more than a century ago. Like Asian American Buddhists more broadly, these Japanese American Shin Buddhists are often erased from the history—and the current mediascape—of American Buddhism. Despite this erasure, the multi-generation young adult Shin Buddhists I interviewed extend the sense of belonging that they feel in their sanghas to people of all backgrounds. In so doing, they continue a lineage of resisting erasure and building a truly inclusive American Buddhism.

Part 2, "Bridge-Builders," focuses on the insights of second-generation Asian American Buddhists whose first-generation immigrant parents raised them within the Buddhist faith. An ethnically diverse group, the second-gen young adults I interviewed confront many shared challenges: language barriers at the temples of their upbringing, generational gaps with their parents' Buddhist practices and beliefs, as well as religious discrimination outside the Buddhist spheres they grew up in. In spite of these obstacles, they find ways to reclaim Buddhism on their own terms: by refusing to denigrate "Asian immigrant" Buddhism, by compassionately reconciling the differences between their own and their parents' Buddhisms.

Part 3, "Integrators," highlights the perspectives of Asian American converts—a group whose experiences are largely invisible within the white-dominated sphere of American convert Buddhism. Raised in Christian, Hindu, Jewish, Muslim, Zoroastrian, as well as nonreligious and mixed-religion households, the Asian American convert Buddhists I interviewed find no easy foothold within the "two Buddhisms" typology of Asian immigrants and white converts. They bear the tension of constantly straddling cultural and spiritual worlds. As "first-gen" American Buddhists (to borrow a phrase from one of my interviewees), these young adults discover an affinity with Buddhism despite a lack of familiarity with majority-Asian temples and a sense of alienation in majority-white sanghas. Their spiritual journeys result in a deepening of Buddhist roots that is inflected—but never predetermined—by their cultural heritages.

Part 4, "Refuge-Makers," draws from the voices of the first-gen, second-gen, and multi-gen interviewees in the previous chapters to explore the possibilities of a pan-ethnic, pan-sectarian Asian American Buddhist identity. Collectively, these young adults harness the energy of anger in the face of injustice as a skillful means to counter underrepresentation and fight misrepresentation. In examining privilege—their own as well as others'—they call for an intersectional awareness of American Buddhism that is keenly attuned to issues of race, gender, sexuality, and class. In sharing their stories, they advocate for solidarity between Asian American Buddhists of different ethnicities—and indeed among Buddhists of all cultural backgrounds.

The Asian American Buddhists featured in this book refuse to be reduced to Oriental monks, superstitious immigrants, and "banana Buddhists." They champion nuanced representations over stale stereotypes. They cultivate sanghas that are inclusive and accessible. They embody the boundless possibilities for interconnection that glow at the heart of American Buddhism in all its dynamism and diversity.

PART 1

TRAILBLAZERS

I often feel like I am trailblazing how to incorporate Buddhism into life ...

—GABRIELLE

ERASURE

The first issue of *Tricycle* magazine hit newsstands on the cusp of the fall of the Soviet Union. In her introduction to the subsequent winter 1991 issue, founding editor Helen Tworkov comments on the recent August Coup, praises the diversity of American Buddhism, and calls for the ongoing protection of political and religious pluralism in the United States.

The penultimate paragraph of Tworkov's introduction includes a remark that would reverberate in Buddhist circles for years to come.

> *The spokespeople for Buddhism in America have been, almost exclusively, educated members of the white middle class. Meanwhile, even with varying statistics, Asian-American Buddhists number at least one million, but so far they have not figured prominently in the development of something called American Buddhism.*

Tworkov ends on a celebratory note about how *Tricycle* subscriptions and sales have exceeded expectations. "As a not-for-profit subscriber-based journal, your response is very important to us," she writes, pleased to be reaching readers in "virtually every state in the union."[1]

One of these readers was a Jodo Shinshu Buddhist minister and a professor at Evergreen State College in Olympia, Washington. He took up the invitation to write a response.

RYO IMAMURA
April 25, 1992

Tricycle

Letters to the Editor

In the Winter issue, editor Helen Tworkov made the inaccurate and racist comment that "Asian-American Buddhists ... so far ... have not figured prominently in the development of something called American Buddhism." I would like to point out that it was my grandparents and other immigrants from Asia who brought and implanted Buddhism in American soil over one hundred years ago despite white American intolerance and bigotry. It was my American-born parents and their generation who courageously and diligently fostered the growth of American Buddhism despite having to practice discretely in hidden ethnic temples and in concentration camps because of the same white intolerance and bigotry. It was us Asian Buddhists who welcomed countless white Americans into our temples, introduced them to the Dharma, and often assisted them to initiate their own sanghas when they felt uncomfortable practicing with us. And it was in our battered and brutalized ancestral homelands that white American GIs and the tourists who followed were introduced to the peace and harmony of the Dharma in the aftermath of our many genocidal wars in Asia.

We Asian Buddhists have hundreds of temples in the United States with active practitioners of all ages, ongoing educational programs that are both Buddhist and interfaith in nature, social welfare projects ... everything that white Buddhist centers have and perhaps more. It is apparent that Tworkov has restricted "American Buddhism" to mean "white American Buddhism," and that her statement is even more misleading than one claiming that Americans of color did not figure prominently in the development of American history.

It appears to me that white and Asian Buddhists live in two discrete worlds and practice different forms of Buddhism, although they may use the same names and terminologies. Do not mistake me to say that white Buddhists do not practice authentic Buddhism; I am not saying that. It is just a very different form, one that is innovative and exciting in its own right. It is eloquent, dramatic, intellectual, impatient, proud, and so very clear. In contrast, we Asians are like Hun-tun (Chaos) and like tofu, seemingly lacking the seven discriminating holes in the head and persisting unobtrusively in new and often hostile environments. White Buddhists treat their teachers like gurus or living Buddhas whereas we Asians regard ours to be fallible human beings who represent an honored tradition and not themselves. White Buddhist centers rise and fall dramatically like the ocean waves whereas Asian temples seem to persist uneventfully and quietly through generations. White practitioners practice intensive psychotherapy on their cushions in a life-or-death struggle with the individual ego whereas Asian Buddhists seem to just smile and eat together. It is clear that, although they may adopt Asian Buddhist names, dress, and mannerisms, white Buddhists cannot help but drag their Western Judeo-Christian identities and shadows with them wherever they go. This certainly makes for an exciting and dramatic new form of Buddhism.

As an eighteenth-generation priest of the Jodo Shin sect and a past (and only Asian-American) president of the Buddhist Peace Fellowship, I believe my perspective is quite unique for this journal. Certainly I may have made some gross generalizations, but they contain enough validity to be voiced here, even though I am neither a white practitioner nor one of their recognized teachers.

I enjoyed reading the Winter issue of *Tricycle* and will encourage other Asian Buddhists to do the same, especially since we would probably never publish such a professional-looking and articulate journal ourselves. In contrast, our publications are quite amateurish-looking and probably uninteresting to those outside our communities. I am sure that *Tricycle* will become a very popular journal for the white Buddhist community and would like to convey my congratulations. In closing, please remember that we Asian Buddhists do exist (if only in the background) and that we have feelings that can also be bruised by unthinking comments.

Gassho,

Ryo Imamura

P.S. Please do not reprint this letter in *Tricycle* if you do not print it in its entirety.

cc: Joanna Macy, Masatomi Nagatomi, and Gary Snyder

Much to Rev. Imamura's sadness and dismay, *Tricycle* never printed his response.[2] Gary Snyder resigned from the magazine's advisory board in protest.

BUDDHISM AND DEATH

The final page of my college transcript lists the one and only religious studies class I took as an undergrad, in the spring quarter before graduation. You'd think I would have come around to it sooner, given the *zafu* in my dorm room, the row of Buddhist books on my shelf, the twenty-eight other departments I'd taken courses in. (You could say I was good at missing the obvious.)

We learned about the Buddha's passing away into nirvana, the veneration of his relics, the cosmologies of samsara and rebirth. We read about hell realms, mummified monks, corpse contemplation, religious suicide, skull rituals. We lightened the mood with the three Pure Land Sutras, which promise rebirth in the heavenly abode of Amida Buddha for anyone who invokes his name by reciting the *nembutsu ("Namo Amida Butsu")*. I delighted in the lavish descriptions of the bejeweled Pure Land, where even the birds sing in praise of the Triple Gem (the Buddha, Dharma, and Sangha).

It never occurred to me that these texts from a class on death underpinned a contemporary—and very much alive—Buddhist tradition right here in the United States. A tradition that immigrants such as Rev. Imamura's grandparents established in this country in the late 1800s. A tradition that persisted through multiple generations in America in spite of intolerance and bigotry. A tradition that survived the incarceration of its Japanese American priests and congregants during World War II. A tradition whose seminary, established in 1949 to meet the postwar demand for English-speaking ministers, would six decades later provide an intellectual and spiritual home for a project on young adult Asian American Buddhists.

On the corner of Durant and Fulton, across from a coffee shop run by a Cambodian American family, sits a City of Berkeley historical landmark. Built in 1930 by the owner of the racehorse Seabiscuit and used in the 1980s as the car dealership of baseball star Reggie Jackson, the classic art deco building came under new ownership in 2003.[3] In the spacious lobby, brass letters on slate tile wall announce the building's twenty-first-century calling:

Jodo Shinshu Center
Buddhist Churches of America

Walking into the JSC for the first time, I feel I've stumbled on a Pure Land. The sweet smell of incense wafts through the wood-paneled glass doors of the BCA bookstore to my left. A summer-cloud-white Dharma wheel hangs from the lofty ceiling, its width easily twice my height, recessed lights embedded like gemstones in the *Dharmachakra*'s outer ring. Beneath its eight spokes, a geometric lotus blooms on the beige tile floor, white-ringed petals against an earthy palette of red-green-brown-blue.

Later I will learn that the carpeted stairs to my right lead to the upstairs *kodo* for lectures and services. It will be months before I realize that the JSC houses not only the Institute of Buddhist Studies—my reason for visiting—but also the BCA's Center for Buddhist Education. It will be years before I discover the dry rock garden tucked away on the second floor, the guest rooms on the third floor.

For now, I stand before a close-to-life-size cast bronze statue of a Japanese monk. The billowing sleeves of his robe reach almost to his knees. He holds a *mala* in his left hand and a walking stick in his right. Split-toe sandals and conical hat complete the pilgrim's outfit.

To my chagrin, I have no idea who he is.

Shinran Shonin was born in 1173 in what is now Kyoto. Orphaned young, he entered temple life at the age of nine. Like his contemporaries Dogen (who founded the Soto school of Zen) and Nichiren (who founded the eponymous school of Buddhism), Shinran began his career at Mount Hiei, the headquarters of the dominant Tendai sect. He practiced for two decades as a monk at Mount Hiei before breaking with tradition by getting married—he and his wife, Eshinni, would go on to have seven children—and eating meat (both marriage and nonvegetarianism were verboten for Japanese monastics at the time).

In 1203, Shinran became a disciple of Honen, a monk who had rejected Tendai, embraced a new path centered around reciting the nembutsu, and founded Jodo Shu (Pure Land sect) Buddhism. Exiled with Honen in 1207 after the imposition of a nembutsu ban, Shinran came to understand himself as "neither monk nor layman."[4] After the ban was lifted, Shinran devoted the next thirty years to teaching in the countryside before returning to Kyoto, where he lived until his death in 1263. In time, Shinran's teachings became the basis for Jodo Shinshu (True Pure Land sect) Buddhism, or Shin for short.

How did Shin Buddhism come to be one of the earliest and most enduring forms of American Buddhism?

The first Japanese community to settle in what is now an American territory arrived as migrant laborers to the sovereign nation of Hawai'i in 1868, the first year of Japan's Meiji government. Over the next four decades, nearly half a million Japanese—more than 99 percent of them Buddhists—would arrive in the Americas to work the sugar plantations of Hawai'i and the railroads of the American West.[5]

As the numbers of Japanese immigrants grew, so too did the demand for Buddhist clergy. A September 12, 1899, report in the *San Francisco Chronicle* announces the arrival of two Shin Buddhist priests:

Missionaries of the Buddhist Faith

Two Representatives of the Ancient Creed Are in San Francisco to Proselyte

Beneath the headline, a black-and-white photograph shows Dr. Shuye Sonoda and Rev. Kakuryo Nishijima standing candlestick-straight in voluminous robes. Clerical stoles identify them as priests of the Nishi (West) Honganji denomination of Jodo Shinshu.

"Our plan here is first to establish a church, then an evening school for our own people, and as we become more proficient in English, to communicate with those among Americans who wish to investigate Buddhism," explains Dr. Sonoda in the news article.[6]

One Buddhist "church"—a name deemed more appropriate for the American context than "temple"—led to many more.[7] Just fifteen years later, twenty-five Jodo Shinshu churches banded together to form a new national organization, the Buddhist Mission of North America (BMNA). It was the second-oldest Buddhist organization in America (the oldest being its sister organization, the Honpa Hongwanji Mission of Hawai'i), and the largest Buddhist organization outside Asia for much of the twentieth century. Members of other Japanese Buddhist sects, including Jodo, Nichiren, Shingon, Soto Zen, and the Higashi (East) Honganji denomination of Jodo Shinshu, built their own sanghas in America.

But as these religious communities became more deeply rooted, so too did animus against them. Seen as members of a "heathen" race and religion, issei (first-generation) and nisei (second-generation) Japanese American Buddhists faced growing hostility in the majority-white, Christian-dominated country they called home.

In 1944, Ryo Imamura was born in the Gila River Relocation Center in Arizona.[8] That same year, the Buddhist Mission of North America officially changed its name to the Buddhist Churches of America at the Topaz Relocation Center in Utah.

Across the United States, 120,000 people of Japanese ancestry—nearly two-thirds of them American citizens—had been forcibly relocated to concentration camps. Like the Pearl Harbor bombing that set it in motion, this massive incarceration would live on in infamy. Buddhist priests were among the first to be arrested. Wartime paranoia facilitated the imprisonment of so many innocents. Racism explains why Japanese Americans were targeted while their German and Italian counterparts were spared.

Pressure to assimilate had already caused Shin Buddhist churches to switch from a lunar calendar to Sunday services by 1910. World War II only heightened the imperative for Shin Buddhists to prove their loyalty to the United States and reduce the stain of being part of the "yellow peril." As a result: the removal of the *manji,* an auspicious Buddhist symbol that unfortunately resembled the Nazi swastika; the creation of hymnals and a "Junior Catechism"; the name change from BMNA to BCA.

After the war, the Imamuras returned to Berkeley. In the spring of 1946, under the guidance of resident minister Rev. Kanmo Imamura, the Berkeley Buddhist Temple reopened after being closed for three years. Jane Imamura founded the temple choir and composed music for BCA Sunday school services. The husband-and-wife team began holding Buddhist study groups that attracted BCA priests and laypeople as well as Bay Area scholars, students, and convert Buddhists. (By the fall of 1955, group members included several writers still at an early stage in their careers: Allen Ginsberg, Jack Kerouac, Gary Snyder, and Philip Whalen.)

By the mid-1960s, the study group had evolved into the Institute of Buddhist Studies (IBS). Rev. Imamura served as the institute's first director. He and Jane practically lived at the original IBS building, a cozy brick house on Haste Street. Their son Ryo entered ministerial training there in 1969. By the time I began my MA at IBS forty-plus years later, the graduate school offered educational programs not just for Jodo Shinshu ministers but also Buddhist chaplains of all denominations and Buddhist studies scholars of any (or no) faith.

When someone asks "Are you religious?" or "What religion are you?," how do you usually respond? If you identify as Buddhist, how do you respond to the question, "What kind of Buddhist are you?"

The Shin Buddhists I interviewed didn't always have straightforward responses to my questions about their religious identity.

"I usually don't say Jodo Shinshu because I don't think that most people know what that is," replies Kaila.

"I'm not Zen Buddhist, which is probably the main sect that Americans know about," responds Kei.

Back in her native Japan, Kumi tells me, Shin Buddhism is "like air—it's there all the time for me!" But even before coming to study at IBS, she had heard that Jodo Shinshu wasn't well known in the United States. Her sect's obscurity in America took some getting used to.

What do you think are the best-known types of Buddhism and/or Buddhist organizations in America?

None of my interviewees, Shin Buddhist and otherwise, answered Jodo Shinshu or the BCA.

David thinks the reason might have something to do with his tradition's failure to live up to "Oriental monk" expectations.

I think when Americans think of Buddhists or Buddhism they think of Zen or Tibetan Buddhism, probably because these two are the ones that come up the most in popular culture. The Dalai Lama is probably the most famous living Buddhist figure in the world right now, so there has been a lot of coverage on his particular sect of Buddhism. Zen seems to have gotten a lot of press as well when Japanese Buddhism is depicted in TV and movies. I want to say that the American idea of Buddhism is focused more on the monastic sects of Buddhism: the "mysterious and mystical" East and their ancient knowledge.

Like Kumi, Nora is the first woman in her family to become a Shin Buddhist minister. It feels fitting to interview these two pioneers in the same classroom at IBS, albeit eight months apart.

Nora's religious and cultural identities are very much intertwined. She feels bad about equating Shin Buddhism with Japanese culture, however, since doing so might unfairly exclude the many non–Japanese American ministers and members in the BCA.

"Of course, Shin Buddhism *did* originate with Japan," Nora muses.

Her comment sparks a thought, and I go off-script from my interview protocol.

"Since Zen also originated in Japan, do you think of Japanese Americans when you think of Zen?"

Nora looks startled. "I don't!" She frowns. "I don't think of Japanese Americans, I think of Caucasians. When I think of Zen Buddhists, I think of the people pictured here."

Nora is pointing to a photo collage of twenty faces that we discussed earlier in the interview. Nineteen of the faces appear to be white. One person appears to be of South Asian heritage.

Credit for this provocative montage goes to—you guessed it—the Angry Asian Buddhist. In a 2012 blog post titled "Why Is the Under 35 Project So White?" Arun writes: "This year, *Shambhala SunSpace* has been posting weekly essays from the Under 35 Project, a laudable initiative to support and highlight the voices of the emerging generation of Buddhists and meditators. As usual, my naïveté never fails to let me down, and I was once again shocked at the whiteness of the lineup. Not a single East or Southeast Asian among them."[9]

Aaron was not a Shin Buddhist, but that didn't stop him from extolling the tradition's contributions to American Buddhism.

In response to a 2008 *Buddhadharma* article that omits Asian Americans from "Next-Gen Buddhism," arunlikhati cites the BCA to emphasize that "we Asian Americans are just as American as any white person (or Barack Obama), and our Buddhist institutions in America are often more American than they are Asian." He adds that the Buddhist Churches of America is more than a Japanese American organization—its president isn't even Asian, its membership is ethnically and racially diverse, its temple basketball teams play against Methodist teams.[10]

Not everyone was willing to accept this integrationist portrayal of the BCA. "From an American [standpoint] there is still an extremely Japanese flavor [to the BCA]," one commenter grouses.

Such complaints are hardly new; in her 1971 book on Buddhism in Hawai'i, Louise Hunter writes about Caucasians who "did not feel at home in most Buddhist 'churches'" because these communities' "Oriental" aspects "were thought to alienate Occidentals."[11]

"The very fact that an organization would be called Buddhist 'Churches' of America and have pews is already off-putting to me and, I bet, most Euro-American Buddhists," gripes another commenter.

Given the internment of Japanese American Buddhists, these seemingly Christian adaptations were, in the words of Gary Okihiro, "a means of survival to maintain their physical presence and culture in the face of white supremacy."[12]

Taken together, the two comments put Japanese American Shin Buddhists between a rock and a hard place. They are either too Japanese (read: overly exotic) or too Christian and Americanized (not exotic enough).

Attempts to contextualize the BCA's history only triggered more pushback. The respondent who is put off by the pews offers this defense: "I really get why immigrants, especially ones in risky situations because of wars or whatnot, would go the assimilative route. I meant no criticism, but was just pointing out why others of us don't relate to it, since what they adopted, for good reasons of their own, is exactly what we rejected, for reasons of our own."

In equating "what they [Japanese American Shin Buddhists] adopted" (Christianized elements) with "what we [white Buddhist converts] rejected" (the Christian faith of one's upbringing), this statement ignores the power imbalance between an ethnic minority defending their religion in response to xenophobia and a racial majority enjoying the freedom to convert out of a dominant religion. The white privilege of the latter group is conveniently obscured.[13]

The respondent who finds the Japanese flavor of the BCA unpalatable accuses the Angry Asian Buddhist of "oversensitivity, something it seems we as Buddhists should strive to avoid in the interests of harmonious coexistence."

In his book *Race and Religion in American Buddhism,* Joseph Cheah objects to this tendency among white Buddhists to avoid discussions of race, challenging "modernist Buddhists of the West" to "honestly acknowledge the Orientalized Buddhist baggage they have been carrying for the short time they have been around."[14]

Is the discomfort of white visitors the fault of the BCA for being too Japanese? Or is this an issue of insufficient tolerance, rather than inadequate Americanization?

For David, Shin Buddhism is a religion "for the everyday person." But as a tradition with noncelibate, nonvegetarian priests—a tradition in which sincerely reciting the nembutsu and listening to the Dharma is far more important than striving for enlightened states through seated meditation—Jodo Shinshu fails to conform to popular expectations of Buddhism.

As David puts it, "When people think of Buddhism, they think of vegetarian, pacifist monks, so when they see a 'normal' meat-eating American Buddhist like me, it kind of clashes with that idea."

"Through the figure of the nonsexual, solitary Oriental Monk, Asian religiosity and spirituality are made palatable—psychologically, socially, and politically—for dominant culture consumption," Jane Iwamura argues in her book *Virtual Orientalism.*[15] The BCA doesn't seem to pass the taste test. But who gets to judge what's unpalatable? Who gets to decide the "acceptable" norm in American Buddhism?

"I do not want to see all Asian American Buddhists represented as bald monks who air-bend," Kaila insists. "I would like to see Asian American Buddhists represented as we are: diverse."

BUDDHISTS' DELIGHT

June 16, 2012

The cheerful title caught my eye, but by the time I had finished reading this *New York Times* op-ed, I was feeling more dejected than delighted.

The op-ed writer weaves his recollections of a four-day Buddhist meditation retreat with information from three American scholars of Buddhism and a celebrity doctor (all of them white men, like the author himself). He then traces the tradition of engaged Buddhism in the West (which he's just learned about) to "early proponents" like Allen Ginsberg, who cofounded "the Jack Kerouac School of Disembodied Poetics at Naropa University in Boulder, Colorado, the first accredited Buddhist-inspired college in the United States."[16]

How easy the erasure of Asian American Buddhists. I too had been an unwitting participant in that erasure, but now I knew better.

Maybe, in Rev. Ryo Imamura's self-deprecating words, the magazine of his parents' Berkeley study group was an "amateurish-looking" publication. But it was the *Berkeley Bussei* that published Jack Kerouac's first poems in the 1950s. The Institute of Buddhist Studies was offering Buddhist higher education in this country a quarter century before Naropa.

As for engaged Buddhism in America? It doesn't begin with the Beat poets in my book.

BELONGING

"Are you going to TechnoBuddha this year?" Aaron wants to know.

"Is that like Buddhist Geeks?" I ask warily, thinking about his blog post on the Geeks' inaugural conference two years ago. As the BG organizers described it:

> *Taking place July 29th–31st, 2011, in Los Angeles, Buddhist Geeks | The Conference brings together some of the most exciting teachers, leaders, and thinkers from the U.S. and beyond as Buddhist Geeks continues its ongoing mission to discover the emerging face of Buddhism. With a vibrant program of presentations, workshops, performance, and participant-led elements and its inclusive nondenominational attitude, #bgeeks11 will be the most innovative, energetic, and relevant event in the Buddhist world. We would love you to join us.*[1]

Ever a champion of the adage "a picture is worth a thousand words," Aaron created a photo collage from the headshots featured on the conference website. The end result is a dead ringer for the collage Nora pointed to upon realizing that she associated Zen Buddhists not with Japanese Americans but with white people.

Aaron wasn't able to attend the Buddhist Geeks conference, but another of my interviewees was.

> *I remember the first Buddhist Geeks conference held at my school in Los Angeles, titled "The Emerging Face of Buddhism in America." I was drawn to its brand as a sangha for young-ish, technology-minded Buddhists. Overall, I enjoyed the conference and valued the motivations of the organizers and participants. Yet I pointed out to the audience that there are actually multiple "faces" of Buddhism in America, and I didn't particularly see that embodied in the content or representatives at the conference. Some people became defensive while others were receptive to my critique.... I noticed that the following year, the conference was amended to a more inclusive title: "The Emerging Faces of Buddhism in America." However, the presenters remain primarily Caucasian.*

Holly, a Vajrayana Buddhist practitioner of mixed Jewish and Japanese American heritage, emphasizes that these reflections are not borne of malice. Her aim is to "help Buddhist Geeks be an ally" to nonwhite Buddhists—in accordance with the organization's own stated value of inclusivity. She hopes her feedback can promote public dialogue about "the homogeneous representation and cosmetic fixes to American Buddhism's lack of diversity"—in this case, adding the *s* in *Faces* without noticeably diversifying the speaker lineup.

In her study of the Buddhist Geeks community, Ann Gleig mentions the lack of racial diversity at the organization's 2012 and 2013 conferences.[2] Capturing the full range of American Buddhism's emerging faces? Easier said than done.

2013 TECHNOBUDDHA CONFERENCE

The Middle Path

Striving for Happiness, Floating with Change

March 8–10, 2013

Jodo Shinshu Center, 2140 Durant Ave., Berkeley, CA 94704

All young adults (21–39) interested in Buddhism are welcome!

Keynote Speaker:

Rev. Inokoji-Kim

(Sacramento Betsuin)

Workshops (tentative):

Tai Chi

Taiko

Buddhism and Hip Hop Culture

... and more!

Judging from the flyer's simplicity, TechnoBuddha, now in its sixth year, had no pretensions of being the most innovative, energetic, and relevant event in the Buddhist world.

While the Buddhist Geeks and TechnoBuddha conferences were both founded by tech-savvy young adults with an inclusive vision of American Buddhism, TechnoBuddha could not boast that their inaugural conference was "received extremely well with nearly two hundred people in attendance, and ended up being featured in several publications, including *Fast Company, Tricycle,* and the *Los Angeles Times.*"[3]

The only publication I could find that featured TechnoBuddha was the BCA's decades-long-running newsletter *Wheel of Dharma.* In the April 2011 issue, Joanne Yuasa, a young adult Shin Buddhist from Vancouver, Canada, glowingly relates her experience at that year's conference ("It *is* worth traveling eight hundred miles for!"). Though coming from farthest away, Joanne was the first to arrive at the JSC, her "temple away from temple." Throughout the afternoon, Gen X and Gen Y Shin Buddhists trickled in from all over California, excited to connect with each other and explore the

2011 conference theme, "The Journey." The weekend's workshops included "Jodo Shinshu Etiquette," "Sex, Relationships, and Buddhism," "Dealing with Death," and the popular "Journey across the Dance Floor."

Naturally, the food was another highlight.

> *And what's a meeting of Jodo Shinshu Buddhists without good eats? There was plenty to be had, from Rev. Umezu's famous curry, to the Korean style "cook at your table" B-B-Q. These delicious meals would have been difficult to put together without the help of our core group of volunteers who seemed to have spent the entire day in the JSC kitchen prepping our food so that we could enjoy it. We are very grateful to them.*[4]

Rev. Imamura might have been on to something in his 1992 letter to *Tricycle* when he writes (partially in jest?) that "Asian Buddhists seem to just smile and eat together." Judging from Joanne's report, maybe this isn't such a bad thing.

Reflecting on the 2012 conference, themed "Who Am I? The Search for the Spiritual Self in the Digital Age," Steven Tamekuni recalls the humble origins of this annual gathering of young adult Buddhists.

> *The TechnoBuddha conference started out as just a networking conference for those who grew up in the Jodo Shinshu community. From there, it was discovered that all of us had the same mentality—that we wanted to be active in the temple still, but that it was very hard to do. This is because it seemed that there was no community for our age group within the larger temple community. People would go to temple up until they graduated from high school and then would disappear until their first child was born. The conference became a way for all of us who existed in this "gray area" to reconnect with fellow Jodo Shinshu Buddhists, and, of course, to make some new friends along the way.*[5]

Aaron was one of these new friends from outside the Shin community. Nobody at TechnoBuddha linked this upbeat young man with his online alter ego.

If Aaron hadn't persuaded me to attend, I'd likely have let my shyness get the better of me, mumbling an excuse about not having been raised in the BCA. But Aaron didn't grow up Shin Buddhist either. He didn't let that stop him from attending—and even helping to organize—TechnoBuddha.

If it hadn't been for the Angry Asian Buddhist, I might never have found out that the very building housing my graduate school was also, for one spring weekend every year, the home away from home for a primarily Asian American group of young adult Buddhists.

True to form, the Angry Asian Buddhist rejected the narrative of decline that hangs like a pall over American Shin Buddhism.

Traditional. Conservative. Static. Insular. Moribund. With assessments like these, it's little wonder that American Shin Buddhists are cast—and cast aside—as clannish foreigners, their sanghas relegated to "ethnic enclave" status.

It's hard not to internalize these negative portrayals. On more than one occasion, I've overheard Japanese American Shin Buddhists worry that their sangha's ethnic affiliation is a liability. All these Japanese elements—language, ritual, food, people—maybe they're unfairly alienating non–Japanese Americans?

These concerns about being insufficiently welcoming or accommodating are more than a little ironic given the long history of racism and discrimination against Japanese American Buddhists who, like Asian American Buddhists more generally, have been "doubly marginalized by virtue of race and religion."[6]

The young adult Shin Buddhists I interviewed, most of whom are fourth- and fifth-generation Americans, refuse to be dismissed as perpetual foreigners in a purportedly white and Christian nation. They see no contradiction in being Japanese and Buddhist and American. They celebrate the inclusive and dynamic sanghas they grew up in—communities that honor but are not reducible to their cultural origins.

"I can't imagine not being a part of my temple ... my heart is there." Dimples bloom beneath Nora's rosy cheekbones as she tells me about growing up in the BCA.

"I never thought of myself as quote-unquote highly religious; it was just a part of my life." She especially loved playing basketball with the church league. Thanks to the BCA's more than sixty temples, churches, and betsuin nationwide, Nora's Dharma buddies weren't just limited to her hometown. Sports tournaments, holiday celebrations, memorial services, and conferences with other middle- and high-school-age Shin Buddhists took her to BCA communities throughout California and even as far afield as New York.

Like Nora, Mari grew up attending weekly Sunday school at a BCA temple in California. She describes her church's summertime programming for youth as a turning point in her spiritual journey. "It was always nice to reflect and have each other during the summer.... That's where all of us got close." These friendships, which Mari has maintained into young adulthood, have kept her connected to her faith after moving away for college.

My conversations with young adult Shin Buddhists revealed a fount of fond memories. Making arts and crafts with kids their age at Sunday school after listening to that week's Dharma talk with their parents. Clasping their *onenju* or *ojuzu* in gassho, colorful prayer beads looped between pressed palms as they chanted the nembutsu. Watching their elders *oshoko* at the *obutsudan* or *onaijin* until offering a pinch of incense and bowing at their temple or home altars became second nature. Dancing at Obon under the summer sun with three generations of family members; learning about the festival's origins in the Japanese Buddhist custom of honoring ancestors who have passed away. Visiting the mother temple in Kyoto on BCA-sponsored youth group trips to Japan.

But these snapshots risk a static portrait. For all these commonalities, the religious journeys of young adult Shin Buddhists are anything but homogenous. Their spiritual paths are ever unfurling, often in unpredictable directions.

"My mom said we had to go to." Growing up, Landon was hardly an enthusiastic youth member of his church. He readily admits he didn't care about Buddhism. "I told the teacher this is stupid; this is not applicable to my life."

Personal challenges led him, rather skeptically and begrudgingly, back to the church. After reading a book about the Shin Buddhist concept of *akunin* (the evil person or one who cannot be saved), Landon came to appreciate the "strong base in Buddhism" his youth group leader had instilled. When he finally returned to his home temple, Landon discovered that "it was nice just to find a place to belong." Pretty soon he was spending most of his free time as a volunteer adviser for numerous BCA youth groups. A few years after our interview, he enrolled in the ministerial program at IBS.

Like Landon, Katrina's relationship with Shin Buddhism shifted from reluctant inheritance to active engagement. She too went to church at the insistence of her mom, who felt she and her sister lacked exposure to their Japanese heritage (their father is white).

In high school, Katrina's YBA adviser recommended that she attend Youth Advocacy Committee (YAC) training. "I went reluctantly—and learned so much about the religion." Katrina became closer to her home temple minister, an avid supporter of the YAC, who convinced her to take "just one class" from Mark Unno, a scholar and Shin Buddhist minister, at the University of Oregon. The result? "Religious studies quickly became one of my minors."

Unlike Katrina and Landon, Mari did not need parental coaxing to attend temple regularly. However, she became less engaged with church after high school, when she and many of her Dharma school friends moved away to more urban areas. Sunday services are no longer a part of her weekly routine, and TechnoBuddha is one of the rare occasions when she can spend extended amounts of time with other Buddhists her age. Nevertheless, Mari still considers Shin Buddhism to be an indispensable part of her life.

"It's okay that I haven't gone to church, because I can always go back to it." Mari came to this realization as a college student. During winter break, she went to an evening class at her home temple after a long stretch of not being back. On the car ride home, she experienced a moment of deep contentment in which she realized: "Whatever I'm doing, it's always there—I can always turn to it when I need to."

Her tradition may not be flashy, but it has stood the test of time. And for that, Mari is immensely grateful.

"The face of Jodo Shinshu Buddhists is changing. We're lucky enough to have a lot of people coming from different religions and different ethnic backgrounds.... It's a stereotype that they're all Japanese or Japanese American." As Nora points out, non-Japanese American converts to Shin Buddhism are diversifying the BCA. (Historians of American Shin Buddhism might add that the BCA has always included non-Japanese American members.)

Mari seconds Nora's observation. "Earlier in the interview I said I grew up in a completely Japanese American community at church, but really it's becoming a lot more diverse now. So it's changed. It's a positive change, in my mind."

Mari pinpoints two driving forces behind this change: "There's a lot of intermarriage and a lot of people who just find it on their own." One of her most influential spiritual teachers fits the latter category. "When I was in high school our minister was Caucasian, and he had great Dharma talks because he broke it down for outsiders." His sermons inspired Mari to reflect more deeply on the tradition of her upbringing. "Even though I had been exposed to Buddhism my whole life, there were things that were part of the ceremony of it but that I had never analyzed."

Mark Unno, the professor and minister who was so influential in Katrina's religious journey, observes that within the BCA, "increase in non-Japanese American participation has at times given rise to friction and contention between groups, but much of it has been energizing and helped to create a positive sense of diversity."[7]

Given the high rates of intermarriage among Japanese Americans and the increasing numbers of non-Japanese American converts to Jodo Shinshu, we would be remiss to assume that American Shin Buddhists are exclusively of Japanese heritage.[8] Three of the thirteen young adult Shin Buddhists I interviewed are of mixed race or ethnicity: Katrina's father is white; David is half-Chinese; Gabrielle's many ways of identifying include "mixed-race Asian American," "*gosei*, or fifth-generation Japanese American," and "second-generation Filipino-American by blood only." Nor is it accurate to assume that Japanese American Shin Buddhists are uniformly born into the religion. Gabrielle, for instance, was raised with an eclectic mix of religious influences but sought out Shin Buddhism in college.

These young adults defy the stereotypes of insularity and sectarianism that are all too often associated with Shin Buddhists. Kaila appreciates the Theravada Buddhist tradition of her Cambodian American fiancé (now husband) for deepening her understanding of Shin Buddhism—and hopes to raise their children with both. She embraces their religious and cultural differences as an opportunity "to think about Buddhism more critically" and find common reference points. Kaila was delighted to discover that she could follow along with some of the chants at the Khmer Buddhist temple—they weren't so different from the Sanskrit chants in Jodo Shinshu that she has long been familiar with.

"Religion for the younger generation is a choice.... It's not that generation Y is faithless, it's just that religion's no longer required."[9] Katrina's comment is fitting for a member of the "least religious" (and most racially diverse) generation in U.S. history.[10]

Landon agrees. "Growing up, my parents didn't have anywhere to go because Japanese people were discriminated against after the war. So the temple was a safe place. All your sports and all your friends were with the youth group, were with the church basketball team or kendo club or judo club." This was even more the case for issei and nisei Shin Buddhists before World War II for whom the BCA offered a spiritual, cultural, and social haven in a nation where many were hostile toward their "heathen" ilk. But nowadays, as Landon puts it, "you just assimilate to whatever your social group is that you're living with, and then there's no need to come back to church, because you have your outside friends, whether it's another Asian group, or Caucasian, or African American, or Latino."

Fortunately, Japanese American Shin Buddhists who came of age half a century after the end of internment do not face the egregious levels of discrimination and segregation their forebears did. There is a flip side to this, however. As Testuden Kashima notes, since "social adversity can help reinforce solidarity," a "more benign social climate" lessens the need for BCA members to stay within the organization.[11] Increased freedom to explore spiritual and social options outside the community explains the absence of sansei (third-generation) and *yonsei* (fourth-generation) Japanese Americans from the BCA's *fujinkai* (Buddhist Women's Association).[12]

Dr. Kashima was interned as an infant with his family during World War II and went on to become a scholar of Asian American studies and sociology. His research on the BCA in the 1970s helped pioneer the budding subfield of American Buddhist studies. Assessing the organization a quarter-century later, Dr. Kashima underscores an additional challenge for the Buddhist Churches of America: pressure to assimilate to a Christian milieu.[13]

Pressure to convert to Christianity may not be as overt for Japanese American Buddhist millennials as it was for issei and nisei Buddhists, but it certainly still exists. Kaila traces a trajectory from past to present in response to the Pew Forum's 2012 statistics on the "net loss" of Asian American Buddhists. "This makes me very sad.... A lot of this could be due to the pressures of Asian American Buddhists to assimilate into American society, which means becoming Christian. I think a lot of this pressure stems from the incarceration of people of Japanese ancestry during World War II and society telling them that in order to be a good American you must be Christian."

It's not just white Americans doing the pressuring; Kaila has met "Asian American Christians who think that Asian American Buddhists are too old-school and haven't really tried to become 'American.'" The Pew Forum presents some striking statistics to corroborate this observation. The 2012 report indicates that 44 percent of Asian American Christians think of themselves as "a typical American" compared to just 32 percent of Asian American Buddhists.[14] Conversely, 59 percent of Asian American Buddhists consider themselves to be "very different" from a typical American compared to 49 percent of Asian American Christians.[15]

What does this bode for the future? Rev. Kuwahara, a Jodo Shinshu minister from Japan who now serves at a temple in the Bay Area, wonders whether diversification within the BCA will eventually result in the attrition of the organization's Japanese American roots. Gabrielle and Kaila's response to this possibility is to redouble their efforts as proud representatives of their ethnicity and faith. Other young adult Shin Buddhists, however, believe preserving the tradition in the United States requires moving beyond its cultural roots. Katrina thinks that "growing this religion in America can no longer rely on the Asian community." Landon concurs, predicting that "it's going to have to be other ethnic populations who keep the religion going in the next hundred years"—though his own extensive involvement with BCA youth is proof to the contrary.

If Landon's prediction pans out and non-Japanese Americans become the primary stewards of American Shin Buddhism, would this be a sign of dilution, decline, and decay—or just another development in Jodo Shinshu's history of adapting to changing circumstances? Would these future members preserve Japanese American cultural traditions within the BCA—or would they make major reforms, such as eliminating Japanese-language chants? These questions encapsulate the tension Japanese American Shin Buddhists face between the ethnically specific, sectarian roots of their religion and the universal nature of the BCA's mission "to promote the Buddha, Dharma, and Sangha as well as to propagate the Jodo Shinshu teachings."[16]

Long hair pulled back in a ponytail, Landon mulls over this tension. Perched on a kid-size chair in a Sunday school classroom, he looks as relaxed as if he were lounging on his living room couch. Landon had proposed that we meet at a BCA church in the South Bay—the very church he had spurned and later returned to. As we walked past the rock garden at the temple entrance, he showed me evidence of his long history with the community: a worn but still-functional bench he built in 1996 for an Eagle Scout project.

It occurs to me that while Landon may not experience the backlash previous generations of Japanese Americans did, he might not be so different from the Shin Buddhist nisei who found in their "religiously sponsored organizations and activities a place where they belonged."[17]

Landon can certainly relate to a Japanese American elder of the sansei generation who attended this very temple in the 1950s and 1960s and went on to study at IBS in the 1970s to become a Shin Buddhist minister. "I felt at home" at the Jodo Shinshu church, Rev. Kenneth Tanaka recalls in his contribution to *Dharma, Color, and Culture: New Voices in Western Buddhism*. By contrast, the conservative Christian church he attended for two years as a child only reinforced his sense of marginalization. "Today, I resist any attempt to identify Buddhism with any particular ethnic or cultural group," Rev. Tanaka emphasizes.[18] Nonetheless, he remains indebted to the BCA for developing his confidence as a person of color and supporting him ethnically, culturally, and religiously in a way the Seventh-Day Adventist Church of his youth could not.

How then, to reconcile the BCA's universalist-particularist tension? Yes, Landon had predicted that other ethnic groups would carry American Shin Buddhism forward into the next century. Yes, he raised his hackles if any Japanese Americans at church seemed unwelcoming toward members who didn't share their ethnicity. Yes, he thought religion and culture were becoming increasingly decoupled for younger Japanese American Shin Buddhists due to intermarriage and Japanese language attrition.

But even Landon cannot imagine—and will not condone—a complete severance of the connection between Jodo Shinshu and Japanese American culture. He defends his community against complaints by Caucasians who think too much Japanese is used in Shin Buddhist services. As Landon explains to me during our interview, many of these Japanese terms contain key Buddhist teachings. *Okagesama desu* reminds him that "because of you, I am who I am." *Ichi-go ichi-e* ("one time, one meeting") reminds him to "be mindful of now."

In discussing the ways that language and history are integral to American Shin Buddhism, Landon cautions against discarding these cultural roots. In arguing that American Shin Buddhism does not belong solely to Japanese Americans, Landon warns against promoting cultural essentialism. In short, Landon advocates for a middle ground between ethnic erasure and ethnic insularity.

As does Gabrielle: "My Japanese Buddhist faith (Jodo Shinshu) often goes hand-in-hand with my Japanese American values and identity," she writes, but this does not diminish her conviction that "Buddhist communities and the Dharma should be open to all people regardless of background or skin color."

When I ask how she would categorize American Buddhists, Katrina responds with an emphasis on interconnectedness. "I wouldn't separate us. That seems to introduce an element of exclusivity that doesn't belong.... I would rather be inclusive."

Her ideal Buddhist community? "A diverse group of individuals that both embraces its Asian history and looks toward its diverse future."

LINEAGE

A few hours before TechnoBuddha 2013 is slated to begin, I am nervously rearranging vegan cookies at the kitchen table. My seventh interviewee is on his way to the Berkeley apartment where Trent and I live. I told our guest to look for the overgrown bougainvillea and apologized in advance for the broken doorbell.

The most recent interview for my master's thesis, conducted a week ago at this very kitchen table, went well. Born and raised in the Bay Area, Alyssa recently started exploring Buddhist teachings and practice. Her religious upbringing had been "very agnostic, at times atheist," though her mother grew up praying to Guanyin. Alyssa was back in California for spring break during a yearlong stint as an English teacher at a college for Buddhist monastics in China. Struggling to understand her place in American Buddhism, she did a Google search and stumbled across my project. Our animated conversation spanned nearly four hours.

A rap on the window announces the arrival of interviewee number seven. It's hard to believe we are finally meeting in person after half a year of exchanging emails.

I open the door to a megawatt smile. Fueled by three hours of sleep, half an hour of morning meditation, and more cups of coffee than he dares remember, Aaron is ready to dive right into our interview.

Five hours later, the table holds a plate of crumbs, a stack of scribbled-on papers, and a voice recorder that ran out of batteries mid-interview. Indefatigable, Aaron heads straight over to TechnoBuddha. I promise to be there right after I finish jotting down notes from our conversation.

"Can you tell me a bit about the importance of Buddhism in your life?"

Aaron half groans, half laughs. "It's so interwoven with everything in my life it's sort of annoying for people ..."

It hasn't always been that way. Aaron's dad went to a Catholic school, identified as Buddhist for a time, then converted to Judaism after marrying his mom. They raised their son Jewish. Aaron started meditating after moving from the Bay Area to Illinois during high school. The meditation led him to read up on Buddhism in an actual encyclopedia.

"The internet in 1998 was not what it is now. Was there even Wikipedia then?" Aaron wonders.

We resist the urge to consult our phones during the interview, so I look it up later: nope, not until 2001. Even without checking his phone, Aaron brings up enough names during our conversation to populate multiple Buddhist basketball teams.

One of Aaron's Jewish classmates in high school was really into Buddhism. Aaron tells me how he went up to Jared during drama rehearsal, having pored over the encyclopedia the previous day, "just to see if I could sort of mess with him."

"Hey Jared, I read about bodhisattvas. I'm a bodhisattva."

Jared paused, then calmly replied, "We all are."

Aaron was stunned. "My mind's like—poof! Explosion! What does that mean? I really had to learn about this ..."

As an undergrad at the University of California, Los Angeles, Aaron helped found the University Buddhist Association. "And the rest is history," he says with a cheeky grin.

Back in college, when Aaron didn't have a car, another UCLA student offered to drive him downtown and show him around. That classmate had grown up in the Sacramento Betsuin of the BCA and introduced Aaron to Jodo Shinshu. Later, while earning a master's degree in Illinois, Aaron connected with the Buddhist Temple of Chicago and the Midwest Buddhist Temple. When MBT hosted the Eastern Buddhist League, Aaron volunteered to shuttle people to and from the airport—and got to know a lot more Shin Buddhists in the process.

Aaron felt an affinity for Japanese American Buddhists: "I come from an Asian American community that also has deep roots in the U.S."—though admittedly he had met only a handful of Toishanese Buddhists. As a mixed Ashkenazi Jewish Toishanese American, Aaron recognized "there isn't really a cultural niche for me." That didn't stop him from volunteering at Shin Buddhist churches. Aaron cherished these multigenerational sanghas even if they didn't emphasize meditation (which was central to his own Buddhist practice). He defended these communities against those who dismissed them as mere social clubs. Something he always appreciated: "There's no cost to entry. You just show up and you're part of the community."

The Jodo Shinshu Center lobby swells with enthusiastic greetings. Beneath the snow-white Dharma wheel, we sign up for workshops. Atop the multicolored tile lotus, we play card games at tables laden with snacks. Before the bronze gaze of Shinran, we volunteer for next year's organizing committees.

After the closing service on the last day of the conference, we line up outside the kodo to sign dozens of thank-you cards. TechnoBuddha is, in principle, run by and for young adults between the ages of twenty-one and thirty-nine, but older BCA members help out every year as keynote speakers, workshop leaders, kitchen volunteers, and logistics coordinators. Their behind-the-scenes support is a reminder of the intergenerational efforts that make this twenty-first-century gathering of young adult Buddhists possible.

This year marked TechnoBuddha's largest gathering to date, with over sixty of us in attendance. Rev. Inokoji-Kim delivered a Dharma talk on applying Buddhism to the challenges of young adulthood. In his write-up for the April 2013 issue of *Wheel of Dharma,* Aaron celebrates the ripple effect of the conference: "The desire to learn more about Buddhism and to be part of a community is strong, and many of the participants are Dharma school teachers and youth minister's assistants. The conference's success has even inspired participants to launch local young adult groups and conferences in their hometowns, including the Central Valley and Los Angeles, just to name two."[1]

In the group photo that accompanies Aaron's article, we each wear lanyards sporting our name and a sticker identifying which cleanup crew we're part of (I'm on Team Sheep). The image shows a sea of smiling faces, a traveling monk behind us. A stark contrast to the collage that had startled Nora into realizing it was not faces like her own that came to mind when she thought of American Zen Buddhism.

"What are three things you would want people to know about Asian American Buddhists?"

It takes Aaron a full ten minutes to work out his answer to this interview question. He would want to make sure that people had an understanding of Buddhism first—but he wouldn't want that understanding to be reduced to a sound bite. "I don't actually know what I want people to know about Buddhism. I think I would want something that all Buddhists would be happy with, and I don't know if you could find that. That's why the diversity is really important."

Aaron ventures a possibility. "Um, maybe the Four Noble Truths?" But then he decides it can't just be reduced to that, given the reaction he's heard in some quarters ("Buddhists are pessimists who hate life!").

Finally, upon further deliberation, Aaron relents and offers a sound bite. "Understand that Asian Americans are interwoven into the history of Buddhism in the United States going back well over a century."

In a 2016 post on her blog *Taste of Chicago Buddhism*, Rev. Patti Nakai, sansei resident minister at the Buddhist Temple of Chicago, applauds an emerging generation of Asian American Buddhists. Watching Asian American youth receive community service awards at the Asian American Coalition of Chicago's annual Lunar New Year banquet, Rev. Nakai observes that while some of the awardees thank God or Jesus for their accomplishments, others express how the Buddha's teachings inspire their community service work.

> *Just as in the past century there were Asian American Buddhists who brought their practice of Buddhist principles into their workplaces and social circles, there's a new and growing crop of young people making their voices heard and organizing for change in society. Let's not dismiss their grounding in the Buddhist teachings as "outdated" because they didn't learn from white teachers who claim transmission from charismatic gurus. If anything, their grounding is more grounded because they have an appreciation of Buddhism as a tradition that goes back many generations, many centuries, not just something that popped up in the U.S. when beatniks started reading D. T. Suzuki.[2]*

Rev. Nakai fights back against the stereotype that "engaged Buddhism" belongs to white convert communities while Asian American Buddhists are "trapped in their old-country modes of rituals and superstitions." She's not the only minister in her tradition to dispute the portrayal of Asian American Buddhists as conservative and passive. In an article on the long-standing acceptance of same-sex marriage in the BCA, Jeff Wilson highlights how Shin Buddhist activism extends beyond the issue of gay rights.

> *Referencing their own history of discrimination, Buddhist Churches of America members have advocated for the rights of African Americans, American Muslims, Native Americans, and other groups, both in their denominational publications and through lobbying the government. This can be seen as part of a long history of pioneering work on social issues by Shin Buddhists, including the creation of the first American Buddhist prison ministries, hospital chaplains, charitable organizations, women's groups, schools, and so on.[3]*

We see an example of this advocacy for marginalized groups in a statement against the January 2017 executive order banning travelers from seven Muslim-majority countries. "We strongly oppose any actions that lead to discrimination against certain groups just because of their ethnicity or faith," BCA bishop Rev. Umezu declares. It's a topic that hits close to home for the Shin Buddhist community: the ban "brought back memories of the unlawful mass incarceration of Japanese Americans during World War II."[4]

Four years after our interview, as the embattled Muslim travel ban wends its way through the courts, Alyssa sends me an email.

> *I was just listening to a podcast on the history of making Manzanar a national monument and about the annual pilgrimage to Manzanar, and found links to Densho, a digital archive of the Japanese American experience from the 1900s onward. Clicking through the collections, there are a lot of old photographs, many of Buddhist church events and social life, buildings, etc.*
>
> *Asian American Buddhism goes deep.... Here are the photographs to prove it.[5]*

How easy it would have been for me to remain ignorant about the depths of this history. How easy it would have been for me not to learn:

Manzanar is one of the ten concentration camps where Japanese Americans are unconstitutionally incarcerated during World War II. Young sansei spearhead the first annual Manzanar Pilgrimage in 1969. In 1992, Sue Kunitomi Embrey, who had been interned at Manzanar, flies to Washington to testify before the U.S. Senate subcommittee on Public Lands, National Parks, and Forests. She successfully appeals to have Manzanar designated a National Historic Site.[6]

A 1944 service for fifty soldiers at Fort Snelling is believed to be the first Buddhist service ever delivered in an Army installation in the United States. A majority of nisei troops are Buddhist, yet nisei units such as the 442nd Infantry Regiment are only allowed Christian chaplains.

A few weeks after Pearl Harbor, ten-year-old Masumi Kimura cries as her father burns her beloved Hinamatsuri dolls and every other Japanese artifact they own: the cost of proving their family's loyalty to America. Mr. Kimura can't bring himself to burn the Buddhist scriptures that have been passed down through multiple generations. He wraps the sacred texts in a kimono cloth and buries them in a tin box on his property. After the war, the Kimuras discover that they have lost their home, their farm, and all the valuables they stored for safekeeping at the Fresno Buddhist temple.[7]

As a ten-year-old in Pennsylvania, I am glued to the TV as Kristi Yamaguchi flies across ice. What holds me rapt is not her sequined dress or her impossible stunts, but the realization that her face is like mine. There is only one other student in my whole elementary school with a face like mine. Our teachers mix up our names sometimes. Much later, an interviewee will inform me that the first Asian American figure skater to win an Olympic gold medal grew up in the Jodo Shinshu community.

Shinjo Nagatomi was a Buddhist priest incarcerated at Manzanar. His son Masatoshi went on to become Harvard University's first full-time professor of Buddhist studies.[8] Upon Masatoshi Nagatomi's death in 2000, his widow Masumi (née Kimura) asks one of Professor Nagatomi's graduate students, Duncan Ryuken Williams, to sort through her late husband's papers. Among the documents are several sermons in an unfamiliar handwriting. Duncan, a Soto Zen priest of Japanese-British heritage who is completing his PhD in religion and has already served as Harvard's first Buddhist chaplain, will go on to become a professor of religion and East Asian culture at USC. But at the moment, he puzzles over the sermons, which were penned not by his PhD advisor but by his advisor's father. Duncan doesn't yet know that these Dharma talks, delivered in a tarpaper barracks in Manzanar, will send him on a seventeen-year research journey to unearth the wartime history of Japanese American Buddhists.[9]

The first commissioned Buddhist chaplain in the U.S. Armed Forces is a Shin Buddhist minister. Lt. Jeanette Shin graduated from the Institute of Buddhist Studies and became an active duty chaplain in 2006.[10]

Learning about Rev. Imamura's letter to *Tricycle* on the *Angry Asian Buddhist* blog, Funie Hsu, a 1.75-generation Taiwanese American Buddhist, feels for the first time a sense of community with other Asian American Buddhists who share her commitment to diversity and social justice.[11] In early 2015 Funie interviews Arun about his blog.[12]

In November 2016, @arunlikhati tweets: "Never in my life did I expect to see @buddhadharma publish a piece on #WhiteSupremacy in #AmericanBuddhism. Wow!" *Buddhadharma* magazine has just published "We've Been Here All Along," with the lede: "Funie Hsu says it's time we recognize the contributions of Asian American Buddhists and address the racism and cultural appropriation that marginalizes their ongoing role in transmitting the Dharma in the West." The article showcases several historical photos, including an image, courtesy of the Japanese American National Museum, of more than fifty members of the Bakersfield Buddhist Church, tots to elders all dressed to the nines. In the course of her research, Funie has extensive conversations with Rev. Imamura.[13]

Angry letters, ad hominem attacks, defensive indignation. The backlash to "We've Been Here All Along" catches *Buddhadharma* editor Tynette Deveaux off guard. She issues a response to critics with a message in support of Funie's article by Ajahn Amaro, a European monk in the Thai forest tradition.[14]

Somewhere in the soil of the Central Valley, swaddled sutras rest in a container meant for rice crackers.[15] Above ground in Fresno's Chinatown,

Lynn Ikeda runs one of the nation's oldest Japanese American businesses. Founded in 1915 by Lynn's grandfather, who managed to continue honing his craft even while interned, Kogetsu-Do ships their popular *manju* (mochi filled with a cornucopia of flavors, from red bean to cinnamon apple to chocolate macadamia) across California (and even, occasionally, across state lines).[16]

At the 2018 TechnoBuddha, I reach into a pink cardboard box expecting a doughnut and pull out a pillowy Japanese confectionary instead. One bite: pure rapture. It takes all my self-control to save the other half for my fiancé. That evening, with rice flour dotting his face, Trent agrees that this has to be the "cake" at our wedding.

Seventy pieces of manju fly out to southeast Arkansas for the 2018 pilgrimage to the Rohwer and Jerome concentration camps. Actor George Takei speaks to the pilgrims about the injustice of the mass removal. He speaks from personal experience, having been sent to Rohwer with his family when he was four years old. Among the audience are twenty survivors of the two camps, some in their nineties; a family of thirteen with four nisei siblings; sansei from across the country; yonsei from London. They leave with accordion-folded books styled after National Park Service passports and temple stamp books in Japan. Covered in Japanese textiles and handmade by volunteers, the books' pages hold commemorative stamps for each visit to a Japanese American concentration camp.[17]

A string of texts from Funie: "Duncan got George Takei to do his book trailer!" "Ryo Imamura told us that it was his mom that got George Takei to consider taking up acting." "Ryo showed us a picture of George Takei in a BCA performance."[18]

American Sutra: A Story of Faith and Freedom in the Second World War hit bookshelves on February 19, 2019, the National Day of Remembrance. Seventy-seven years ago on this date, President Roosevelt signed Executive Order 9066, authorizing the internment of 120,000 Japanese Americans.

On July 20, 2019, thousands of paper cranes fly to Fort Sill, Oklahoma. Braving 102-degree heat, hundreds of protestors—including representatives from the Japanese American group Tsuru for Solidarity (*tsuru* meaning "crane"), the American Indian Movement, United We Dream, and Black Lives Matter, as well as twenty-five Buddhist clergy and lay leaders—march with the cranes. Fort Sill Army Base, the World War II concentration camp where two Japanese immigrants had been shot to death by U.S. Army guards seventy-seven years ago, is now slated to confine 1,400 asylum-seeking children from Central America who have been separated from their families.[19]

Strings of colorful tsuru surround a makeshift altar that holds a framed photo of Kanesaburo Oshima—who was shot in the back of the head by a guard at Fort Sill in May 1942—alongside a Buddha statue carved at Manzanar in 1943. The Buddhist contingent, Duncan Williams among them, leads a memorial service for the Japanese and Native Americans who died at Fort Sill and the migrant children who perished under Border Patrol custody. Rev. William Briones, grandson of Mexican immigrants and head minister of the Los Angeles Hompa Hongwanji Buddhist Temple, leads the chanting of the *Juseige* (Three Sacred Vows) of the Jodo Shinshu tradition as protestors bring forth paper *ihai,* memorial tablets with the names of loved ones who have died or are suffering due to family separation, indefinite detention, and deportation.

Four days later, plans to house migrant children at the facility are put on hold. The organizers put out a call for further action. "One camp closed. There is still work to be done. Turning up, speaking up. Cranes to be folded."

Thanks to Funie's unstinting efforts, Rev. Imamura's letter was finally printed in its complete, uncensored form in 2017. It had taken a quarter of a century. Introducing the letter on the Buddhist Peace Fellowship website in an article titled "Lineage of Resistance: When Asian American Buddhists Confront White Supremacy," Funie writes:

> *We want to preserve the integrity of the statement in its entirety as a political act of recovery. Although BPF may not necessarily share the sentiment of every statement in the letter, we stand behind the importance of making it available for public consideration. Thus, we encourage dialogue about*

*thoughts and different perspectives on the letter. For example, though I
am greatly appreciative of the letter, I disagree with some assertions made
about Asian American Buddhists, as they don't ring true with my experience. (Such is the diverse reality and complexity of the category "Asian
American.") However, being able to access and read these thoughts from
a fellow Asian American raised in the Buddhist tradition makes possible the very opportunity to disagree and be in conversation.* It makes
community possible, and for Asian American Buddhists, such pan-
sectarian, sacred spaces are very much needed.[20]

Accompanying her words is an image bearing the caption: "Grandfather
and grandson of Japanese ancestry at the War Relocation Authority center
in Manzanar, California. Photo by Dorothea Lange, censored by the U.S.
government until 2006, now public domain."

Matching black hair and white shirts. Salt-and-pepper mustache on
the wizened face of one, small scabs on the otherwise smooth face of the
other. The grandfather carries his grandson; the posture should be one of
joy (what child doesn't love a piggyback?) but the boy is draped with eyes
downcast, lips unsmiling, hands hidden beneath the older man's wrinkled
fingers. A sense of sorrow. And also, of buried hope.

Reading his 1992 letter to *Tricycle* for the umpteenth time, I still can't
figure out what Rev. Imamura means by "we Asians are like Hun-tun
(Chaos) and like tofu, seemingly lacking the seven discriminating holes
in the head and persisting unobtrusively in new and often hostile environments." To me, *hun-tun* are a celebration: flour on my mother's arms,
a tongue of dough stretching from the silver mouth of a pasta maker,
an inverted drinking glass biting the dough into coaster-size rounds, a
mountain of freshly made filling swallowed into parcels, the sweet tang
of Zhenjiang vinegar, the tough choice of which dumpling I will sink my
chopsticks into first.

That doesn't seem to be what Rev. Imamura is referring to. It is Funie who
persuades me to reach out to him directly. Voilà: in less than twenty-four

hours, mystery solved. Hun-tun is a reference to Chuang Tzu's collected works, from Burton Watson's 1968 translation:

> *The emperor of the South Sea was called Shu [Brief], the emperor of the North Sea was called Hu [Sudden], and the emperor of the central region was called Hun-tun [Chaos]. Shu and Hu from time to time came together for a meeting in the territory of Hun-tun, and Hun-tun treated them very generously. Shu and Hu discussed how they could repay his kindness. "All men," they said, "have seven openings so they can see, hear, eat, and breathe. But Hun-tun alone doesn't have any. Let's trying boring him some!" Every day they bored another hole, and on the seventh day Hun-tun died.*[21]

Rev. Imamura interprets this story as a "myth of de-creation" that cautions against the dangers of excessive ego. To him, hun-tun symbolizes the unconscious as the creative matrix of life, which is constantly under attack by conscious interference as represented by the emperors Shu and Hu.[22]

"It appears to me that white and Asian Buddhists live in two discrete worlds and practice different forms of Buddhism." So begins the long paragraph that presents the "two Buddhisms" story in a nutshell in Rev. Imamura's 1992 letter. Twenty-five years later, this story no longer seems to be able to contain the hun-tun of American Buddhism. Still, I admire the balance of humility and forthrightness in the letter. "I may have made some gross generalizations," Rev. Imamura acknowledges—but he asserts his perspective nonetheless, uncowed by the prevailing white Buddhist voices.

When Rev. Imamura wrote to Helen Tworkov in 1992, I didn't yet know that the stuff at the center of the hun-tun I loved had an English name. I knew the filling only by its Chinese name: *xinzi*. The heart.

To me, the last sentence of Rev. Imamura's letter perfectly captures the heart of his message: "We do exist, and have feelings that can be bruised by unthinking comments!" A call for recognition. An appeal to kindness.

Enduring incarceration. Resisting marginalization. Fighting for freedom. I think of the tireless efforts of countless Japanese American Shin Buddhists and their allies. People past and present who have trailblazed—are trailblazing—a path for future generations of Asian American Buddhists to practice their faith as racial and religious minorities. The largely unheralded efforts of these mostly anonymous individuals are a gift whose reach extends far beyond the bounds of their own communities.

Gassho.

PART 2

BRIDGE-BUILDERS

The volunteers who are running the Buddhist youth group—we were that youth at one point. We are there because we think it's important. We're bridging that gap. We're creating that space.

—LARENE

GAPS

Los Angeles: some say it's the most diverse Buddhist city in the world.[1] Yet in 2014, UCLA undergrad Mara Guevarra was having trouble with her field-based research project for a class on Buddhism:

> *I wanted to study second-generation Korean Americans, people my age. In the traditional temples there's a concentrated demographic of first-generation Koreans aged sixty-plus, but at Dharma Zen Center it was a mostly white American community with Korean American teachers. This surprised me—you know they exist, but where are the second-generation Asian American Buddhists?*[2]

Five years earlier, Rohan Gunatillake was wondering the same thing in a February 2009 blog post titled "Second Generation Practitioners ... Where Are You?"

> *If you are (or know of) a practitioner of Sri Lankan, Thai, Burmese, Japanese, Tibetan, Chinese, Cambodian, Vietnamese, etc. origin but*

were born and brought up in the West, I would be endlessly grateful to hear from you. I know how precious my heritage is to my practice and feel there is much joy to be had in the connection with others in my rather unique position—this band of second-generation meditators stuck in the middle as the clashing rocks of East and West smash beautifully together.[3]

Reading Mihiri Tillakaratne's 2012 master's thesis about the Sri Lankan youth members of two Theravada temples in LA, I saw that Rohan wasn't alone in yearning for greater attention to the unique issues second-generation Asian American Buddhists face. As one of Tillakartne's interviewees puts it:

Sometimes I wish there would be a more explicit recognition of the collective experiences of second-generation Sri Lankan American Buddhists. Growing up in the United States, race is an overwhelmingly powerful factor for me, but I'm often grouped, as someone still learning about [the] basics of Buddhism, under the same rubric as young white Americans who are simply "exploring" Buddhism, and who haven't had to suffer any of the burdens growing up with the Buddhist faith in a racialized context. At the same time, I'm occasionally critiqued for not knowing how to be "Sri Lankan Buddhist," while young whites are praised for just being at the temple. There are completely different sets of expectations, and I just wish someone would recognize this.[4]

I wasn't raised in a Buddhist household, but I can relate to these "completely different sets of expectations" based on race. When I began exploring Buddhism in college, at the very meditation centers where I was taught that attachment to racial identity is a hindrance to enlightenment (race is illusory, bringing it up is divisive, talking about it signals a lack of wisdom and compassion, and so on), I was never allowed to forget my race. Kindly white folks marveled at my "unaccented" English, asked where I was *really* from, assumed my parents were Buddhist—which they did not do to their fellow white practitioners.

But then, the "two Buddhisms" typology wouldn't have me attending these predominantly white meditation centers in the first place.

"Two Buddhisms" divides "Asian immigrants [who] maintain practices coincident with ritual activity or Pure Land observance, depending on the nature of the parent tradition of their community" from "American converts [who] gravitate toward the various meditation traditions."[5] As an Asian American immigrant whose parent tradition is atheism, and whose Buddhist practice has spanned chanting, ritual, and meditation, which of the two camps am I supposed to belong to?

As I would come to learn, even young adult Asian Americans who *are* Buddhist by inheritance feel alienated by these dichotomized portrayals.

Thirty-six of my eighty-nine interviewees are second-generation Asian Americans whose first-generation immigrant parents raised them within the Buddhist faith. They represent all the heritages on Rohan's list (Burmese, Cambodian, Chinese, Japanese, Sri Lankan, Thai, Tibetan, Vietnamese) and more (Indonesian, Korean, Laotian, Malaysian, Taiwanese). Even so, the group hardly exhausts the diversity of Buddhist Asian America (I didn't interview any second-generation Bangladeshi, Bhutanese, Dai, Kalmyk, Mongolian, Nepali, or Shan Buddhists, for instance).

These second-generation young adults differ from their first-generation parents, who share their children's status as racial and religious minorities in America but typically grew up in an Asian country where they enjoyed majority status. They differ from white Buddhists, who may be religious minorities but are still the privileged racial majority in America. They differ from multi-generation and convert Asian American Buddhists, who are the focus of part 1 and part 3 of this book, respectively.

"Two Buddhisms" would have us look for second-generation Asian Americans in temples with others of the same ethnic, linguistic, and Buddhist background. But what about the young adults whose chosen Buddhist communities don't mirror the ethnicity, language, or denomination of their upbringing? What about those who don't feel a sense of belonging in their parents' temples—or in majority-white sanghas either?

As I would come to learn, articulating and asserting Buddhist identities of their own is no simple feat for second-generation Asian American Buddhists.

Birdsong. A man in a short-sleeved shirt and khaki shorts walks his golden retriever under a cloudless blue sky. They pass by single-story suburban homes, palm and oak trees.

A manga poster. Next to it a handmade poster reads "Badminton 2003" in neat handwriting and NATHAN in cutout letters alongside construction paper-mounted photos of a teenage boy.

Three Taoist deities. The colorful ceramic gods share the shelf with a small golden statue of a seated Shakyamuni and a framed photograph of an elderly Asian woman in black robes.

A woman's voice in Mandarin. "他們到了高中就比較不跟我到寺廟去." English subtitles translate her words: "When they were in high school, they stopped going to temples with me." On the screen, a middle-aged woman sits next to her mustachioed son on a two-seater sofa. A magnet-covered refrigerator and Costco-size boxes of cereal and granola bars peek out from behind their heads.

"不過他們也知道寺廟, 去是拜佛, 知道自己父母親是愛佛教的. 然後後來他自己 find out, 他自己的一些朋友又去 volunteer, 他們就是做義工. 我就是說, 你同學做義工了, 你為什麼不去跟著做義工? 他就跟著去了."

("But they knew that you pray to the Buddha at temples and that their parents are Buddhist. And then later on, he found out that his friend was volunteering at a temple. I told him that he should go volunteer with his classmate. So he went to volunteer.")

"也許他們懂得佛教比較多, 因為他們去法印寺, 也許師父會告訴他們, 就是說解釋, 告訴他們一些佛教的東西, 也許他比較深入了解, 多過於我了!"

("Maybe they know more about Buddhism. Maybe the *shifu* [monastics] at Dharma Seal Temple explain Buddhist teachings to them. Maybe now he knows more than I do!")

The woman giggles. Nathan shakes his head from side to side and responds in English, a quizzical look on his face. "I'm not sure, Mom, what do—what do you mean by the last, well, the last, like, thirty seconds? What was—what did you mean about ..."

His mom switches from Mandarin to English.

"Well, I mean, it's like, you going to temple and volunteer, right?"

"Yeah," Nathan affirms.

"So maybe you know more than me now, because right now, you know, you meet the shifu and the shifu will be tell you, explain to you a lot about the Buddha or whatever."

"Oh, Mom, I don't talk to the shifu about the Buddha," Nathan responds, laughing.

"No?" His mom leans back, surprised. "So, I don't know, you go volunteer—I don't know what you doing over there ..."

Fade to black.

What exactly has Terry Shwe Tam's son been doing over at Dharma Seal Temple in Rosemead, California? The remaining twenty-five minutes of *Youth Group,* a 2015 documentary film by Wanwan Lu, devotes itself to this question.

We learn how Nathan and his fellow BOCA youth group advisers Larene, John, and Andrew guide weekly meditations, icebreakers, and Buddhism-related lectures in English for the temple youth.[6] We meet more than a dozen other members of the predominantly Asian American group, who do community service and take field trips together in addition to their Sunday gatherings at Dharma Seal. Andrew and Larene are former youth group members who became advisers. Nathan got involved after hearing about BOCA from his high-school buddy John, who is white.

"The congregation at Dharma Seal is of a certain generation," Larene explains. Cut to an image of older Asian congregants sitting on a bench by the temple parking lot, one of them holding a cane.

"And it might not be something that translates quite as easily to youth." Inside the main hall, rows of clay-colored kneelers perch largely unoccupied on polished gray tile. An older Asian woman in black and brown robes sits on one of the kneelers, studying a Chinese sutra. In front of her, another woman—also Asian, also older, also in layperson robes—performs three full-body prostrations.

"There's so many differences, and there's so much gap in language, culture, etcetera," Larene continues.

Which is why it's all the more important that young adults like Larene—who were those puzzled temple youth not so long ago—are there to support a new generation of Asian American Buddhists. Because there is no shortage to the challenges they have to face, the gaps they need to bridge, the spaces they want to build.

"How could we retain and learn new sutras if we could not understand the language in which they were expressed?" asks Dedunu.

Though she grew up as an active member of the Sri Lankan Sinhalese American Buddhist community in Staten Island, Dedunu found herself attending temple ceremonies less frequently because of the language barrier. Despite consistent encouragement from one of the monks at her temple, Dedunu's motivation to become fluent in Sinhalese was outweighed by her embarrassment over having an American accent, shame about being a slow learner, and "desire to assimilate into white America."

Ratema can relate. She and her older sister grew up going to a Cambodian Buddhist temple in Oakland, California, but their visits tapered off as they get older. "It's hard being around people who speak your language when you don't understand them.... It's kind of shameful. So I guess that's one of the reasons why we stopped going." But Ratema didn't give up hope of one day being able to understand the temple chants and communicate with older temple-goers, including her own grandparents. In her freshman year, she enrolled in a Khmer language class at UC Berkeley; I was cross-registered in the course as an IBS grad student. By our second semester, Ratema was glad to be speaking "less broken Cambodian" compared to the "really, really broken Cambodian" of her childhood.

It wasn't just Dedunu and Ratema. For most of the second-generation young adults I interviewed, language is an obstacle to connecting with their parents' Buddhism. Lacking fluency in their parents' native tongue— Burmese, Cambodian, Mandarin, Sinhala, Tibetan, Vietnamese, and so forth—they find everything from understanding sermons to socializing with temple elders to be more of a challenge.

David Kyuman Kim, a scholar of race and religion, stresses the deeper implications of these language woes.

> *The acquisition of an Asian mother tongue may be an impassable barrier to the recognition and reappropriation of Asian religious traditions. In short, since many Asian Americans have been raised with English as their "mother tongue," our conscious moral and spiritual identities may have been more informed by the religious traditions of the American linguistic universe—namely, through some form of Christianity—rather than by Confucianism, Buddhism, Taoism, ancestor worship, Hinduism, and so on.*[7]

Larene agrees. Language-wise, it's often easier for the Asian American youth she works with to understand Christian sources than the Buddhism they learned at home or temple.[8] Confronted with a profusion of Buddhist texts in different Asian languages, it can be overwhelming to know where to start. As Connie, who was raised in the Taiwanese Buddhist humanitarian organization Tzu Chi, points out: "Unlike Abrahamic religions, Buddhism in English-speaking countries does not have standardized, widely distributed English translations for many of its sutras."

A five o'clock shadow dusting his face, Michael pours me another cup of tea at his parents' Monterey Park home. "I've been a Buddhist all my life," Michael tells me. "I was born into it. But I've become the most devotedly Buddhist member of my family." An elaborate altar anchors the room, its three tiers heavy with statues and offerings from the wide range of Buddhist traditions that Michael practices in. My host chuckles as he explains that he is considered "the baby" (he's twenty-eight years old) at one of the temples he attends. Most of the members are over fifty. The oldest is ninety-six.

"Most of the demographic is my mom's age or older," Anthuan laments as he reflects on the temples he grew up attending. Born in Vietnam and raised in the heart of LA, Anthuan struggled to meet other young adults at local monasteries and temples until he discovered Thich Nhat Hanh's tradition: "Deer Park has young adult retreats, teen retreats—so I identify with that." He spent three months at the Vietnamese Zen master's monastery in Southern California before enrolling as a Masters of Divinity student in the Buddhist chaplaincy program at University of the West. At UWest, Professor Jane Iwamura's class on Buddhism in America inspired Anthuan to gather narratives of young adult Buddhists of color. He reached out to the Angry Asian Buddhist, and Aaron put him in touch with me. Which is how Anthuan came to drive the six hours from SoCal up to the Bay Area for our interview.

For many second-generation Asian Americans, Buddhism can seem like a religion of their parents' generation. "It might seem archaic and superstitious to younger Asian Americans, especially since a language barrier can be difficult to overcome when explaining something as complex as a religion," Larene remarks. "This is why I think having English-speaking groups available to young Asian Americans and making Buddhism relevant to their lives as young Asian Americans is crucial to retaining interest."

But retaining that interest is easier said than done. The parents of second-generation Asian American Buddhists often lack the time and resources to immerse their children in Buddhist practices and teachings. The Buddhist temples they attend rarely have programs tailored to English-speaking youth.

Ratema marveled upon hearing about the youth programs her Japanese American friend had enjoyed growing up in the BCA. It was a privilege she could only imagine. Of course, her friend's Shin Buddhist community has had over a century to root itself in America. It remains to be seen how the Buddhist temples established by post-1965 Asian immigrants like Ratema's parents and grandparents will find ways to thrive for generations to come.

In "Homage to Ancestors: Exploring the Horizons of Asian American Religious Identity," Jane Iwamura proposes that many Asian Americans feel ambivalent about their spiritual heritages, which can feel "both foreign and familiar."[9] Iwamura illustrates this point in an article that features interviews with Japanese Americans about their Buddhist home altars. "Plagued by a high standard of religious and cultural authenticity, they felt they did not possess the 'right knowledge' to engage in proper *butsudan* practice and expressed anxieties about their abilities to pass on the tradition."[10]

Her observation brings to mind a story Landon told me about buying a butsudan at a BCA church fundraiser—and then having no idea how to set it up. Many of the second-generation Asian American Buddhists I talked to defer to their parents as better stewards of the home altar. They hesitate to take ownership over tending the sacred space themselves.

For Sarah, who occasionally went with her parents to Vietnamese Buddhist temples in Northern California as a child, the home altar is a source of both comfort and anxiety. She values the familiarity of lighting incense and saying prayers at the altar the way her mom taught her, but worries she's not following the "official protocol" for worship. Dawa sympathizes. "I always worry that I'll do something 'wrong,' particularly when I don't have an older relative to guide me, which does make me feel a bit more distant from the religious community." Dawa knows other second-generation Tibetan Buddhists feel this religion-induced anxiety as well.

Eric was born in Taipei and immigrated with his family to Southern California at the age of four. The familiar Buddhism of his childhood began to feel increasingly foreign as he got older.

I grew up with my father exposing us to a lot of Buddhism at home. He is a devout practitioner and he would take us to local Chinese immigrant temples in Southern California such as Hsi Lai Temple, as well as neighborhood temples established in residential households.

Under my father's guidance, the rest of our family passively went to Buddhist events and participated in praying, chanting, burning incense, burning paper money, wearing Buddhist necklaces and bracelets, and connecting with our ancestors through Buddhist practice. It was just something we did because our father wanted us to, not something we were necessarily personally passionate or knowledgeable about. Besides superficial explanations from my father, I never learned what I was actually doing, why I was doing them, or what Buddhism actually taught.

Even though I always had relatively positive experiences with Buddhism throughout my childhood (I always found the monks to be friendly and the temples to be interesting places to visit), I decided by the end of high school to stop wearing a Buddhist bead bracelet and stop calling myself Buddhist because I realized that I knew nothing about Buddhism. While many of my other friends (mainly of Christian faith) seemed articulate in explaining to me the basic concepts of Christianity, I found myself unable to give even the simplest explanation of what Buddhism was.

Reading Eric's words, I recall something Nora said when describing her relationship to Jodo Shinshu: "I was born into the religion, so a lot of the things that I did growing up, I did by rote." Leslie, who considers Buddhism to be a component of the Taiwanese folk religion she grew up with, had a similar experience. She remembers mimicking her grandfather's nightly ritual of "going through the motions of lighting incense and bowing and praying."

But it's one thing to go through the motions. It's quite another to find meaning in them.

"我有時候佛誕節我也是去這些佛堂, 這樣啊, 就求平安, 對我來講是求平安."

Back on the living room couch, Ms. Tham is explaining that she goes to temples in West Covina on Buddhist festival days to pray for happiness.

Nathan asks her about a Chinese phrase she has just used. "What is *qiu ping'an*?"

His mother switches to English to clarify. "Pray for everything, you know, healthy and safety and smoothly ... and then, *shangxiang* [offer incense]."

Nathan nods, "Okay, yeah, I remember a lot of that, that my mom did when we were at Hsi Lai temple."

He grins. "What I never understood was who was going to do that."

Who was going to answer those prayers? Later in the *Youth Group* film, Larene expresses a similar conundrum. "The element of faith in Buddhism is actually something I struggle with. I think my mom's Buddhism—if there's such a thing to really differentiate in that way—is different from my own." For example, Larene strains to accept her mother's "otherworldly" belief in the Pure Land, a celestial realm of Buddhas and bodhisattvas. In much the same way, Eric grapples with what he calls "the superstitious practices that my father taught me."

"What are you doing here?" jeered the other students at Charlini Somaweera's private Catholic elementary school. In Mihiri Tillakaratne's short documentary *I Take Refuge*, Charlini, a young adult Sri Lankan American Buddhist, recalls the painful experience of being marginalized on account of both her race and her religion. "I always understood that I was neither this nor that—I was never going to be American. I'm not white, I don't have blond hair, I don't have blue eyes, and you know just by looking at me that ... I have a different identity."

The second-generation young adults I interviewed understand Charlini's pain. Growing up Asian American Buddhist is no cakewalk. To wit: being criticized for not believing in God (Heather). Discovering the brief lessons on Buddhism at her middle school bore no resemblance whatsoever to her family's Buddhism (Sarah). Having her Buddhist faith dismissed as a system of "idolatry" and a "tribal set of rituals" (Heather again). Being told by Christian classmates that they are going to hell (Yeeshen and Emily). Getting mocked in eighth grade for wearing a jade Buddha pendant: "Don't wear that; Buddha is ugly" (Wenli).

Kevin, who identifies as an American of Burmese Chinese descent and a Theravada Buddhist, can think of several reasons why second-generation young adults like himself might shy away from their Buddhist identity. For starters: "I think part of it has to do with self-consciousness. If they don't have a good grasp of their own faith, it's difficult to give themselves that label."

Sarah can relate. Growing up, she and a friend wore the same Buddhist pendant, though they called the bodhisattva by different names: Quan Âm in Sarah's case, Guanyin in her Taiwanese American friend's case. They had just gotten back to her friend's house after grocery shopping when her friend reminded Sarah not to eat the fruit just yet—they had to leave it in front of the Buddha altar first. It was a practice Sarah's family followed too. Yet in spite of their shared religious connection, Sarah never talked about Buddhism with her friend "because I don't really feel secure in how I should present my beliefs."

Kevin highlights another reason second-generation Asian Americans might be reluctant to come out as Buddhist. "Another issue is that labeling oneself as Buddhist certainly deviates from the norm, the American norm. When we still see blatant cases of religious discrimination in modern-day America (the recent Louisiana school case that rightfully ruled in favor of the Buddhist student comes to mind), it's easier to understand why people don't want to raise eyebrows or go against the grain." Kevin is referring to the ACLU's lawsuit on behalf of a Thai Buddhist sixth-grader who was "ridiculed in front of his classmates for his religious beliefs until he was physically ill." School officials allegedly denigrated the boy's Buddhist faith as "stupid" and suggested he transfer to another school with "more Asians."[11]

Social stigma. Generational gaps. Language barriers. All of these can alienate second-generation Asian Americans from the Buddhism they were raised with. Some may stop identifying with Buddhism altogether— though the young adults I talked to did not. How did they stay connected to the religion of their upbringing in the face of these formidable obstacles?

RECLAMATION

After high school, away from the orbit of his father's Buddhism, Eric started exploring the faith of his upbringing on his own terms.

After I left home to attend college at UCLA, I took an "Introduction to Buddhism" class and joined the University Buddhist Association at UCLA student organization. This is where I learned broadly about the teachings, history, and practices of Buddhism in both a classroom and student group context. I finally felt like I was learning about Buddhism and understanding what it taught.

However, my acquisition of Buddhist teachings was often processed in comparison to acquisition of Christian teachings that my friends had exposed me to. At the time, I was definitely seeking a religious identity, some set of teachings I could follow that would fill a spiritual gap I had. Yet, I found myself feeling wary of too easily accepting Buddhism back into my life, and so I actually attended my friend's Christian fellowship, where I went to their weekly meetings, Bible study sessions, and social events.

Though I found them to be incredibly welcoming and kindhearted, our interactions always led to my religious search and whether or not I'd made any progress in accepting Jesus into my life. Even after reading parts of the Bible and trying to learn more about Christian teachings through Bible study sessions, I found myself unable to understand and accept the teachings of the Bible. While I enjoyed them as metaphorical stories, I could not bring myself to understand them as the ultimate, universal truth, and more importantly, I could not bring myself to believe in "God."

In contrast, the teachings of the Buddha seemed very practical and useful to me. I found concepts such as compassion, attachment, mindfulness, impermanence, and suffering to be intellectually stimulating, logical, and practical in applying them to my own life. I also started becoming more involved and meeting other young adult Buddhists, both Asian American and non-Asian American, who were experiencing similar journeys.

Broadening his religious horizons away from the Buddhist contexts he grew up in. Exploring other spiritual traditions. Transforming his faith from a carryover of previous generations to a personal choice in the here and now. Eric's story etches an arc traceable in the spiritual journeys of the other second-generation Asian Americans I talked to.

This path of learning and discovery shifts Buddhism from an "ascribed identity" inherited from family to an "achieved identity" constructed in response to change, to borrow sociologist Wendy Cadge's terminology.[1] Through this process, young adult Asian Americans forge Buddhist identities influenced by—yet also distinct from—those of their parents.

Quite the transformation from a high schooler who removed his mala beads and renounced his Buddhist identity to an undergrad actively engaged with Buddhist study and community. What changed?

I think one of the most important factors in being able to reinvigorate and reclaim my Buddhist identity is language. Before attending

"Introduction to Buddhism" and the University Buddhist Association at UCLA, I was exposed to Buddhism in Mandarin through my father and the Chinese-speaking immigrant Buddhist community in Southern California. While I definitely think that learning some of the basic interactional sayings of Buddhism in Chinese (such as "Guanyin Pusa" or "Oh mi to fou") is important, I think it's impossible for me to grasp more abstract and philosophical ideas such as impermanence and mindfulness through the Chinese language. My Chinese abilities were limited to everyday conversations with my parents, and so my knowledge of Buddhism through Chinese was limited to its simplest nature. Being able to learn more about Buddhism through English, the language that I had already used to understand more abstract concepts such as race and gender, was the major factor that changed my relationship with Buddhism.

Like Eric, many second-generation Asian American Buddhists find English-language resources to be invaluable for reconnecting with the religion of their upbringing.

Connie went from copying what her mother did at temple, to questioning her faith, to volunteering extensively in the Taiwanese Buddhist organization she was raised in. She credits English translations of Tzu Chi's books for helping bridge the gaps in her understanding.

Heather's parents were active Buddhists in Taiwan but largely abandoned the religion when they immigrated to the United States. Lacking fluency in Chinese, Heather struggled "to rediscover the Buddhism that I once knew, that my parents passed on to me." After she encountered English-language materials on Buddhism in undergrad and graduate school, Heather began calling herself a "born-again Buddhist," a phrase she uses with a touch of irony given its Christian connotations.

Sarah distinguishes between "the Buddhism that I was introduced to as a kid, and the Buddhism I started learning more about as a young adult, during and post-college." The second form, readily available in English, was more accessible than the Vietnamese Buddhism of her childhood. When Sarah and I first met in 2008, as roommates in a study abroad program in Cape Town, the pendant she wore hinted at her early Buddhist influences (Quan Âm worship at the family altar, ceremonies and Tết cele-brations at Vietnamese temples). Five years later, a plate of vegan cookies between us, Sarah relates how these influences have expanded to include a class on mindfulness-based stress reduction in the Bay Area, graduate student friends in Buddhist studies whom she met while living in Hong Kong, the Dalai Lama's Facebook page, and more.

"Two Buddhisms" aligns Asian American Buddhists with the "ritualistic" and "devotional" practices of bowing, chanting, and relic worship. Yet the second-generation young adults I interviewed have mixed emotions about being associated with these practices.

Anthuan was keen to distance himself from the "cultural baggage" of the Vietnamese Buddhist temples of his youth when he began "experimenting with religion" through reading books by the Dalai Lama and Thich Nhat Hanh. At times he still feels the impulse to justify his faith to others.

Eric also finds himself on the defensive when people ask about his reli-gion. "Often I will add the disclaimer that 'I don't do the superstitious stuff, such as burning paper money and praying for a wish to come true,' even though I actually *do* do those things when my father wants me to as a way of appeasing him. I think the disclaimer is a way for me to vali-date the kind of Buddhism I practice (a more philosophical and scholarly Buddhism) in a social context (such as America) where the superstitious aspects of Buddhism are not well understood or welcomed."

Claire, who grew up thinking her Taiwanese mother's bowing and chanting at their home altar was just "one those weird things my mom does," has an ambivalent relationship with the term *relic worship*. "It sounds fishy to me. But then at the same time, you know, I think stupas mostly have relics in them, and certainly I've related to those as objects of devotion. So I'd say, yes, I've done that ... but at the same time it's a practice that I wouldn't want to tell people right away that I do." I ask Claire why she doesn't want to tell people that she pays respect to Bud-dhist relics as part of her practice. Fear of judgment, she admits.

It saddened me to hear these stories. Stories in which second-generation young adults hide the full breadth of their Buddhist practices. Stories in which Asian American Buddhists posture—not to impress or mislead, but as a way to preemptively deflect negative stereotypes. Stereotypes foisted on them by virtue of their Asian faces.

And then I realized: I had done exactly the same thing. Though I wasn't raised Buddhist, I was familiar with this hiding and posturing. I had cloaked my Buddhism in caveats. Assured others that I'd sat my share of retreats (as if entrée into the ranks of "authentic" Buddhism required passing a meditation résumé check). Kept silent on the ways my heart has been touched by chanting and bowing, ceremonies and relics.

Clad in a gray BOCA T-shirt, John is arranging kneelers in Dharma Seal Temple's sunlit main hall.

Cut to footage from John's interview. "I feel like I am a Buddhist," he says, brows knitted beneath a mop of curly brown hair. "And, I don't feel like anyone—or even anyone in youth group—should have to feel like they *need* to be a Buddhist."

Cut to an image of a youth group member unfolding the sutra bookrests, long black locks obscuring half of the letters on her "Everything Is Fabulous" shirt. She stands in the same posture as the sparkling gold statues on the altar behind her, Shakyamuni flanked by two bodhisattvas.

Back to the interview. "But also the opposite, which is, sometimes it breaks my heart a little bit when people feel like they *can't* be a Buddhist because of different things about them"—on-screen, John and a few other BOCA members are placing the red liturgy books on the sutra holders—"like, I don't do this, therefore I am not a Buddhist."

New scene. Sitting in a circle with the youth group, Jennifer Lüc haltingly confesses that she doesn't think she qualifies as a Buddhist because she doesn't apply the teachings every day. "So I don't feel like I have the right to be a Buddhist," she concludes, with an apologetic smile.

Others in the circle chime in. "There are flaws in anything, so instead of claiming Buddhism, I say I practice Buddhism but I am not religious," explains Maxwell Ta, his blue baseball cap worn backwards. He is flanked by Mason Wong (who is sporting a BOCA shirt) and Kathy Chen (who is hugging a beige zafu like it's a teddy bear). Mason pipes up: "As I started coming to youth group I learned what Buddhism actually was. Buddhism is more than just that boring, ritualistic form of worship. Rather, it's a way of thinking."

Sharing their insecurities and skepticisms. Expressing their complicated feelings about a familiar-yet-foreign faith. Finding ways to make Buddhism relevant to their lives. There's a sense of camaraderie among these young adult Asian American Buddhists as they come to terms with their betwixt-and-between identities.

The soothing sound of running water.

A white bowl with a sky-blue rim, ringed by flamingo flowers, filled with fragrant liquid the color of oolong. A cherubic baby Buddha rises from the amber pond, right arm pointing to the heavens, left arm to the earth—a classic gesture of his birth.

In the upper reaches of the San Gabriel Valley, Shin Buddhists in Pasadena will be celebrating this Vesak (better known in their community as Hanamatsuri) by showering the infant Buddha with sweet tea.

Here at Dharma Seal, Mason (wearing a black hoodie over his BOCA shirt today) and Maxwell (varsity jacket, backwards baseball cap) hold their ladles with aplomb, pouring with perfect synchrony before bowing in unison.

John again: "One of the things that concerns me too is when people say, 'Oh, *I'm* a Buddhist, I do it this way. These *other* people are less Buddhist.' 'Oh, my parents just go to pray, therefore they are less Buddhist.'"

I've seen this attitude among some second-generation Asian American Buddhists. It's the inverse of fearing they will never measure up to their parents' devotions.

A white-haired temple member clasps the ladle in veined hands. She gingerly spoons the holy water over the Buddha while three younger temple members watch, transfixed.

Cut back to John's interview. "No, no, no, no!" he exclaims. "They get to be Buddhist too. You know, just because you decide—or you're comfortable in—your kind of Buddhism, doesn't mean you can take other people's practice away from them."

Aaron emphatically agrees. As he explains in a November 2014 film interview with Wanwan Lu that didn't ultimately make it into *Youth Group,* Aaron fears young Asian Americans may internalize racialized stereotypes and start to look down on their Buddhist elders.

Unlike most of the Asian American youth at Dharma Seal, Aaron wasn't raised Buddhist—but he was close to his grandmother on his father's side, who *was* Buddhist. "She was a full individual, full of color, with her own quirks and idiosyncrasies," he remembers, eyes twinkling. But seen through the lens of stereotypes, she is reduced: "To this old Asian immigrant woman who's concerned with things like money—honestly, who *isn't* concerned about money?—and not really concerned about or into Buddhism. In some ways, she's like an inferior Buddhist. And the way she practices is not 'real' Buddhism. So she's this immigrant superstitious Buddhist."

It's one thing if this disdain is directed at racial "Others." But it's heartbreaking to aim it at your own family. "Who wants to think about their family that way? Who wants to think about their communities that way?" Aaron asks. "And who wants to think about their *self* that way?"

Back at Dharma Seal, there's a line of people waiting to bathe the baby Buddha. Larene pours the water, joins her palms, dips her head. A woman with short-cropped salt-and-pepper hair clatters on crutches toward the altar. She joins her palms, bows her head, pours the water, her movements just a beat behind Larene's.

Raised in a residential Chinese Buddhist community in Northern California, Monica intentionally moved across the country to attend a secular college. A philosophy class at her Buddhist high school had inspired her to experience "another way of looking at the world." Her desire to learn from "other forms of Buddhism, other interpretations, and other practices" led Monica to temples in the Thai Forest tradition and a predominantly white meditation center in Massachusetts (not to mention Buddhist temples in Taiwan and pilgrimage sites in India).

Anthuan is also an intrepid explorer. "My sanghas are all over the map," he announces with pride. His choice to engage with a wide range of Buddhist communities is in part an act of resistance against stereotypes of Asian American Buddhists. He refuses to be pigeonholed by his race or relegated to an ethnic enclave. "I want to diversify my experience. I don't want to be involved strictly in a people of color sangha, or strictly just a sangha that has predominantly Caucasian forty-year-olds.... I want to be mainstream, I want to just attend any sangha and not be *ooh that Asian, ooh that Vietnamese guy,* I want to be just Anthuan who could attend any sangha, could read any Buddhist magazine and publication."

In broadening their spiritual horizons, second-generation young adults venture beyond the Buddhist communities they were raised in— and even beyond Buddhism altogether. Christianity in particular offers an obvious alternative to the faith of their upbringing. Christian college groups abound; their Buddhist counterparts are paltry by comparison (or, on many campuses, nonexistent). America's dominant religion presents a route to shedding the unflattering associations of "Asian immigrant" Buddhism. It offers a promise of belonging, a way out of being forever Other.

When I presented interviewees with the Pew Forum statistics that "One in ten Asian Americans (10 percent) were raised Buddhist and have left the faith, while 2 percent of Asian Americans have become Buddhist after being raised in a different faith (or no faith), resulting in a net loss of eight percentage points due to religious switching," our ensuing conversations often revolved around comparing Christianity and Buddhism.

Eric has witnessed this "net loss" firsthand, beginning in childhood and continuing to his UCLA years. He has many close friends who are Asian American Christians; he might have become part of the statistics himself after attending an Asian American Christian fellowship for ten weeks. Eric sees several reasons why Asian Americans might leave Buddhism: "language (it's difficult to want to stay in a religion that doesn't use the language you're most familiar with), lack of inclusion in the overall social and cultural landscape of America (Christianity has a presence in many social and cultural institutions across America—many high schools have Christian youth groups, many private schools are Christian or Catholic), and inability to cater to what interests young people (Christian concerts, Christian-themed pop songs, etc.)."

Lan, a Vietnamese American whose parents are devout Buddhists, presents a small but telling example that illustrates Eric's point about Buddhism's marginal status in society. Just by watching American TV shows and movies, Lan has a sense of how to talk to Catholic priests. By contrast, he has "no outline" for approaching monks at the Vietnamese temple, and often feels shy to do so.

Kevin also attributes the "net loss" of Asian American Buddhists to Christianity's dominance in American society. Christianity is the established norm in America; non-Christian politicians still turn heads in America. Also, Kevin adds, "Christian churches offer the networking and community that many Asian Americans are drawn to." He was surprised to learn about Christian apologetics, which offers Christians a systematic framework to defend the tenets of their faith.

Kevin thinks Buddhism is more accepting of Christianity than vice versa, a viewpoint shared by many of the other second-generation young adults I interviewed.[2] Several interviewees point out that Buddhism encourages individuals to be flexible and avoid holding too tightly to any single concept. Kevin concedes that this flexibility can be "a double-edge sword": it cultivates open-mindedness, but it hardly pressures second-generation Asian Americans like himself to remain Buddhist.

"Especially in America, some Asian Americans might feel left out." I can just make out Brian's soft voice over the clanking of the espresso machine.

"So they need a place where they can feel loved, where they feel like they're equal with everybody. And churches, that's what they offer: a sense of belonging that many temples don't give." The din from the barista station echoes off the industrial-style exposed ceilings as Brian ponders Christianity's competitive edge in attracting Asian Americans.

Brian was one of the first people to contact me for an interview, having heard about my project from the *Angry Asian Buddhist* blog in January 2013: "I am a Laotian American Buddhist who attends a Korean Buddhist temple on a weekly basis. However, I live in Orange County." As luck would have it, a Buddhist bibliographic project at USC (under the direction of Professor Duncan Williams) would bring me to LA that summer. And so, five months after receiving his email, I am sitting across from Brian in a Koreatown coffee shop.

Born and raised Theravada Buddhist in Chicago, Brian started attending a temple in the Jogye order because it was easily accessible by public transportation (he didn't have a car). Upon moving to Anaheim (where he still didn't have a car), he walked past a Buddhist temple one day. To his astonishment, it turned out to be the sister temple of his Chicago sangha. What are the odds, Brian thought, given that Buddhists make up a tiny fraction of Korean Americans, who are overwhelmingly Christian. He was used to the exact opposite in the Laotian American community ("I only figured out this year how to say 'Jesus' in Lao. My parents didn't know. My grandparents didn't know. Pretty much nobody knew, except for one of my cousins, because he knows a Laotian Christian"). Temple members were convinced this young Laotian American must have been Korean in his past life.

Not immune to the appeal of Christianity, Brian agreed to attend a Christian church with a friend. Though he kept an open mind and felt genuinely glad that his friend found so much value in Christianity, the process helped Brian discern that Buddhism is more aligned with his worldview.

With his buzz cut, prayer beads, and Buddhist T-shirts, Brian is a frequent target of conversion attempts, especially by other Asian Americans who insist he would be a great "asset" to their Christian churches. His reaction to their intense recruitment efforts? The promises of free food and the opportunity to meet other young people were enticing, but Brian was "shocked" when they advertised attractive girls—a "wrong reason to go" in his view. Eventually, he was put off by the "incentives" of food, friends, girls, part-time jobs, and help with homework, though he recognizes that his choice to remain Buddhist can be an isolating one. "They said, 'There's just one of you, and there's so many of us.' They said, 'Eventually, you're going to have to join us, sooner or later.' And I was like, nah. I mean, I already thought about it. I feel that, in a way, we are like a very tiny platoon in this huge world where everybody has big armies."

Wanisa, a Thai American Buddhist, is no stranger to these kinds of interactions. Nor is she a fan of them. "Coming from a Buddhist background, I didn't feel that one had to be vocal with one's religion. I do not appreciate people who try to force their religion on others." Wenli's strategy for countering the "big armies" of other religions? "By understanding more about my own faith as well as others' faith, I grew wiser in dealing with those who attacked me for my faith." Deepening her understanding helps Wenli "respectfully decline" when others try to convert her—and enables her to enact the Buddhist value of compassion "for those who are not like us." In a sense, Wenli's spiritual explorations have been a valuable training in Buddhist apologetics.

Kevin grappled with whether he was missing out by choosing to remain Buddhist. Ultimately, he embraces his skepticism as "a healthy part of being religious." That double-edged sword he mentioned? Kevin reappropriates it to strengthen his ties with Buddhism and resist the overtures of his Christian peers.

While some of the second-generation young adults I spoke to are wary of Christianity, others appreciate it as a gateway to invigorating their relationship with Buddhism. As Jane Iwamura notes:

> Although Asian American Buddhists have a unique identity, grounded in a specific worldview, this identity can assist them to transcend the boundaries of their particular cultural, ethnic, and religious groups. By following the Buddha's injunction to cultivate wisdom, one must associate with wise people, and these people may be found both inside and outside the Buddhist community.[3]

For Claire, these wise people were members of a college Christian group. Before embarking on a volunteer trip with the group, she wasn't really interested in becoming Buddhist. But in the company of young adults who were sincerely studying the Bible and applying it to their lives, Claire began to rethink her "superficial idea of what religion was." Quite unexpectedly, she came away more open to Buddhism.

For me, these wise spiritual friends were South Africans working in various nonprofit organizations, most of whom were committed Christians. Interviewing these Capetonians for an undergraduate thesis that had nothing to do with religion, I came away humbled by the faith that sustained their social justice work—and more willing to embrace my own spiritual leanings.

Andy, who was raised by Taiwanese parents in Tzu Chi, is grateful for a college interfaith retreat on spirituality and sexuality he attended—despite being the only Buddhist. At the retreat, Muslim, Jewish, and Christian members of the LGBTQI community shared their struggles to redefine their faith after being ostracized from their religious communities. These conversations challenged Andy to ask tough questions about his own religion (for example, "What does Buddhism say about sex?") and inspired him to reanalyze his relationship to the faith he was born into.

Venturing beyond the sanghas they grew up in gives second-generation Asian American Buddhists an opportunity to situate themselves within the broader Buddhist and religious landscape of America. Apart from their families and the temples of their upbringing, they seek out the spaces they need to redefine Buddhism for themselves. Along the way, many discover how other aspects of their lives—race and ethnicity, sexual orientation and gender, service and social activism—intersect with their Buddhist identities.

"I was like, *yes!* I want my voice heard!" Andy starts our interview by relaying his exuberance over hearing about my project via Aaron's blog.

An hour ago I was sitting in a café in Koreatown, listening to a calm college student with a buzz cut talk about his relationship with Buddhism. Now, déjà vu—except replace Koreatown with USC, calm with literally bouncing out of his seat, and buzz cut with tousled black hair.

Meeting other Buddhist youth at an international conference in Taiwan was a pivotal point in Andy's spiritual journey. The conference proceedings were translated from Chinese to English, greatly aiding his comprehension. At the Tzu Chi headquarters in Hualian, Andy met members of the organization's collegiate association, Tzu Ching. The encouragement of these newfound friends prompted Andy to start a Tzu Ching chapter at USC.

Andy had always had a hard time relating to the Chinese-speaking adults at Tzu Chi. Hearing other Buddhist youth explain the organization was a revelation: "I realized it's not just a middle-aged women thing." He used to avoid telling his friends that the community service organization where he spent his Tuesday nights was a Buddhist one. After the conference, he wasn't shy to talk about the Buddhist values underpinning his volunteer work at Tzu Chi.

Andy acknowledges that his dad (a devoted practitioner who urged his son to take a gap year to live in a Taiwanese Buddhist monastery) has long been a driving force for his Buddhist practice. But as he takes a more active role in weaving his Taiwanese American, Asian American, and Buddhist heritages with his passion for service and social justice, Andy's stance is shifting. "I'm slowly starting to take it as my own. In college, I've started to reclaim it.... I'm starting to do it more for myself than just for my dad."

Though Eric is several years older than Andy, the parallels in their Buddhist journeys are striking: Being at odds with their family's faith. Grasping Buddhist teachings through the medium of English. Establishing friendships with young adults from diverse spiritual backgrounds. Beginning to see Buddhism not as a "superstition" of their fathers but as a religion they can proudly call their own.

COMPASSION

"Yeah that's me! That is me."

Nathan taps a photo with a pinkish-red date stamp from more than two decades ago: a pair of young kids sit snuggled close with their elbows resting on a table, her chin resting in her left palm, his chin in his right, perfect mirror images of each other. Some of the other photos in the album are just visible in the frame: mom and daughter in front of three giant Buddhas; mom and dad in front of the same trio of golden statues.

"Aw man, what was I thinking with that haircut?" Nathan laughs. "Shoulda had better style!" (On the screen, we catch a glimpse of his current look: mustache with a hint of handlebar, wavy black hair extending past his sideburns and beard.) "I didn't choose the haircut, my grandma cut my hair," he explains.

Another page in the album contains a triptych of young Nathans standing on a straw doormat in front of a white front door, his bowl cut barely reaching the doorknob. He's covered in a black Manchurian tunic from neck to toe.

"I actually remember taking this photo! I killed some ants right before I took this photo. Yeah, there were some ants, and I remember stepping on 'em, and then I remember somebody telling me: 'Don't do that. This is life, and this wasn't bothering you.' I don't know who taught me that. It might've been my uncle or something."

Nathan turns the page, nodding.

"Good times," he murmurs.

This scene in *Youth Group* always makes me think of the chorus of appreciations I heard from second-generation Asian Americans who are grateful to have been steeped in Buddhism growing up.

Thao calls her mother "the gatekeeper to my involvement in Buddhism" because "she opened the door for me to be grounded in my own beliefs." Her parents attended a Vietnamese temple in San Francisco until a Chan Buddhist monastery opened closer to home. They brought four-year-old Thao along, and she's been going ever since. Thao was a regular at the monastery's Saturday evening youth group until the end of high school. "While we have all grown up and chosen different paths, we still consider each other family," she notes. It's a family bonded by many years of meditation, calligraphy, and tai chi; many seasons of circumambulating the Buddha hall and memorizing mantras; many semesters of studying languages and making arts and crafts; many evenings of storytelling after the Saturday-night lecture. Tragically, in seventh grade, Thao was going home for winter break from the temple's boarding school when she and her parents got into a car accident; her mother was killed instantly. The Buddhist principles and morals her mom instilled remain a bedrock of Thao's life to this day.

Camilla, a Taiwanese American who grew up in the same religious organization as Thao, also traces her deep connection to Buddhism to her devout mother, who read sutras to her daughter until the teachings of the faith (and the intricacies of the Chinese language) became second nature. "It would not be an exaggeration if I were to say that I spent about a third of my childhood at the local temple," Camilla relates. Her temple activities run the gamut "from ceremonies to lectures to volunteering (which for me mostly consists of consecutive translation, running errands, and sometimes doing odd jobs like cracking walnuts)." Camilla continues to read Buddhist texts daily and finds it hard to imagine a life without the religious teachings and community that have so profoundly influenced her.

Born and raised in America, Dawa finds it nearly impossible to disentangle Buddhism from her Tibetan heritage. The religion was woven into the daily rhythms of home life with her parents, who taught her how to make offerings and recite prayers. Dawa continues some of these traditions in the home she shares with her husband, who grew up in Tibet. Visiting them in San Francisco, I am nearly bowled over by their newly adopted mastiff puppy before being ushered into the sanctuary of their living room. Colorful *thangkas* grace the walls. Display cabinets house scrolls and prayer books. Stately Buddha statues from their recent trip to Tibet, consecrated by a local *geshe* upon returning to California, bless the space.

At the age of twenty, following in the footsteps of his father and uncles, Kevin temporarily ordained at a Burmese monastery in California. He had his head shaved by the abbot, took on the eight requisite possessions (including the monastic robes and alms bowl), and vowed to follow the code of conduct for novice monks. He also received a new Pali name in accordance with the Burmese naming system. His cousins joined him in the rite of passage; their family celebrated the meritorious occasion by serving Indian *biryani* to hundreds. Kevin's weeklong ordination was shorter than those in Burma, which often span several weeks to a few months. Despite this shorter time frame, the temporary ordination still had a powerful impact, giving Kevin a sense of belonging he hadn't previously felt.

Gratitude for the religion they inherited is especially strong among the second-generation young adults I interviewed whose families came to America as refugees. Knowing that Buddhism sustained his parents "through the hardship of dodging bullets" is an extra impetus for Brian to maintain the faith as a Laotian American. To Sarong, Buddhism is the tradition that her family carried from their home country of Cambodia; to the Thai refugee camp where she was born; to Nashville, Tennessee, where she and her siblings were raised. She loves to wear traditional temple attire and chant in Pali during ceremonies—practices that connect her to her family's heritage.

I should note that the scene in *Youth Group* where Nathan is browsing the album doesn't end on "good times."

The camera hones in on a photo date-stamped "26 11 88": Nathan next to two young girls and two elegantly dressed women in front of a building that seems to stretch the length of a city block. Other Asian families mill about in the background. Double-eaved roofs with upturned corners tower above them.

"Ah, Hsi Lai temple. The same temple where I was taken for Chinese school. The temple was cool. It was big. I ran around a lot."

Nathan's chuckle gives way to a slight frown.

"But I knew that I always dreaded the place, 'cause I didn't really like Chinese school."

Gratitude and pride are not the entirety of the second-generation Asian American Buddhist experience. Ambivalence and critique are part of the picture too.

As much as Dedunu appreciated the religious rituals she grew up with, they sometimes felt like an imposition from her mom, who "was keen on having me participate in this way, in fear of losing my cultural (i.e., Sri Lankan Sinhalese) identity."

Claire sees the gap between second-generation Asian Americans and their parents as an unavoidable corollary of the immigrant experience. "There's a disconnect with the values of your parents, especially in a context where you're adopting different values."

Second-generation Asian American Buddhists are not carbon copies of their parents. They are not inert vessels receiving the unhindered transmission of a timeless faith. Their intergenerational relationships are not without conflict.

Sometimes the conflicts are unexpected. Anthuan's parents disapproved of his "impractical" decision to study religion in college, though they are regular temple-goers. Lan's parents didn't want him to be vegetarian, fearing it would compromise their son's health, though his father is a strict vegetarian for religious reasons. Claire's mom criticized her choice to live in a Buddhist meditation center full time, though her mother is deeply involved with a Taiwanese Buddhist group.

Sometimes the conflicts occur outside the homes and temples of their upbringing. Feeling "visually and culturally different" at a meditation center whose members were primarily white, middle-age, and middle-class, Monica was struck by the contrast with the "social, cultural, very close-knit connections" of her home community, where other young adult Asian Americans—Thao and Camilla among them—engage in contemplative and devotional Buddhist practices. At the meditation center, Monica couldn't help but wonder: "Where are all of the other young Asian American Buddhists? And why aren't they here? Where is everybody else going?"

Those were the very questions that propelled this book into being. Though not a direct answer, what comes to mind is a phrase that Lan said three hours into our interview together. (I never imagined that five years after that conversation, Lan would surprise me and Trent by joining photographer Wanwan in capturing our wedding with stunning artistry; that the following year I would officiate his and Jenny's wedding; that both occasions would resound with chants of *metta:* loving-kindness in English and Vietnamese, soaring over evergreen forests to Mount Rainier; loving-kindness in Pali and English, floating across the Santa Cruz mountains to the Pacific Ocean.)

It's a phrase that lingers with me even now, when our conversation on the palm-studded campus of our alma mater should be a distant memory: "Our faith is complicated."

It has certainly been complicated for Eric.

> *Overall, I still find my relationship with the English-speaking, non-immigrant version of Buddhism and my Chinese-speaking, immigrant version of Buddhism (both through personal identification and community involvement) to be very nuanced and a conflicted part of my Buddhist identity. Just the fact that I am even posing them as two separate, opposing entities is telling of how I conceptualize these two parts of my relationship and experiences with Buddhism and in Buddhist communities.*
>
> *Even though I sometimes find myself feeling distrustful and cynical about the immigrant Chinese-speaking Buddhist community that my father had exposed me to early on (for its inability to really teach me what Buddhism was), I still understand that it is a part of who I am as a Buddhist and my Buddhist origins.*
>
> *I have definitely experienced feeling awkward at an only-English-speaking Buddhist event and more comfortable at an immigrant, Chinese-speaking Buddhist event. I've also experienced in Taiwan feeling like I was not just a tourist or spectator at the popular Longshan Temple but rather one of the local Taiwanese practitioners who was there to genuinely participate in the Buddhist community at that temple (even though I was a tourist!). I felt proud that I wasn't a confused visitor trying to figure out how to light and hold the incense, how to properly address the Buddhist icons, or how to buy packaged snacks used for prayer. I was proud that because of what my father had taught and exposed me to, I felt qualified for a sort of automatic, unofficial membership into the local Buddhist community there.*

Even as he struggles with a kind of internal "two Buddhisms" divide, Eric casts doubt on the dichotomy he's constructed in his mind. Are "Asian" and "Western" Buddhism diametrically opposed entities? In conceptualizing them as such, Eric had disdained the "immigrant" religion of his father. But as he brings skepticism to bear not only on his father's faith but also on his own ways of thinking about Buddhism, Eric begins to reconcile the tensions he's experienced as an Asian American Buddhist. Eric's narrative contains distrust and cynicism, but also three unequivocal words that never fail to move me: "I was proud."

"If you are a young Asian American raised with American culture ... open your heart and learn about your original roots and the country of your parents and grandparents. Growing up in the United States, you have received a culture, an education, a way of carrying on your activities, but do not think that it is superior."[1]

The second-generation Asian Americans I interviewed may not be familiar with these words by Thich Nhat Hanh, but they have largely followed his compassionate advice. In seeking to understand the Buddhism of their elders, they move beyond dismissing it as "superstitious" and "backwards." With open-mindedness and humility, these young adults come to recognize the wisdom their Buddhist parents have imparted.

Thao believes that "younger Asian American Buddhists who want to form a more stable sangha" would do well to look to older generations for lessons about building and maintaining Buddhist communities.

Sarah remembers being admonished by her parents for treating a singing bowl as a souvenir: "You can't just play with sacred objects!" She took their advice to heart and donated the bowl to a temple. "It has so much power and significance," Sarah realized. "It shouldn't be something that you just take out for party tricks, which is what a lot of prayer bowls are sold as."

Sarah's respect for Buddhist icons doesn't translate into an uncritical exaltation of all things Buddhist, however. American Buddhism may project "calm" and "Zen," but "nothing is ever as serene as it looks," she notes. Sarah doesn't fall for the romanticized views of Buddhism purveyed by the American media (the unflappable Oriental monk, the blissful white meditator). Anthuan doesn't buy into these illusions either—his parents have taught him to place Buddhism into a broader historical context.

The second-generation young adults I interviewed aren't prone to exotifying their religion or putting it on a pedestal. Buddhism in Asia isn't perfect—why would Buddhism in America be an exception? Dawa celebrates having a realistic, culturally rooted relationship with Buddhism:

> *My experiences and interactions with my religion have become more complex as I've gotten older. I've seen some religious leaders for the (flawed) human beings they are and discovered that a prayer will not solve everything. But I still do find religion to be a comfort in times of difficulty or transition—I'm not ashamed to say that is when I find myself in front of the altar, mumbling the few prayers I know!*
>
> *And I've also grown to see the value in having religious teachers whom you know closely and respect as a result of this relationship—seeing how they interact with their followers, the way they treat those around them, the guidance they give to others, whether they give back to the community, etc. The geshe-la who did the statues for us fills this role for my husband and me—he is in his seventies, still inspires the sense of nervousness that all religious leaders do for me, but is someone I deeply respect and whose guidance I gladly follow because of the good, learned, sincere person we've seen him to be. He is not an all-holy, perfect being, but he is a good teacher that we will turn to for help and guidance, and who we will wholeheartedly support however we can.*
>
> *So I feel like I've reached a good balance of religion in my life, for now, at least. I don't need to be the most knowledgeable—perhaps someday I'll learn more—and I don't need to make a public display of it by attending all the community religious gatherings or prayers that just make me nervous anyways! My observance is mostly private, in my home, where I feel most comfortable, with a few close teachers I know and respect. And that is good enough for me.*

Embracing their capacities to accept and question, respect and resist, honor and critique, second-generation Asian Americans come to appreciate that they are not carbon copies of their parents—and that their parents are not caricatures. From this vantage point, reciprocity blooms.

For instance: Thao was the one who convinced her father to become more involved with Buddhism. He used to drop his wife and daughter off at the monastery and sit in the car all evening until they were finished. With Thao's coaxing, her dad started attending Saturday lectures. Eventually, Mr. Phi took refuge in the Three Jewels, became vegetarian, and started following the five precepts. He even went on a pilgrimage to India to visit Buddhist sites and meet the Dalai Lama, and now regularly brings Buddhists texts to temples in Vietnam. "While he is grounded in his own practices, he also supports my involvement, because he understands how important it is to me," Thao observes. Despite their differences, she is grateful to her father for affirming her ongoing spiritual explorations. I suspect the feeling is mutual.

In striving to find common ground with their parents, these young adults embody the compassion, acceptance, and open-mindedness that many of them consider to be the hallmarks of Buddhism.

Leslie relates an anecdote that epitomizes this inclusive approach: "When my mother once asked a Buddhist monk if she could pray for a friend who was Catholic and not Buddhist, the monk immediately said it was fine, and explained that the emphasis of Buddhist teachings is on conscious decisions to be a better person, not on staunch belief in one god or another. I found that take very refreshing and very welcoming, especially compared to the exclusivity of some other religions."

In a testament to her open-mindedness, Monica returned to the primarily white meditation center where she had felt so out of place. Why go through that discomfort again? Because "rubbing shoulders with people who are really different" is indispensable to Monica's Buddhist practice.

In a time of divisiveness and rancor, what a humanizing stance.

"White Buddhist for Asians." Aaron could have written this August 2010 blog post as the Thankful Asian Buddhist.

Over on Dharma Folk, *kudos posts about largely Vietnamese immigrants in Orange County who have "hired a white American man to*

teach Buddhism to their kids." This man is a Buddhist monk, Ven.
Kusala Bhikshu.

There are a number of white Buddhist teachers who have ordained and
now minister to multicultural communities, especially here in the United
States. There's Ven. Heng Sure and Thanissaro Bhikkhu, to name just
two. What sets Kusala Bhikshu apart, in my opinion, is that he has not
made the same effort to thoroughly immerse himself in another culture.
While Ven. Heng Sure speaks flawless Mandarin and Thanissaro Bhik-
khu speaks fluent Thai with a mastery of slang that would make my
own mother blush, Kusala Bhikshu is a happily monolingual American
Midwesterner—who also happens to reach out to Asian American Bud-
dhist communities.

In my opinion, this is a most beautiful manifestation of Western Bud-
dhism, where Western Buddhists of different stripes and colors come
together in spite of—even because of—their differences. Here are people
who are leveraging their community's diversity to strengthen it! Kusala
Bhikshu's not the only white guy working in this vein. For example, I
often talk of Richard [Harrold]'s assistance to a local Lao temple.
My hope is that, one day, self-styled Western Buddhist institutions
can outgrow their cultural insularity and follow in the steps of these
multiculturally-minded individuals.[2]

kudos was one of the people Aaron started the *Dharma Folk* group blog
with. John was another—as in John of the BOCA youth group. It was only
several years after our interview that I put two and two together: "kudos"
was none other than Eric (Ku)! The final paragraphs of Eric's essay about
his Buddhist journey suddenly shimmered with new valences.

The main person I consider to be my Buddhist teacher is Ven. Kusala, who
regularly attends the University Buddhist Association meetings at UCLA
and serves as a discussion facilitator and our guide. One of the reasons
why he has played an integral part in the development of my Buddhist
identity is because he helped me better understand the role "my father's
Buddhism" plays in the greater Buddhism I was learning about from class.

As you might be able to tell from what I've written about "my father's
Buddhism," I really didn't think it was "real Buddhism"—I often felt like

they were just a set of made-up, superstitious beliefs and practices that he associated with Buddhism. However, after having discussed it with Ven. Kusala, he helped me redirect my focus not so much on what was authentic, but what path helps each individual person on their journey to detachment, compassion, and mindfulness. I think it's become clear to me that my father and I find different approaches to be useful for our different needs. That realization is something Ven. Kusala helped guide me to.

While I do think that my interest in the more philosophical and scholarly aspects of Buddhism are a reaction to what I felt were the inadequacies of "my father's Buddhism," in the end, I don't think that they necessarily have to be at odds with each other. Simply put, I think I can have the best of both worlds, and in my opinion, that is one great benefit of being an "Asian American Buddhist."

I feel like this is the current phase of my Buddhist journey that I'm in. One example is that as my Chinese has been gradually improving, I've attempted to incorporate Buddhism more into my conversations with my father. I'm trying to find the similarities we do have in our practices. If I'm able to find and connect related beliefs we have that come from our Buddhist practices, I think it can bridge the disconnect that I've long felt between "my father's Buddhism" and mine.

It's a challenging and ongoing process, bridging the gaps. But it's a worthwhile journey, one that traverses the dichotomies of "two Buddhisms" and opens up the possibility of transcending those dualities altogether.

Like Eric, Buddhist values helped Larene shift from disparagement to kindness. "I personally struggled with coming to terms with my 'mother's Buddhism' and 'my Buddhism' when I first delved into Buddhism seriously," Larene confesses. "I finally came to an understanding by looking at a couple of key points: the fact that we both believed in the existence of impermanence in life, and the concept of something deeper and farther reaching than the idea of 'self.' I also asked myself if I thought she was becoming more peaceful, wise, and compassionate in her practice. If yes, even if we might practice differently, she is getting out of Buddhism what she needs, and I am getting from Buddhism what I need. The other details are not as important."

After pooh-poohing her mom's "weird" bowing and chanting, Claire was enjoying a class at her mother's temple and planning to take lay precepts with her mom at the time of our interview. Even before this change of heart, Claire used to instinctively chant *"om mani padme hum"* in times of stress. Her mom had taught her the mantra as a way to alleviate anxiety.

Sarah is glad she and her mom are at least "somewhat on the same page"; it would be harder if one of them wasn't Buddhist. "What she believes is Buddhism is not really the same as what I believe is Buddhism. But, it's nice that we can still talk; I can still go to temple with her. And we both find comfort in it, in different ways." And sometimes in similar ways: Sarah occasionally lights incense and does prostrations on her own because these simple acts give her a sense of familiarity and comfort, even if she doesn't know the "actual official protocol" around these rituals.

When I ask Ratema what object best represents her Buddhist practice, she knows exactly where it is, if not precisely what it means. Ratema pulls out the small square of paper with the photocopied yantra. I've seen the sacred diagram hung over doorways and inked on bodies in Cambodia. "My mom gave it to me a while ago," Ratema tells me. "She keeps a copy in her wallet too. I think she mostly gave it to me 'cause she was probably worried, 'Why are you out so late?,' etcetera, etcetera."

Ratema's yantra reminds me of a scene in Wanwan's documentary where Nathan is reflecting on the age-old wish of parents to protect their children. It's Lunar New Year, and the BOCA youth group is talking about their parents' occasionally mystifying cultural practices around the holiday.

"My mom totally believes in this. Should I believe in this too?" Nathan asks.

One of the group members recounts how she went a step too far in following her mom's instructions not to wash her hair on Chinese New Year, whereupon her mom teased, "You have to *shower;* just don't wash your hair!"

Nathan joins in the group's laughter before his tone takes a turn for the serious. "I mean, that is the origin of their compassion. They really want the best for me."

He concedes that young adult Asian American Buddhists have the option to reject the cultural and religious traditions they don't believe in, but wonders if it might not hurt to participate "as a sort of understanding and ... self-sacrifice on your end. I mean, you could make your mom happy and provide joy for her." After all, he concludes, "This whole season is about giving."

There's another moment in the film where Nathan is pondering his religious identity.

"My parents call themselves Buddhist. And they called me Buddhist, 'cause I asked them, like, 'Well, what am I?' *'You're Buddhist.'* 'Oh!'"

"So," Nathan continues, "I don't feel like I'm Buddhist, because I don't put any effort into it, or any work. And the work and effort I'm talking about is like chants. And meditation. It's just hard to call myself Buddhist without doing anything at all. Yeah, I dunno."

From behind the camera, we hear Wanwan's voice for the first time. "You help out every weekend at the youth group."

"I help out every—oh!" Nathan's left hand flies up to his face. He laughs nervously, stroking his chin in thought, then aims his index finger at camera.

"Yes. Yes. Great point. I do help out at the youth group." He sounds skeptical.

"But that—that doesn't sound like something a *Buddhist* person does? You know what I mean? Like, I'm just helping out. I'm a-helpin' out. If I can help out here, I can help out there, I can help out...."

When representations of individual meditators dominate the American Buddhist mediascape, it's all too easy to undervalue the more community-oriented practice of serving others.[3]

I think of Camilla, doing everything from interpretation to cracking walnuts for her community. Or her fellow sangha member Tiffany, who enjoys washing dishes and planning events for the temple—and considers these practices to be just as important as meditation and chanting. "My Asian Buddhist background encourages me to have this service-oriented mindset that might not have been there if I was just learning Buddhism from an academic or more intellectually investigative Western perspective," Tiffany explains.

Over at the Korean temple in Anaheim, Brian is a jack-of-all-trades: recording the monks' dharma talks and uploading them to the temple's YouTube page (which he helped set up), putting up posters to advertise events, cleaning bathrooms, acting as an ambassador to other temples, accompanying temple members with limited English proficiency to city hall. Having been born in the United States and grown up with close connections to Asian culture, Brian finds that he can alleviate tensions between American-born and Korean-born sangha members because he "gets along with both sides." Like Nathan, Brian is humble about his contributions. He prefers to "help out behind the scenes, when people are not looking."

Self-promotion clearly isn't the point. No wonder it's so easy to overlook these second-generation young adults' tireless efforts in service of others.

Before moving to California, Brian formed a Buddhist club at his high school of four thousand students in Chicago. Many of the people who came to the club only wanted to meditate, which came as a shock to Brian. Growing up Laotian American Buddhist, the emphasis was on community service, prayers, and ceremonies. For Brian, Buddhism had always been a religion; this was his first encounter with those who saw it as "just a philosophy that you use to enhance your meditation." Not wanting to privilege any one viewpoint over others, he worked hard to build a community that made space for diverse and even divergent ways of relating to Buddhism.

Wenli's high school had a Christian organization but no Buddhist group, so "it was very lonely" being Buddhist when she wasn't at home or temple. As an undergrad, she led the Buddhist Association at the University of California, Irvine, and cofounded the Southern California University Buddhist Association. SCUBA faced hostility from other students; some even tore down the Buddhist group's posters. Undeterred, Wenli took this as urgent proof that young adult Asian American Buddhists need safe spaces to "seek the belonging that we so need."

Michael always makes an effort to engage those who denigrate bowing and chanting as "idolistic." He invites people to respect these ego-reducing, equanimity-building practices rather than dismissing them as inferior to the more "philosophical" aspects of Buddhism. "What I deeply hope is that people at the very minimum acknowledge that there is a ritual component in Buddhism," Michael reflects. "For me personally, it's quite important, because that was what I was built up from."

Michael might be heartened to hear how Andy's relationship with ritual shifted from disparagement to greater appreciation. "I played off the ceremonies as just Chinese superstition, as unnecessary to Buddhism," Andy admits. "But after talking with some other Asian American Buddhists, I realized, this is as much a part of Buddhism as everything else is. This is how they found Buddhism. So I can't just throw it away and disrespect it."

Recently, Andy reached out after seeing that I was one of the many contributors to *A Thousand Hands: A Guidebook to Caring for your Buddhist Community:*[4] "I am considering getting the book because I'd love some resources on caring for Asian American youth, especially training our summer camp counselors with resources grounded in counseling and Buddhism." It didn't take him and his camp coleader long to decide. Andy sent me a Facebook message the next day: "We work with Ven. Bhikkhu Bodhi, and when we saw his rave review, we knew we had to get it!"

In the summer before college, Larene attended an English-language retreat at a Buddhist monastery in New Jersey. It was a formative experience of many firsts, including meeting Bhikkhu Bodhi, hearing the words "Mahayana" and "Theravada," receiving meditation instruction, meeting Mahayana and Theravada monastics under one roof, and meditating daily. The retreat made a huge impact and solidified her faith and interest in Buddhism. As an adviser for BOCA, Larene draws on her experiences as a past youth group participant to create open, safe, and welcoming environments to delve into Buddhism. It's evident from Wanwan's documentary that the youth group is succeeding in its aim of fostering Buddhist leaders, being of service to the community, and promoting strong friendships.

It's not just the BOCA youth group that has fostered new Buddhist leaders. Though her mom was her gatekeeper to Buddhism and her dad remains an important supporter of her practice, Thao considers the Dharma Realm Buddhist Youth (DRBY) to be the greatest influencer of her Buddhist journey. She vividly recalls meeting the down-to-earth group members during DRBY's first winter retreat when she was nine years old (they were discussing the Shurangama Sutra with Rev. Heng Sure, director of Berkeley Buddhist Monastery). These college students and young working professionals instantly became her role models for how to apply Buddhism to everyday life. By senior year of high school, Thao was one of three leaders planning the annual DRBY spring conference—"I was the youngest person to be a leader, and I had been waiting for it since I was nine." While the group has since disbanded, some members are now her mentors, others are her good friends, and a few are even her coworkers at Dharma Realm Buddhist University.

Andy, Brian, Larene, Nathan, Thao, Wenli. Just some of the many unsung Asian American Buddhist leaders who are creating spaces for Buddhist youth to explore their cultural and religious identities—in the company of supportive peers, on their own terms. Leaders who are reciprocating and extending the generosity and compassion they have received from their parents and teachers.

In the penultimate scene of *Youth Group,* Nathan and his mom are once again sitting on the couch.

"When Mommy had surgery, I even prayed inside," Ms. Tham explains to her son. She taps her hands to her heart. A jade bracelet adorns her left arm; brown mala beads encircle her right wrist.

"I've done that before too," Nathan interjects.

"觀世音菩薩, 保佑平安, 保佑平安," his mom continues. ("I asked the Goddess of Mercy for blessings.")

We hear Wanwan's voice for the second time. "Have you done that before too?"

Nathan looks sheepish. "Well, I mean, like—it wasn't Guanyin Pusa that I was praying to, but I was just channeling, you know, those good, virtuous thoughts that my mom is really good at doing. Which I probably picked up from her at a young age."

Mother and son nod in unison.

"And who I was calling out to was just this—powerful being; I don't know who it be. I really don't know. I mean, I can't say that it is Guanyin Pusa, or God, or the Buddha himself, or anything." Nathan throws his hands up. "I was just crying out to whoever's out there, if there is someone, something there. So, that was like *my* internal prayer." Nathan puts his hand on his mom's shoulder. "Mom, I know you, you pray to Guanyin Pusa inside. But I'm saying, we do the same thing, except, you call her Guanyin Pusa, I call her 'the benevolent being.'"

Mother and son behold each other, smiling.

PART 3

INTEGRATORS

Buddhists like myself face challenges in integrating and expressing multiple cultural identities—as young, American, Buddhist, and Asian. Yet I think we are all moving toward a more pluralistic world in which multiplicity of identity will be the norm.

—HOLLY

7

TENSION

May I be filled with loving-kindness
May I be well
May I be peaceful and at ease
May I be happy
May you be filled with loving-kindness
May you be well
May you be peaceful and at ease
May you be happy
May we be filled with loving-kindness
May we be well
May we be peaceful and at ease
May we be happy

Our voices rise to the wooden rafters, the simple tune cresting at *filled,*
I–you–we, happy, a song made sweeter by days of communal silence.
Years later I will sing this melody of metta with patients on the oncology

unit, but right now I am a college student on winter break who doesn't even know what a hospital chaplain is, much less that I will eventually train as one.

This, my first meditation retreat, has not been all honeyed tones and herbal tea. I expected to struggle with pain in my inflexible hips, to fight my penchant for nodding off, but there's another discomfort I'd forgotten to anticipate. In a room of more than a hundred people, I can count on one hand those of us who aren't white. Also few and far between: those of us who aren't baby boomers.

I should be used to this by now. The insight meditation center I've been going to for evening Dharma talks and daylong sits has been good practice for feeling conspicuously Asian and markedly young. ·

I know this retreat center, which is also in the insight meditation tradition, is trying to diversify. There are scholarships available for people of color and young adults; I'm here under the auspices of one.

Still, given the demographics, it's hard not to think of these sanghas as white spaces. I am on my best behavior because I want to be a good meditator, a polite guest, a harmless interloper. I say "thank you" when white sangha members praise my "unaccented" English, swallowing the temptation to snark that five-year-olds tend to have pretty good language acquisition skills, especially in the aggressively monolingual public-school environment of 1990s America. I say "China" when asked "Where are you from," because responding with "Pennsylvania and Washington State" will only trigger a "Where are you *really* from?" I'm sure my questioners mean well, even if their curiosity about my ethnic origins curiously doesn't seem to extend to their fellow white meditators. I doubt they are trying to remind me that Asian Americans have long been painted as perpetual foreigners even if their families have lived in this country for generations.

This is hardly the first time I've fielded compliments on my English or queries about my origins, but "your parents must be Buddhist" catches me off guard. I suppress the urge to blurt out "are you saying that because I'm Asian?"

Having lived through the tumultuous Cultural Revolution, my parents are staunchly areligious, if not antireligious. I suppress the urge to point out that U.S. Asian adults are more likely to be Christian (42 percent) or religiously unaffiliated (26 percent) than Buddhist (14 percent).[1]

"I practiced with a Korean Zen community for four years, and white members tended to assume I was Korean and grew up within that school," Catherine observes. "Neither is true." Like me, Catherine was born in Shanghai, raised by nonreligious parents in various parts of America, and gravitated toward Buddhism in college. Yet people assume we have inherited an "ethnic" form of Buddhism from our parents—our stories predetermined before we have a chance to speak them ourselves.

Where are we to stake our tents in the dual, dueling camps of "Asian immigrant" and "white convert" Buddhism?

All my ancient twisted karma,
From beginningless greed, hate and delusion,
Born through body speech and mind,
I now fully avow

A dozen voices echo in the room where I have come to memorize this chant, our solemn monotone reverberating off pine floors, absorbing into black *zabutons,* awakening wintry morning air as *avow-w-w* constricts into a haunting, hallowed silence. Years later Trent and I will intone these words before exchanging wedding rings, but for now we are living in our first apartment, juggling multiple part-time jobs (me) and a fellowship (him) while applying for grad school (both of us).

At this Zen temple just down the street from us, the practice style differs from the insight meditation center where I learned the loving-kindness song. The demographics do not. After a month of morning *zazen,* I work up the courage to ask the vice-abbot where I might find other young, nonwhite Buddhists and meditators.

His frank reply: "You should look elsewhere."

Avalokiteshvara Bodhisattva, when deeply practicing prajña
paramita, clearly saw that all five aggregates are empty and thus
relieved all suffering.

It's no problem following along with the English version of the Heart Sutra on the page in front of me, but I get lost in the clump of roman letters rendering the Japanese:

Maka Hannya Haramitta Shingyo
Kan ji zai bo satsu gyo jin han nya ha ra mit ta ji sho ken go on kai
    ku do is sai ku yaku …

I can't help but wish the service book included kanji and hiragana in addition to the romaji, like I've seen at the Shin Buddhist temple a mile north of this Bay Area Zen center.

まか はん にゃ は ら みった しん ぎょう
摩 訶 般 若 波 羅 蜜 多 心 経

かん じ ざい ぼ さつ
観 自 在 菩 薩

ぎょう じん はん にゃ は ら みった じ
行 深 般 若 波 羅 蜜 多 時

しょう けん ご うん かい くう
照 見 五 蘊 皆 空

ど いっ さい く やく
度 一 切 苦 厄

I can decipher the meaning of the kanji because they are virtually the same as the Chinese characters, and reading hiragana is one of the few things I've retained from high school Japanese. But even if I couldn't make sense of these glyphs, there's a beauty to the depth of history they convey. In a tradition so focused on lineage, it's odd to see these roots erased.

Of course, it's this Zen center's prerogative to print the chants only in roman letters. Maybe there wasn't enough space on the page. Maybe they assumed their sangha members wouldn't feel any cultural connection to the kanji and hiragana.

"It's very rare to find Asians in these communities," Manoj acknowledges. Raised Hindu in southern India, Manoj began exploring Buddhism after moving to America and discovered an affinity for Soto Zen. He reached out after hearing about my project from another Zen practitioner, though he wasn't sure if he qualified for an interview: "I am Indian and hope it counts in the Asian category." After assuring him that Indian very much counts as Asian in my book, here we are, braving blustery winds at an outdoor table in a café by the bay.

Over the chatter of the Sunday brunch crowd, Manoj reflects on the time he has spent in Zen communities in the Midwest and California. "I would love to have more Japanese people, even just for things like pronouncing" (Manoj admits that he gets annoyed when fellow practitioners "mangle Sanskrit words"). He recalls a cringe-worthy occasion where his Zen temple in Minneapolis printed out cards for a special function and a Japanese man pointed out the calligraphy was upside down. "Diversity's always good because you know it's going to give you more ideas—it's going to be a more enriching experience," Manoj argues.

In the online anthology "Making the Invisible Visible: Healing Racism in Our Buddhist Communities," a twenty-seven-year-old Asian American Zen practitioner considers how she, "a yonsei, came to find out about Zen Buddhism through a 'predominantly white Zen Center' rather than through a 'local Japanese American temple.'" Writing anonymously, she reveals some of the "more charged" moments in this environment: "An older white female practitioner patting me on the head and petting my hair while speaking to me in what I perceive to be patronizing tones." "Hearing residents comment to me that my parents, who recently visited, are 'so-o-o cute' and feeling as if they are describing a teddy bear." She tries to relate to these encounters as "fertile ground for practice," though it's rarely easy to do so.

When I have felt like residents are putting down Asian people and things, how to be fully present for the initial fuzziness, the disbelief, and then the hurt and annoyance? How to make contact when sensations and remembrances arise of past experiences when Asians have been relegated to the category of subhuman (often in order to deny opportunities or resources) and to not get stuck or lost?

When I feel like young men are looking at me through their stereotype-pumped lenses, how to be present for the arising disdain and for the remembrance of other not-so-pleasant encounters I have had with certain men (being told such things as "You are so exotic. I really like special, exotic things"). How to make space for the rising impulse to close off and become "all business like" as well the deep desire to be open and to meet each person in the moment as human? How to be present for all of these things and neither suppress or over-emote? And when I can't do this, how to remember to just give myself a hug and to notice?[2]

These words were published in 2000, but every time I read them, it feels like they could have been penned yesterday. I'm always struck too by how startlingly rare it is to hear voices like hers. I know she's not the only Asian American experiencing racial tensions in her sangha.

Following the advice of the vice-abbot, I went further afield—or more precisely, I circled back to the bigger Zen temple where I first learned the Maka Hannya Haramitta Shingyo. I told the abbot about my desire to connect with other Asian American Buddhists. He offered to introduce me to a sangha member, thinking she (a Chinese American) would be better equipped to discuss these issues than he (a white man).

The interaction didn't go quite as expected. (A good lesson in beginner's mind?) The practitioner cut off the conversation with a curt "She's a banana" and walked off. The dumbfounded abbot quickly excused himself. I was unsure how to parse the situation, though the encounter certainly disabused me of any notions of Asian American Buddhists being a unified, harmonious bloc.

She's basically a white person who happens to be Asian. She speaks English surprisingly well and barely a word of whatever Asian dialect her parents spoke. She cooks nonethnic food, uses the dishwasher, and

crosses her chopsticks. She may have been raised by Superstitious Immi-
grants, but she's renounced that backwards and foreign worldview. She
probably doesn't even identify as Asian. You can find her at yoga Thurs-
days and your zendo's weekend sits, where she'll sit quietly in the back
and not make much of a fuss. It really doesn't matter if she doesn't speak
up because whatever she says isn't going to be any different from what
the white Buddhists are saying.[3]

A carefully crafted caricature of the "banana Buddhist," courtesy of the
Angry Asian Buddhist. Some might take offense at the flippant tone. Others
might consider the racial slur egregious.

What I see is a satirical extension of the logic of "two Buddhisms." In
a typology that separates American Buddhists into Asian immigrants and
white converts, where do people like Manoj, Catherine, and me fit in?
Are we essentially white converts who "happen to be" Asian, our culture
merely a sidenote, baggage to be unburdened from?

For ethnic Asians in the West, it is really not a matter of "conversion" to
Buddhism, even if one's family or ethnic group was not Buddhist in Asia
in recent times. It is rather a matter of reversion ...[4]

Reading sociologist Paul Numrich's scholarship on American Buddhism,
I'm often left with the impression that when it comes to Asian Americans
and convert Buddhists, never the twain shall meet. (Numrich did, after
all, coin the term "parallel congregations" to underscore the separation of
the two groups.[5]) In addition to suggesting that Asian Americans can only
revert to Buddhism, Numrich also contends:

Non-Asian Buddhist converts in Western societies adopt a religious
worldview different from that of their ethnic heritage and of the main-
stream culture in which they were raised. An argument can be made
that the term "convert" still applies to the children of the original cohort
since this new generation must at some point consciously choose to per-
petuate their parents' rejection of their former religious worldviews.[6]

This perspective unleashed a flurry of questions in me. So if a white convert raises their children Buddhist, these children would also be "converts"? But why wouldn't the children of, say, an Asian American Christian who converts to Buddhism also be considered converts? Don't they also have to consciously reject their parents' former religious worldviews? And if an Asian American whose family has been Christian for multiple generations converts to Buddhism, are they actually "reverting"? Is the opposite of a convert a revert?

In an interview about her book *Virtual Orientalism,* Jane Iwamura talks about being raised Jodo Shinshu, attending Seventh Day Adventist and Mennonite schools along with Catholic and Episcopalian summer camps, and considering herself a Christian in college before realizing an affinity for Buddhism in graduate school.[7] Has Iwamura converted to Buddhism? Reverted? Switched? Done something else entirely that we have yet to find a good term for?

In the introduction of a book by a Buddhist studies scholar, the author defines North American convert Buddhism as "the Buddhism of Americans who are not of Asian descent."[8]

In retrospect, it wasn't entirely fair to decontextualize this quote before posing it to my interviewees. The full sentence ("A case in point is the phenomenon of modern North American 'convert' Buddhism—the Buddhism of Americans who are not of Asian descent") marks the start of a long, incisive paragraph in an academic book whose main focus is medieval Chinese Buddhism. With due apologies to Professor Robert Sharf for cherry-picking, I can certainly say the quote prompted plenty of discussion.

"Ha-ha-ha! That's really funny. I can see that." Claire responds to the quote in good humor. "If you're not happy with, say, Christianity, or the dominant meaning of whatever you grew up with in the U.S., then sometimes you want something that's *other.* I think Buddhism currently serves those purposes really well." Claire wonders if Asian Americans, especially those who grew up in Buddhist households like she did, "don't see Buddhism as something new to turn to"—perhaps it's "more of a cultural thing" for them.

Kiet also offers an explanation in support of Professor Sharf's statement. From his vantage point as the son of Vietnamese Buddhists, Kiet hypothesizes that religion is secondary to economic advancement for Asian American immigrants. By contrast, Caucasians who have lived in America for a long time "may be very wealthy; they may have nice cars, big houses, but they are not happy"—so they might embrace Buddhism as a solution to their suffering. In this line of reasoning, Buddhism is at best incidental for Asian Americans, at worst an obstacle to success.

Nora agrees that "there's this assumption that new Buddhists are Caucasian American." But she is not entirely unfazed by this assumption, "which does a disservice to this group as well as to Asian Americans." Regrettably, "there are a lot of stereotypes that come along with a lack of knowledge." As a Japanese American Shin Buddhist born into the religion, Nora chastises herself for unwittingly perpetuating these stereotypes. She often assumes that non-Asians at her temple are converts from Christianity who encountered a personal crisis that made them turn to Buddhism—even though she can immediately think of a counterexample: "I have a friend who grew up in the temple, and she's not Asian American.... People always thought that she and her mother were converts to the religion—but that's not how it was."

I guess I would be missed in that definition, as you can say I "converted" to Buddhism and am also of Asian descent.

Bhikshu Jin Chuan's response to the North American convert Buddhism quote is diplomatic. "Maybe the scholar didn't interact with too many convert Asian Buddhists who met the Dharma in America?"

Bhikshu Jin Chuan is among the thirty or so young adults I interviewed who might be considered Asian American convert Buddhists. Some were raised Christian. Others grew up Hindu. Some, like Bhikshu Jin Chuan, come from nonreligious families. Still others come from Jewish, Muslim, Zoroastrian, or mixed-religion households. The group represents a wide range of Asian ethnicities, including Chinese, Filipino, Indian, Iranian, Japanese, Korean, Nepali, Turkmen, and Vietnamese. A third of the group is multiracial, thus expanding the list of ethnicities to include Ashkenazi, Belarusian, Danish, French, German, Irish, Mexican, Spanish, and more.[9]

I say thirty "or so" because deciding who counts as a "convert" isn't always straightforward. Gabrielle, introduced earlier in this book along-side multi-generation Jodo Shinshu Buddhists, grew up with various religious influences, including a Zen grandfather. Wanwan identifies as agnostic but might be considered a Buddhist sympathizer: "I have been exposed to very different forms of Buddhist practices and am curious about why people adopt different approaches to Buddhism." Supraja, who grew up Hindu and began reading books on Buddhism in college, could also count as a sympathizer: "I'm attracted to Buddhism, but I wouldn't identify as a Buddhist."

Ambiguities around categorization aside, this group by and large pushes back against the idea that North American convert Buddhism is "the Buddhism of Americans who are not of Asian descent."

Vince, who "grew up without any real religious or spiritual upbring-ing," though his parents are now Catholic, asks: "Why isn't there an acknowledgment of those of Asian descent who convert to Buddhism from another religious or spiritual tradition?" He worries these individ-uals are being neglected out of ignorance or lack of intellectual interest.

Wanwan expands on Vince's line of questioning. "What about second- or third-generation non-Asian American Buddhists?" She worries this definition of convert Buddhism implies the existence of essentialized differences between "Asian" and "non-Asian" Buddhists when the real-ity is much more interconnected: "Many Asian American Buddhists learn about Buddhism through texts written by 'convert Buddhists' and 'con-vert Buddhists' study with Buddhist teachers in Asia or of Asian heritage."

"As a convert American Buddhist of Asian descent, I'm feeling pretty alienated by this," exclaims Anthony, who was raised in a Christian family.

"How exactly would the scholar describe Asian American Buddhists who do convert? Which 'American Buddhism' is ours?" Manny, who identifies as a "third culture kid" (his father is Iranian, his mother Hispanic), asks an analogous question: "Who qualifies as a true and blue North American after all?"

Cristina also objects. "Of course Asian Americans are going to also be converts to Buddhism—whether it's from Islam, Christianity, or indigenous Asian religions (Hindu, animist, Shinto, etc.) or between Buddhist sects. My family came from Korea. Though my maternal grandmother is Buddhist, I never had much exposure to her lineage of Korean Buddhism. My parents were married in what was originally an Anglican chapel. We went to church when I was growing up. As a convert to Buddhism myself—first Theravadan and now Rinzai Zen—I find this definition to be incomplete."

Lola's reaction is even more impassioned. "Argh, this immediately strikes me the wrong way.... Asian Americans have had a large impact (albeit invisible) to 'the Buddhism of Americans.' Needless to say, again, we are not seen as Americans." Lola's parents are among the many immigrants from Asian countries who had already adopted Western religions before coming to America. Her mother went to Christian schools in Hong Kong and the United States; her father's background is similar.

Although I was not baptized or christened, I consider myself a convert Buddhist ... and I was born here, in North America, in the States. So I guess I can't be included in this scholar's definition, simply because I'm of Asian descent—I believe this is a pretty clear case of discrimination and racism. (And I'm quite aware that I'm assuming that this scholar is white.)

Lola's frustration calls to mind Rick Field's observation that white Buddhists have done most of the defining in American Buddhism—and have been largely defining it in their own image.[10]

There's a pressure for us to choose an identity, when we feel our identity is something in between.

This comment from Aaron's videotaped 2014 interview with Wanwan hints at the tensions Asian American convert Buddhists face as they navigate multiple religious and cultural worlds.

Sometimes the tensions are familial. "I experience quite a bit of conflict with my family.... They constantly tell me to convert and that I need to come back to Jesus." Unfortunately for Matthew, a Korean American who was raised Christian and now practices in multiple schools of Buddhism, it's not just his relatives who give him grief about his new religion: "The Korean Christians that I've met have not been understanding of my religion, and they criticize my religion at every opportunity." His story reminds me of the painful account of another interviewee who left the Chinese American evangelical church that formed the fabric of her childhood religious life. Eileen's family members were far from thrilled when they learned about her newfound Buddhist practices.

Bhikshu Jin Chuan's journey to becoming a Buddhist monk after growing up in a secular Chinese American household was also marked by family tension, as he details in a series of blog posts.[11] His mother bought him a Bible and gave him books on Buddhism to support his exploration of both religions, but when her son announced that he wanted to become a monk, she began to regret encouraging his religious interests. After many tense years, the young man who would eventually become Bhikshu Jin Chuan was at an impasse, wanting to pursue his monastic aspirations but not wanting to make his parents unhappy.[12]

Sometimes the tensions are felt most keenly in Buddhist communities. As a person of South Asian Indian descent, Kirthi sits with the paradox of how Buddhism is both "of my culture and of my people, but not something I grew up with." As someone whose spiritual practices combine Hinduism, yoga, and vipassana meditation, she often feels a sense of "belonging and not belonging" in various sanghas. Kirthi clarifies that "these ruptures of belonging surface mostly in sanghas that are white-dominant"—sanghas that often fail to acknowledge Buddhism's South Asian roots, sanghas that too often ignore the structural oppressions contributing to the lack of people of color in their communities.

Raised in a South Asian household, Shubha now practices insight meditation—but hesitates to identify as Buddhist. This is partially because they don't want to reject their Hindu upbringing (though Shubha doesn't mind identifying as a Hindu who practices Buddhist meditation), and partially because they fear that proclaiming themselves a Buddhist would signal an embrace of "all the exoticized fantasies that people have." Though they feel bad about it, Shubha associates the term "practicing Buddhist" with white people who hold romanticized notions about Buddhism.

In a blog post titled "Meditation and Diversity" on their blog *Ganesha's Scarf,* Shubha puzzles over feeling "out of place" on noticing they were one of only three "visible minorities" at a meditation retreat.[13] "What makes me feel 'in place'? I know that being around a group of Indians doesn't suddenly put me at ease. I guess it's the mix of people—it's easy to feel out of place when you're one grape in a bowl of apples, but a grape in a bowl of mixed fruit feels welcoming."

Shubha goes on to acknowledge that Buddhism's Asian origins contribute to their discomfort at meeting so few Asian Americans at the retreat—yet they also believe Buddhism should be available to all people regardless of racial background. Supraja, whom I met at the 2013 TechnoBuddha conference, felt a similar ambivalence upon seeing only white faces on the website of a Zen group she considered visiting. She told herself, "I shouldn't be racist; I know those people are really committed," but couldn't shake the thought that "I just want to see some Asians there too." Shubha and Supraja's reflections bring to mind the tension between cultural particularism and religious universalism that I heard Landon and other Japanese American Shin Buddhists grapple with.

"I find myself in the middle in a lot of ways," Alyssa comments: in the middle of cultural worlds, in the middle of Buddhist worlds, and also, she says with a chuckle, "in the middle of learning." Alyssa was finishing up a year of teaching English at a Buddhist college in China when we first met. As an example of her betwixt-and-between status, Alyssa explains that on the one hand, being a layperson and native English speaker sets her apart from the Chinese-speaking, majority-monastic community at the college;

on the other hand, she is not fully at ease in predominantly white Buddhist communities.

Case in point: on a visa run from China to Hong Kong, Alyssa decided to attend a series of Dharma talks at a Zen center. Listening to renowned teachers from around the world, she had the jarring realization that almost all of them were white males. To her dismay, she realized she was being more critical than usual as she listened. Seeing herself as an open-minded person who doesn't prioritize one ethnicity over another, Alyssa was baffled by her visceral reaction, especially since she was used to being the minority in the largely Caucasian environments she grew up in. "In the context of Buddhism, maybe I feel like I *should* have some more connection to this religion *because* my family came from the same place where Buddhism is primarily practiced?" Alyssa surmises that practicing in a predominantly white sangha "would feel uncomfortable because maybe there are certain assumptions they'd have about me"—that Buddhism is a product of her ethnicity or family background rather than a personal choice, for instance.

In "Making the Invisible Visible," an anonymous Chinese American practitioner writes frankly about the discomfort she feels in both majority-white sanghas and majority-Asian Buddhist temples in America. "As an adult child of Chinese immigrants who married in a Protestant church, I've come to Buddhism only recently, as part of a several-years-long attempt to learn more about my heritage.... My experience with Buddhism somewhat mirrors my life as an Asian American—I don't fit in with first-generation Asians, I don't fit in with white America, and so I have to find my own way."[14]

I suspect many Asian American Buddhists who weren't raised in the faith can resonate with these words. I certainly do. When faced with simplistic assumptions, unrealistic expectations, and general ignorance about what it means to be an Asian American convert Buddhist—indeed, when our very identities seem to be an oxymoron within "two Buddhisms"—how do we find our way?

AFFINITY

It's hard to pinpoint an exact moment when I "converted" to Buddhism. It was more of a gradual steeping, Buddhism suffusing my life the way tea remakes water, a subtle flavor intensifying over time.

To borrow an insight from one of my interviewees: You connect the dots in retrospect. I might trace a line beginning from high school (clawing my way out of a suffocating depression, seeking relief from burnout and despair, finding no comfort in my secular upbringing) to a gap year in Australia and Asia (the couple who introduced me to meditation on their farm in rural New South Wales, a beloved uncle whose death from cancer made my months in Shanghai a tear-soaked lesson in the *dukkha* of impermanence, the Buddhist art and architecture and devotions that awed me in Thailand and Nepal and Tibet).

A fallow time followed those early seeds of interest, my spiritual leanings forgotten in the busyness of starting college. And then, in the fall of junior year, I chanced to meet a religious studies major who had taken a gap year to study Buddhist chant and temporarily ordain as a monk in Cambodia. He also happened to be the president of the Buddhist association at our university, though (not wanting to proselytize, perhaps?) he kept mum about this for months. Eventually, I joined Trent for the Buddhist club's early morning sittings. Though slightly baffled by the what and why of it all, I persisted at this new practice, in part out of a spirit of inquiry, in part because my presence usually brought the number of meditators to a grand total of two. (The evening sittings may have been better attended.)

That spring, I left for a study-abroad program in South Africa, a stack of Buddhist books in my suitcase (Sister Chan Khong's *Learning True Love,* Sogyal Rinpoche's *The Tibetan Book of Living and Dying,* Joanna Macy's *Widening Circles,* Shunryu Suzuki's *Zen Mind, Beginner's Mind,* something by Jack Kornfield, or was it Jon Kabat-Zinn?). Reading made me curious to visit actual communities. I managed to visit a few sanghas (who would have guessed my introductions to Soka Gakkai International and Tzu Chi would be in Cape Town?) when I wasn't conducting interviews at various nonprofits for my undergraduate thesis.

Back in the Bay Area after my time in Cape Town, a cascade, a smorgasbord, call it what you will: meditating at insight and Zen centers. Visiting Cambodian and Taiwanese and Vietnamese and Thai and Chinese American temples. Taking the refuges in Khmer-inflected Pali. Chanting repentance rites in Japanese and English. Paying homage to the Buddha in Cantonese-tinged Mandarin. Listening to Dharma talks in a profusion of languages. Poring over Buddhist books, wondering why they all seem to be authored by white converts or Asian monastics. Feeling out of place at both "Asian immigrant" and "white convert" sanghas, yet more connected to these communities than any of the Christian spaces I'd ever been to. Feeling an odd sense of familiarity with Buddhist teachings and practice, though all of it was strange and new. Feeling, nevertheless, hesitant to call myself a Buddhist, and even more reluctant to identify as a "convert"— though isn't that what I was?

Overall, Buddhism had the greatest net loss due to changes in religious affiliation within the Asian American community. One in ten Asian Americans (10 percent) were raised Buddhist and have left the faith, while 2 percent of Asian Americans have become Buddhist after being raised in a different faith (or no faith), resulting in a net loss of eight percentage points due to religious switching.[1]

It didn't occur to me to include myself in the purview of these Pew Forum statistics, even after I'd presented them to eighty-nine different interviewees, even though I could practically recite these two sentences in my sleep.

Dan, however, did see herself reflected in the numbers. "That's interesting, is my first thought—I wasn't expecting to read that Buddhism among Asian Americans was declining. I'm definitely a part of the 2 percent who have converted; I was formerly Catholic." Dan was born in Vietnam and grew up in California; thanks to our mutual friendship with Aaron, she and I would meet first via email and later in person at TechnoBuddha 2015.

Luke, the last person I interviewed, also resonates with the Pew report. "I am really glad you've cited this statistic. Really glad. I classify as part of the 2 percent. I grew up in a Methodist family. My mother wanted to raise me as Japanese Buddhist, but my father disagreed.... I technically 'converted' to Buddhism at age twenty-four. I took refuge vows in the tradition after identifying as atheist for many years."

Aaron's reaction to the Pew statistics is that his dad—having traveled through Catholicism and Buddhism to Judaism—would fall into both categories, the 10 percent *and* the 2 percent. Aaron was raised Jewish, but Buddhism was woven into his "ambient environment" growing up: through pop culture, his mom's "Bu-Jew" friends, the closet his grandmother repurposed into an altar room, and so forth. When I ask Aaron where he would fit in the ethnic versus convert divide within "two Buddhisms," he furrows his brows.

"I would be a problem. You could make a pretty good argument either way." The jury is out on whether Aaron qualifies as a convert Buddhist.

"I think 'conversion' is so contextually rooted in European theistic histories that I find 'convert' ill-suited to describe the way that people newly take up Buddhist practice." Holly is hardly alone in this line of thinking. As Vince memorably puts it: "We can't equate the act of taking refuge with conversion in the Judeo-Christian sense. There's no stress test either."

The young adults I interviewed repeatedly installed scare quotes around the word *convert*. For one thing, "conversion," with its Christian connotations, often brings to mind a sudden transformation. Consider, for example, the dramatic events—complete with divine revelation—that converted Saul, persecutor of early Christians, into the apostle Paul.[2] By contrast, Gabrielle describes a less dramatic shift: "I don't really think one 'converts' to Buddhism. To me, becoming a Buddhist was more like a slow realization."

Aaron Huang relates a similar experience: "I can't actually pinpoint a seminal event in my life.... I just started meditating and reading more about Buddhism, and at some point I'd been inoculated by enough of the Dharma that I was comfortable calling myself a Buddhist." Aaron, who grew up Catholic, can't think of an official ceremony that inducted him into Buddhism. I laugh in recognition when he tells me the story of going to the East Bay Meditation Center and asking someone how he could learn more about Buddhism. "She gave me, like, ten books to read—you know, for Catholicism, they're like, well, just read the freaking Bible!"

Like Aaron, Vinod cannot name a pivotal conversion moment. "It's been an organic process.... I was raised in a Hindu household (and still identify as Hindu as well), but have admired Buddhist hagiography and imagery for as long as I can remember." As a child, the Amar Chitra Katha comics whetted Vinod's appetite for Indian history, mythology, and religions; anytime a Buddhist documentary came on TV, he would watch it with his folks. Vinod began reading Buddhist and Hindu texts at the end of high school and started listening to talks by the Dalai Lama and Matthieu Ricard in early college. After taking several courses on Asian religions, he decided to form a daily meditation practice.

Manny's Buddhist journey was also a gradual unfolding. Raised Muslim, his introduction to Buddhism came through a college class. "The exposure to Buddhist philosophy really shook me and forced me to rethink and reframe my values. I found tremendous resonance with the Buddhist emphasis on training the mind, the wisdom of emptiness of the self and ephemeral reality, and the necessity of compassion. It awoke a voice for feelings that I'd had for years—I felt like I'd been Buddhist my whole life and didn't know it." Though deeply affected, Manny still considered his relationship with Buddhism to be an "intellectual dalliance," more of a philosophical identification than a lived practice. This all changed after he participated in a study-abroad program in Bodh Gaya that incorporated contemplative practices in the Burmese, Zen, and Tibetan meditation traditions. Manny established a meditation practice, began to read more Buddhist literature, and sought out spiritual teachers. Two years later, while working in Bhutan, he met the *rinpoche* who would become his primary Buddhist teacher.

Manny, Vinod, and Aaron would all fit comfortably within scholar Peter Gregory's capacious definition of American convert Buddhists as "Americans (regardless of ethnicity) who are not Buddhist by birth but who take up various forms of Buddhist practice without necessarily undergoing a dramatic experience that could be characterized as a religious conversion."[3] Yet none of them use the term *conversion* to describe their journeys from Muslim, Hindu, and Catholic upbringings to Buddhist practices.

I spend the summer after graduation learning the limits of the bachelor's degree I've just earned. Trent's research has connected him to Rev. Beth Goldring, founder of a Buddhist chaplaincy organization in Cambodia. A decade later this American Zen nun will officiate our wedding, but that humid and humbling summer, her blessing is to place me under the tutelage of Brahmavihara's Cambodian staff, whose diligent and warm-hearted care for the dying make them living embodiments of the organization's name. As we offer what we can to meet the needs of our patients in each moment—whether Reiki or chant, food or presence, consolation or silence—the work itself becomes a cultivation of the divine abodes of loving-kindness, compassion, empathetic joy, and equanimity. Every Wednesday the staff gathers at Beth's Phnom Penh apartment for a morning of meditation and Dharma study. An annual retreat provides space for deepening their practice. For that year's retreat, we steal away to a temple in nearby Prey Veng Province. Emerging from ten days of meditation and chanting with the Brahmavihara bodhisattvas (as I'd come to think of them), Beth announces to all of us: "Your feet are firmly on the path."

Maybe I didn't locate myself in the "2 percent of Asian Americans [who] have become Buddhist after being raised in a different faith (or no faith)" because I didn't experience this process as a form of "religious switching," to use the parlance of the Pew report. It wasn't like I flipped a switch from off to on.

Then again, switches come in different forms. A dimmer gently gliding, a room slowly brightening—now that feels like a more apt metaphor.

"I think that conversion to Buddhism happens very subtly," Manny reasons. "No coercion is involved, but the offer is always on the table."

"Buddhism is not so much a religion of proselytization," Luke argues. "People come to it if it is in their karma."

Yima, my first interviewee, thinks "you can contribute to another person's liberation without converting the person."

"We propagate the Dharma, which is different from converting others," Matthew insists.

"Conversion—I have mixed feelings about it because I was raised Catholic," Aaron Huang admits during our Skype interview. "Even the Dalai Lama—I don't know if he's necessarily had the effect of converting people to Buddhism as much as he's just been agnostically inspiring people." Aaron relates to Buddhism as a "catalyst to uncover the truth" and is reluctant to invoke the word *conversion* because "that excludes other religions that also have fundamental truths to them."

Camilla, introduced earlier in this book alongside other second-generation young adults, provides a Buddhist scriptural interpretation to corroborate Aaron's viewpoint.

> *In the Diamond Sutra, the Buddha says: "This Dharma is level and equal, without superiority or inferiority." This means that any Dharma (teaching, in this case) that gets you to liberation is equal. So if different religions serve to fulfill the needs of different people, there is no reason why people have to believe in Buddhism necessarily.*

Camilla doesn't think conversion plays as big a role in Buddhism as in other religions such as Christianity.

> *In Chinese thought and culture in general there is the concept of affinities* (yuan), *which can be loosely explained as ties that connect you to things. So if you have affinities with a certain religion, it will click for you, even if you've never been exposed to it before, but if you do not have affinities with a certain religion, it will not click for you even if you've been exposed to it for most of your life.*

Though Buddhism would not have survived to this day without missionaries, the young adults I interviewed resist associating the religion with proselytization. Another reason for using those scare quotes: to distance themselves from evangelical Christianity's mandate of converting others.

Matthew points out that if you don't believe in Buddhism, it's "not that serious; you will be reborn based on your karma," whereas "in Christianity, if you don't believe, you will go to hell."

In Bhikshu Jin Chuan's estimation, Buddhist teachings should be sought out rather than imposed: "One has to embody the Dharma to have it really benefit others—they see something that they think will help them, so they ask about it."

Karma and contribution, propagation and inspiration, catalysts and affinities and embodiments. A bevy of alternatives for reframing "conversion." A kaleidoscope of possibilities I might have missed had I not listened closely to the voices of Asian American Buddhists.

Noel offers yet another alternative for talking about "convert" Buddhists.

> *I might suggest generational categories. Many Asian people might say, "I'm first-generation American" or "I'm third-generation American." I think we can use this for Buddhism. By indicating a "generation," one can still value one's Buddhism (just like a first-gen American is as much an American as a fifth-gen American), but it also gives insight into where a person falls in the induction of Buddhism in one's life and background.*

Noel, who was born in the Philippines and raised Catholic in LA's Historic Filipinotown, explains that he would call himself a "first-gen" American Buddhist under this schema. Camilla would be "second-gen." Landon, Mari, Nora, and the other Japanese Americans I interviewed might call themselves "multi-gen" American Buddhists to indicate their families' long history of being Shin Buddhist in America.

"Conversion" in Christian contexts often implies the renunciation of one's former faith, but many of the "first-gen" Buddhists I interviewed prefer to take a more inclusive stance toward the religions they grew up with. For Gabrielle, it really was religions, plural, that shaped her upbringing:

> *As the child of a teen mother and someone of mixed heritage, I grew up with many different influences in my life. I was raised by both teenagers and older people. I was introduced to various religions, professions, and ways of life from a young age. While in many ways this diversity was beneficial and eye-opening, the lack of structure made me crave the formality and tradition of religious life. I was raised to be politically liberal and secular; while believing in God never felt right to me, I saw those around me with faith and longed to have the meaning, purpose, connection, and community in my life that often accompanies religion. It never occurred to me that theism and religion were not mutually synonymous, and so, for a long time, I thought that the realm of spirituality wasn't one in which I belonged.*

The multitude of influences in Gabrielle's childhood included her mom (raised Catholic) and stepfather (raised Jehovah's Witness), who instilled in their daughter a suspicion of organized religion; her "spiritual and even new-agey" grandparents, who criticized her parents' decision to raise Gabrielle without religion; her formerly Methodist and now-Jewish step-grandmother, who first piqued Gabrielle's interest in religion; and her Zen grandfather, whom she sought out after realizing she wanted to become Buddhist.

Gabrielle found in Shin Buddhism a religious identity and community akin to what her boyfriend had with his Christian friends in college. By the time I interviewed Gabrielle, this boyfriend had become her fiancé, and they were planning to incorporate Buddhist, Christian, Shinto, Japanese, and Irish elements in their wedding to honor their diverse spiritual and cultural heritages. Gabrielle celebrates the respectful, participatory way they engage with each other's religious traditions:

> My fiancé has gassho-ed before the Buddha and danced at the Obon with me. In return, I enjoy going to church with his family on Easter and Christmas. In some ways, our children will have the same diverse religious experience I had; the only difference will be that everything will be positive and supportive (I hope), rather than conflicting (like how my Catholic grandmother clashed with my atheist parents). I also want my children to be allowed and encouraged to find their own truth—unlike me, who was pretty much told by my parents that God isn't real. Granted, I think I've come to my own conclusion about God, but still.

Vinod may hold differing beliefs about God, but he shares Gabrielle's integrative approach toward spirituality. He is proud to identify as "a practicing Hindu-Buddhist and a student of all religions," though he worries whether the mainstream can understand and accept this identity when misconceptions of both Buddhism and Hinduism run rampant in popular culture. "At times, I wonder if my belief in God—a central piece of my Hindu philosophy—is compatible with Buddhist practice. My personal answer is yes; I don't think one has to renounce other beliefs or faiths in order to practice Buddhism."

Manoj couldn't agree more. "I definitely practice Buddhism ... and I celebrate all of my Hindu festivals as well," he informs me, just minutes after we've sat down for our interview. "You can be multiple things: you can be an atheist and a Hindu; there's no problem at all—same thing in Buddhism too." Much of our conversation on that gusty Sunday morning centers around Manoj's relationship to the Hinduism he grew up with in India and the Buddhist practice he adopted after moving to America. Since Buddhism largely accords with his preexisting beliefs, Manoj is reluctant to call himself a "convert," which he fears might come across as antagonistic and exclusionary. He prefers a more inclusive and complementary approach to religion.

Indeed, Manoj's Buddhist practice has enriched his understanding of the traditions that infused his childhood. For instance, he had always shrugged off pre-meal chanting as the province of orthodox Hindu grandfathers. "When we were kids we were forced to do it on some level on some days, but we never paid attention to why or how." But after doing similar chants in Buddhist settings? "Now I'm thinking, *wow,* you know, it makes sense!"

Altan credits the Dalai Lama for helping him realize that "Buddhism can enrich people without necessarily taking away from what they already have." Born in Turkmenistan when it was still part of the Soviet Union, Altan considers himself a "person of multiple religious belonging" since he grew up in a secular Muslim family, was baptized Christian, and now practices Buddhism. "Five years ago I didn't think I was going to be a Buddhist, Christian that I am," he laughs. On a grassy lawn a short walk away from the Jodo Shinshu Center—we had decided it was a pity to stay indoors on a sparkling summer day—Altan tells me about the meditation retreat that served as his gentle introduction to Buddhist practice, as well as a recent trip to Bodh Gaya, where he was deeply moved by the reverence of the thousands of people who had gathered to chant beneath the bodhi tree.

Like Altan, Yima's openness toward different Buddhist practices has evolved over time. "When I was first being exposed to Buddhism, I never would have imagined I'd be practicing my bowing routinely, or using prayer beads. Even three years ago, I wouldn't think chanting would be for me." Yima was born in California and raised in an Iranian Zoroastrian family, though his parents were both interested in meditation (when he was younger, his mom would visit Hindu ashrams and Zen centers). Reading *Zen Mind, Beginner's Mind* in high school was Yima's first exposure to Buddhist thought. Toward the end of high school, he took a course on mindfulness-based stress reduction; in college, he practiced at various vipassana centers. When Yima first attended a retreat at a Tibetan Buddhist center, he left early, overwhelmed by the ritual elements and unfamiliar cosmologies: "I told the teacher I don't think I'm ready for this. I may come back."

Yima did eventually go back, and has been returning for regular retreats ever since. He has developed a greater appreciation for the practices (bowing, chanting, prayer breads) and stories (such as loving-kindness meditation's origins as a method for pacifying forest spirits) that he previously dismissed as "superstitious."[4] In spite of his deepening affinity for Buddhism, Yima struggles to answer questions about his religious identity since it is not "something that is solid and always there." His Buddhist path is always interacting with the Zoroastrianism, atheism, and agnosticism that have shaped his spiritual beliefs. "I don't think you can take away how your upbringing and your background influence who you are. I don't think I can say I've totally given up on my Zoroastrian heritage; I think it's something that's always going to be with me and filter my experience."

In Yima's room, images of Tibetan teachers share space with a photo of his Zoroastrian grandfather.

Among the sacred objects gracing Altan's cozy abode: Mala beads blessed by lamas in Bodh Gaya. A small figure of Saint Francis. Artwork by a Lhasa-based Tibetan painter: half Buddha head, half Statue of Liberty, all on a prayer-flag canvas.

Manoj sometimes practices Zen meditation in front of a statue of the Hindu goddess of learning.

Three home altars that beautifully epitomize how first-gen Asian American Buddhists make room for multiple faiths in their spiritual lives.

Lest I paint too rosy a picture, it's important to acknowledge that integrating disparate faith traditions is not without limits.

I think of Zoe, who was raised Catholic but left the church in protest of its oppressive beliefs and teachings around abortion and sexuality: "I was and am still filled with irrational guilt, which I am working on unlearning with metta practice."

I think of Matthew, whose dissatisfaction with the Christianity of his upbringing led him to Buddhism, after which his uncle declared that he wouldn't attend Matthew's wedding if it was a Buddhist one: "I've actually thought about changing my name to a Buddhist one, lol."

I think of Eileen, for whom leaving her childhood church was no simple matter: "I've suffered a lot from the Christian community really trying to impose itself on me; I don't want to do that to other people."

I think of Altan recalling his time in an evangelical Christian group: "It divided my world into us and them, and I don't want to be in that situation again."

Even Vince, who generally has a good relationship with adherents of other religions (including his Catholic parents), recognizes that mutual respect doesn't guarantee a complete absence of tension. He and his parents might never agree on certain religious concepts or how best to practice them in daily life, but Vince is "learning to have equanimity about that and still have a sense of goodwill toward them and others I disagree with."

Vince advocates for maintaining a skillful response in the difficult but important work of interfaith dialogue. While mutually enriching conversations are possible, sometimes "noble silence is the best response ... in order to protect yourself from saying or doing things that you may regret." He cites conflicting beliefs about God as an example where "sometimes you can't overcome differences" and may need to decide that disengagement is the most respectful choice. "I would be very interested to know about the experiences of those who grew up in mixed-faith families—for example, one parent was Buddhist, but the other was Jewish. Did they choose one path over the other? Was this even an issue because Buddhism is more open to syncretism? Or is Buddhism not as open to syncretism as people think it is?"

A month before graduating from IBS, I had a chance to visit Aaron Lee in Los Angeles. A couple weeks later, Aaron sent me an email. "I want to know how young Asian Americans find comfort, confidence, and strength in Buddhism—if they do at all," he writes, before his message takes a turn for the melancholy. The cousin of a close friend had recently converted to evangelical Christianity. "I felt sad—and I felt bad that I felt sad—particularly because I interpreted her conversion in part as an indictment of how Buddhism is presented to Asian American youth," he confesses.

For all their open-mindedness toward other religions, for all their willingness to interweave different traditions, for all their unwillingness to impose Buddhism on others, the young adults I interviewed are not indifferent about the Pew Forum's "net loss" statistics.

Altan wonders if those 10 percent of Asian Americans who have left Buddhism might return in the future. "As we grow, we get to appreciate what we might have lost, or have not yet discovered, and hopefully get a chance to do this little homecoming." He considers the 2 percent of Asian Americans "who either came back home or found home in Buddhism" to reflect "a bit of a natural process."

Manoj also predicts that people who have converted out of Buddhism "will come back" as it becomes more firmly rooted in America. As Supraja humorously puts it, "Just give it some time. Give it a few generations. Asian Americans are going to get real screwed, and then everyone's going to be like, we need Buddhism. They're going to come back, I promise!"

Sitting across from Supraja at a coffee shop in Sunnyvale, I fail to keep an interviewerly poker face as she responds with characteristic candor to the Pew report.

"A net loss?" she exclaims, incredulous. "Okay, I know sociologically maybe they are interested in quantifying it ... but it's kind of offensive to use terms of capitalism—you know, like companies and just making money, like it's an ROI or something. Why are they using these terms? It just seems weird to quantify people in this way." Citing her concerns about the rise of Hindu nationalist groups, Supraja critiques this kind of language for miring Buddhism "in ego on a bigger scale."

Bhikshu Jin Chuan makes an analogous point, if more reservedly. "I don't think there is any need to get into a competition for converts. That was one of the aspects of Buddhism that really attracted me—namely, it wasn't about going out and converting others to my way of seeing things." He introduces a completely different timescale to the conversation. "My sense is to look long, look to a thousand years. Five thousand years. Ten thousand years. Or in Buddhism, we talk about *kalpas.* There is no rush. The Bodhisattva makes vows to spend endless eons simply to help even one living being from his or her suffering." Bhikshu Jin Chuan is quick to clarify that taking the long view is not an excuse for inaction, however. "At the same time, I do not think this means we can be apathetic or just let things go. There is a lot to do—Buddhism has a lot to offer our generation, but it can be hard to see through the layers of ritual and ceremonies, which are very meaningful, but often not explained."

Noel also invokes Buddhist teachings to steer clear of treating religious identity as a numbers game. "Impermanence is part of Buddhist philosophy. Change happens. I don't think Asians leaving Buddhism for Christianity or atheism is necessarily a bad thing. I think Asians should be everywhere in American society, including various faith traditions. Asian Americans as a whole will receive less racism, I believe, if we are seen in all sectors of American life."

Like Noel, Dolma hopes that Asian Americans will find affinity in a wide range of religions. Dolma, who was raised by a Sherpa Nyingma mother and a culturally Jewish American father, reminds us of the freedom that can arise when we loosen our fixation on conversion:

> *At times, I think tension arises between Asian American Christians and Asian American Buddhists. I have two stories for you on this.*
>
> *A relative of mine converted to Christianity, and at first, many of my family members were upset. I think this may stem from feelings of betrayal—by choosing to be Christian he was "abandoning" our culture and community, which translated into an abandonment of the family. I don't personally agree with this perspective on conversion, but I understand why this tension is present.*
>
> *A colleague I've worked with is an Asian Canadian Christian convert and she had a similar experience. Her family didn't accept her religious beliefs, and they rejected her decision. They were hurt. But for her, the first time she went to church with her Christian uncle, it just made sense to her. She felt at home in a way she never had in temple.*

Ultimately, Dolma's reaction to the Pew Forum's "net loss" statistics begins with a healthy dose of skepticism and arrives at a hope born from observation and personal experience.

> *My first honest thought is that these data may not be accurate. Religious and spiritual identity and affiliation are difficult to quantify, and the Pew Forum is a notoriously inaccurate source when it comes to Buddhism.[5]*
>
> *Nonetheless, this doesn't worry me. In my interfaith work, I've found that every tradition is terrified about "losing numbers" and about how the "young people" aren't attending service. The Dharma is alive in our communities, whether it goes by that name or not. I have faith that it will thrive and continue to grow.*

Connect the dots, cause and conditions, a trail of affinities, call it what you will: Starting a job in Boston, quitting to spend time with my grandmother in California before she died. Venturing into realms I hadn't considered:

hospice volunteering, a Buddhist chaplaincy training program. Applying to the Institute of Buddhist Studies, since the chaplaincy training program counted for class credit there. Taking summer trips to Asia: a Buddhist women's conference in Thailand, a Buddhist studies conference in Taiwan, a Guanyin workshop in China. Interviewing Asian American Buddhists, finishing my master's thesis (though the project wasn't quite finished with me). Completing a hospital chaplaincy residency, recovering for a semester at a Buddhist college in Taiwan. Moving to Southeast Asia with Trent. Spending much of the past four years in Theravada Buddhist countries. Feeling, somewhere along the way, that spurning the label of Buddhist was getting to be more trouble than it was worth.

At what point does water become tea? It's hard to say when I became a Buddhist, though the Triple Gem has left its indelible mark on more facets of my life than I could ever have imagined.

ROOTS

At the temple named Compassion in the little beige house in San Francisco, after the chanting and the shower of candies, we are shepherded to the basement, where a vegetarian feast awaits. The folding tables and chairs are as densely packed as the food on our plates. Proximity and deliciousness fuel a hubbub of lively chatter.

Plied with goodies by kindhearted temple-goers from across the Asian diaspora, Trent and I eat way too much. We leave with enough leftovers to last another several meals. Nestled between the broccoli, tofu, and spring rolls in our take-home box is an onion-shaped item I've never seen before, too big to eat in one bite, crunchy on the outside and starchy on the inside. I take a photo and email it to my mom, who promptly solves the mystery.

It is called cigu 慈姑 *[arrowhead]. It's available around this Chinese New Year season. My grandma and I used to cut it very thin and deep-fry it like a potato chip.*

When I point out that *ci* 慈 is the word for compassion, my mom off-handedly mentions another memory from her childhood in southern China: listening to her grandmother recite Buddhist chants in Cantonese.

I had always been told that atheism was rooted in both sides of my family several generations deep. Were it not for this edible tuber from a diasporic temple in San Francisco, I might never have learned that Chinese Buddhist chants had reverberated in the ears of my great-grandmother, my grandmother, and my mother in China—chants that had somehow found a way into my life in America.

I'm not the only Asian American convert to belatedly connect with the Buddhist roots in my family tree.

Catherine, who grew up nonreligious, discovered on a post–high school family trip to western China that her family was Buddhist before the Communist Party banned religion. Though she became interested in Buddhism as part of her heritage, Catherine's subsequent explorations of the religion were not limited to Chinese forms. Freshman year of college, she discovered the teachings of Thich Nhat Hanh and took a religion class that included a Buddhism component. She began to integrate Buddhist teachings into her daily life and later joined the Buddhist group on campus.

"My mama told me of her memories of my grandma praying at an altar," Zoe recalls. "Those practices surely diminished over time as she assimilated into her Filipino and multicultural community." Raised Catholic before claiming agnosticism for several years, Zoe began to take an interest in the Buddhist beliefs that had guided her grandmother's upbringing after hearing a eulogy on the Five Remembrances at her grandma's funeral.[1] It wasn't all smooth sailing from there, but Zoe eventually found a supportive spiritual community where, she writes, "I felt like I finally arrived home."

You wouldn't expect someone from a Jewish family to celebrate Buddhist roots, but Aaron Lee often did just that.

An August 2016 tweet from his Twitter handle, @arunlikhati, reads: "My parents didn't raise me to be Buddhist. They raised me with Buddhist values and let me choose—all without being converts."

"Yes, I come from a Buddhist family, but I'm also a convert in the sense where I grew up in a Jewish family," Aaron tells Wanwan when she interviews him in November 2014. Earlier that year, after talking with his brother for hours about meditation, he had tweeted: "So grateful to come from a #buddhistfamily."

The jury is still out on whether Aaron qualifies as a convert Buddhist. When I ask Aaron what object best represents his Buddhist practice during our 2013 interview, he pauses. "Maybe my necklace? I think what makes the necklace representative is that it's a Buddha figure.... It was given to me by my grandmother. The cultural connection for me is very deep, the connection to my family." Half an hour later, almost as an afterthought, he adds: "My father was Buddhist before meeting my mom. He used to wear a Buddha necklace around his neck too."

One of my favorite pieces of Aaron's writing is a blog post he wrote for *Dharma Folk* before he started *Angry Asian Buddhist*.

Running in the Family
May 18, 2008

Tonight is the last of three nights that I'm staying at my brother's place in the Bay Area. I came back up here for the first time in two years to run a race and see family that I don't usually get the chance to see. This weekend has also made me realize the comforts and importance of having a Buddhist family.

Not all of my family is Buddhist. Five generations ago, everyone was supposedly Buddhist or followed our indigenous religion. Many converted to Catholicism and later to Protestant Christianity when they came to the United States in the years before and just after World War I. My grandmother clung steadfastly to the "old ways," and some aunts and uncles "reverted" to Buddhism. But it was the Buddhist practices of my grandmother that left the strongest imprint on me and my siblings, who have come to embrace our Buddhist heritage.

Buddhism was never forced on me, but neither did it hang as some sort of background tapestry on the wall. It was the little symbolic things that I built my practice on later in life, even if I didn't know what they stood for.

On New Year's Day, we would wake up at midnight and eat a vegetarian meal as an auspicious opening to the New Year. This established my profound respect for vegetarianism (in addition to growing up in the Bay Area), even though I may not keep this diet all too strictly.

I remember receiving my first soapstone Buddha statue when I was about ten. I found some lion action figures and toy flowers. I then meticulously arranged these into an altar on top of my dresser, copying the placement that I often stared at in my grandmother's shrine room.

When I was young and tore into a fit, it was my father who would quickly and eloquently point out that the source of my anger was within. So was the power to overcome it. While I couldn't appreciate this wisdom at the age of five, my father's anger management tips have since grown into one of the fundamental aspects that I most appreciate about Buddhist philosophy.

Now I sit in my brother's living room, and I realize that we are living on the fruit of Buddhist traditions that our parents and grandparents passed down to us. In the morning my brother, his wife, and I take turns before the altar to supplicate and pay our respect to Lord Buddha, the Dharma and the Sangha. While eating dessert, we look over pieces of Buddhist art and discuss the meanings embedded in hidden symbols. And for my trip back to Los Angeles tomorrow, my brother's wife has given me two additions to the altar in my own home.

With my family, doctrinal issues fall to the wayside. I may attend a mostly Vietnamese temple, and practice according to Theravada tradition, but my brother and his wife are steeped in Mahayana practice and attend a Japanese temple with a mostly Japanese congregation. Nevertheless, we judge each other by our actions: the respect for life, possessions, social customs, honesty, and sobriety.

I feel my experiences contrast sharply with other young Buddhists who I've met. For one, most don't share my ethnic and cultural heritage (although I've met a few who do). Many never really had much of a Buddhist upbringing either. Even for many "heritage" Buddhists, they will sidestep their Buddhist identity with a simple, "Well, my *family* is Buddhist ..."

In the end, I am so deeply thankful for all the little bits of Buddhism that have been passed onto me and nurtured by my family. Before, I have discussed

Buddhist identity, especially in the Asian American context, but with my family this label dissolves completely into practice. Each family having its own practice, this reflection on the thread of Buddhism in my family really makes me wonder how it runs through other Buddhist families in America. And maybe for a future post: What is a Buddhist family?[2]

Every time I read this post, I marvel at how Aaron's ethnicity remains enigmatic. But his love for Buddhist family—in all its diversity, complexity, and perplexity—comes through loud and clear.

I wish I could ask Aaron about the scare quotes around "reverted" in the part of his post where he alludes to "some aunts and uncles [who] 'reverted' to Buddhism."

I wonder what Aaron would think about Paul Numrich's take on the issue.

> *For ethnic Asians in the West, it is really not a matter of "conversion" to Buddhism, even if one's family or ethnic group was not Buddhist in Asia in recent times. It is rather a matter of reversion, or of reenvisioning their Buddhist heritage, even if that heritage has suffered hiatus for some time, or has to be created in response to the social pressures involved in minority group identity formation.[3]*

The idea that Asian Americans can only "revert" to Buddhism seems to imply some sort of Buddhist default setting that ignores the complex histories of various Asian diasporas and the myriad ways Buddhism has or hasn't developed in different parts of Asia. It contains hints of biological determinism, as if Buddhism was not just culturally but genetically transmitted among people of Asian heritage. Does this mean that white Americans can only revert to Christianity? What religion would other racial groups revert to?

Like Aaron Lee, Aaron Huang mentions his Buddhist grandmother during our interview—though he says that "her version of Buddhism is much more mixed in with Taoism and ancestor worship" than his. Eileen remembers a godfather who would take her to Buddhist temples to burn incense and pray, but she considers that to be "a very different kind of Buddhist tradition" than the "very American strain" she practices now. Alyssa recalls having gone to temple once or twice as a kid: "It was more about respecting ancestors, not so much about Buddhism," though her mom also took the family to church on Christmas Eve because she enjoyed singing Christmas songs.

It hardly sounds like Aaron, Eileen, or Alyssa are "reverting" to a "heritage" form of Buddhism.

I join Wakoh Shannon Hickey in respectfully disagreeing with Numrich: "Because we cannot link nationality or ethnicity to religion so tidily, we cannot assume that any ethnically Asian person who begins to practice Buddhism in the United States is reverting to a heritage faith."[4]

But the latter half of Numrich's statement intrigues me. If "reversion" seems like too deterministic a concept, "reenvisioning their Buddhist heritage" does capture an important aspect of the experience of Asian American convert Buddhists: the need to grapple with a Buddhist heritage, whether that heritage is real or imagined, assumed or discovered, sought out or wished for.

I think of Aaron Lee and Zoe honoring their Buddhist grandmothers.

Or Catherine and me unearthing Buddhism in our family histories.

I think of Gabrielle, who feels a self-appointed responsibility to make sure her Japanese American and Jodo Shinshu heritages continue to thrive in the future: "As a gosei, or fifth-generation Japanese American, I carry a deep reverence for my ancestors, and the roots that have made me who I am today—even five generations removed from 'the homeland' in Japan."

Or Anthony evoking hypothetical Buddhist ancestors: "The Korean side of my family were all nonpracticing Presbyterians, but I figured that several generations back at least some of them had practiced some kind of Buddhism." Anthony considers himself to be "like a lot of American converts" in that he started exploring Buddhism in college—which was also the same time he became more interested in his Asian heritage.

I think of Lola as she reinterprets her Christian family's history through a Buddhist lens.

> *I did not come to Buddhism by way of my family, who mostly identify as either Christian or Catholic, though I now know and see how many of my family's ways of being are Buddhist. The practice of Buddhism came to me by way of white Americans and non–Asian Americans of color bringing it to the forefront of my immediate observable universe— which is through my work as a therapist and health provider....*
>
> *Psychologically (and politically) I have to admit that I judged the devotional practices of Asian Buddhists, looking at their spirituality through the white-dominant male lens of patriarchy and the fear that has been forced upon me as a person growing up in this country. Now, as I'm more able to lift that oppressive lens and see things with less of a dominant culture bias, I see just how much my family (although they did not identify with it) practiced (when we could) Buddhism in many ways, such as respect for all life; minding our impact on others; having compassion for suffering and doing what we can to decrease it; generosity with friends, neighbors, and family; and trying to appreciate what we have.*

By aligning her family's values and behaviors with Buddhist principles and practices, Lola counters the denigration of "devotional" Asian Buddhists and asserts the importance of non-Christian, nonwhite, nonmale voices like her own—an act of religious, cultural, and political reclamation.

Cultural heritage is clearly more than just a sidenote for these young adult Asian Americans. But they are not "heritage Buddhists" in the sense that "two Buddhisms" usually portrays, whereby Asians are assumed to practice a type of Buddhism consonant with their ethnicity. In which case one might expect Aaron Lee to practice Toishanese Buddhism, Aaron Huang to practice Taiwanese Buddhism, Catherine and Lola and Zoe and Anthony to practice Chinese and Hong Kongese and Filipino and Korean Buddhism, respectively. Not so.

"I'm not connected to a branch through my heritage," notes Catherine, who practiced Korean Zen in college and later joined a people of color group at an insight meditation center.

Virtually all of the first-gen Asian American Buddhists I interviewed had, like Catherine, practiced in multiple Buddhist traditions. And—you guessed it—they didn't just attend sanghas with people of the same Asian ethnicity.

"I was going through a very difficult time in my life and I felt that I needed spiritual answers for the suffering I was experiencing. My Christian background was not satisfying." Matthew's search for answers began with reading books by the Dalai Lama and other teachers. He checked out Shambhala and the New Kadampa Tradition, but found the former prohibitively expensive and the latter's criticism of the Dalai Lama objectionable. Undeterred, Matthew started "going to multiple centers at the same time to see what fit," a journey that led him to a Korean temple of the Taego order, a Drikung Kagyu group where he practiced deity yoga and the *ngondro,* a Thai temple that he had to stop attending once their English-language sessions ended, and a Sri Lankan temple that he still goes to.

Like Matthew, Anthony discovered that "the worldview of Buddhism just made sense in a way that the Christianity I grew up with never did." A college intensive class where he learned about Buddhist history, teachings, and meditation techniques from several different traditions set the foundation for personal practice and further exploration. After graduation, Anthony faced economic struggles, personal illness, unexpected deaths of relatives, and other challenges. Buddhism was his lifeline through these tumultuous times. "Without the mental training I received from my teachers, and without the strength I gain from devotional practice, I would really be a lesser person in every respect and might not have survived or surmounted some of the challenges that I've faced.... It's the peace I have found through the Dharma that has carried me through everything I have faced and inspired me to seek a life of service as a medical provider."

Nathan also points to personal suffering as a gateway into Buddhism.[5] Though he first became aware of Buddhism in high school when his mom started practicing in the Pure Land tradition (before that time, his family was completely secular), Nathan's own Buddhist journey began in undergrad. "I had a pretty serious bout of depression. The stuff I was learning in my core classes was way over my head, there was a lot of family drama, finances were really tight, I was in a long-distance relationship (still am), and overall just didn't feel like I 'fit in' with being an undergrad. Naturally, I started looking for answers to broader questions about life, and that's when I looked more closely at Buddhism." Nathan began reading Mahayana texts in Chinese and accompanied his mom to some rituals at her temple (though he was always afraid of unwittingly breaking the rules, having accidentally worn the black layperson robes into the bathroom once). Since some of the more abstract topics were harder to grasp in Chinese, Nathan expanded into English-language sutras and Dharma talks from the Theravada tradition.

Holly's Buddhist journey contains many of the threads in Matthew, Anthony, and Nathan's stories: An appreciation for a wide range of Buddhist traditions. A deepening relationship with Buddhism after personal hardship. A choice of profession guided by dharma teachings and practice.

I had scattered Buddhist influences during childhood. My dad knew some Buddhist prayers in Japanese from his father, and I remember reading a Tibetan Buddhist children's book about reincarnation and feeling at peace with the notions and values of Buddhist teachings. I also remember as a little girl hearing a story of how Zen began in Japan, after I received a popular Japanese children's toy of Bodhidharma. I remember thinking that this meditation master was somehow magical as I made wishes on his eerily wide-open eyes.

Neither of my parents were religious, so I grew up with some cultural exposure to Buddhism but never learned about it overtly. As a teenager, I became interested in philosophy, and after high school, I attended the Buddhist-inspired Naropa University in Boulder, Colorado, because I wanted an education wherein I would learn about both European and Asian philosophy.

At Naropa, I began a shamatha meditation practice and got my degree in religious studies, studying Judaism, Japanese Zen, and Tibetan Buddhism (mostly the Kagyu tradition). I did several short meditation retreats and kept up a simple, daily meditation practice for several years.

During and after college, I was engaged in social work, activism, early childhood education, and hospice, and found my Buddhist practice increasingly important for sustaining myself and better serving others in the helping professions. I gradually became more of a Tibetan Buddhist practitioner, meeting rinpoches and lamas for teachings and empowerments, and beginning a daily sadhana practice. While I appreciated the Buddhist teachers and practitioners I met at Naropa and in sanghas I visited after graduation, I was never able to find a sangha where I felt I "belonged." At this time in my life, my Buddhism was kind of casual; it was mostly about the ritual of daily meditation, about doing good work for others in the community, and about feeling a vague loyalty to the philosophy and principles behind the teachings.

Eventually, my involvements in social service propelled me to see how deep and profound the Dharma was. I experienced intense suffering both through my work as a caregiver to others and for myself through personal trauma and loss, and these intense experiences prompted me to make Buddhism more central in my life. I began to realize that I was becoming "religious," and I wanted to seek a profession where I could combine my commitment to deeper spiritual development with a career in service of others.

I found chaplaincy as a fitting vocation, a right livelihood, and pursued a graduate education in Buddhist chaplaincy at University of the West, in a suburb of Los Angeles. There, I continued in my Tibetan Buddhist practices associated with teachers from the Gelugpa and Kagyu lineages, and also started community groups where Buddhists of varied backgrounds and from various countries could share our practices together. In my academic journey and in these community groups in Los Angeles, I learned a great deal about the variety of Buddhisms in the world, and about shared values in all the traditions. This was the first time in my life where I felt "at home" in a sangha, surrounded by a remarkably diverse community of varied ages, cultures, nationalities, primary languages, and Buddhist traditions. During graduate school, I attended sangha groups regularly to offer incense and prayers, chant, and do group meditation in varied Buddhist traditions. I also studied about women in Buddhist history, and gained an awareness of and respect for many female Buddhist leaders of the past and present.

Since graduation, I now work as a health care chaplain, and I see chaplaincy as a form of Buddhist practice, especially as it relates to my bodhisattva vows. I attend a local Shangpa Kagyu sangha and meet with the lamas there for guidance, and I began a Young Adult Group to foster spiritual community. I still study other forms of Buddhism, often relying on teachings of Japanese Zen and Thich Nhat Hanh in applying Buddhist practices to a chaplaincy context.

"What is a Buddhist family?" Aaron asks at the end of his "Running in the Family" blog post. I find in Holly's narrative an expansive possibility, an answer to Aaron's question that isn't contingent on bloodlines: *A remarkably diverse community of varied ages, cultures, nationalities, primary languages, and Buddhist traditions.* A place to feel at home.

Given the diversity of their spiritual practices and communities, questions of religious identity are anything but straightforward for these Asian American convert Buddhists.

Lola used to identify as "spiritual rather than religious," though she's become increasingly comfortable talking about Buddhist teachings and meditation. Nevertheless, she doesn't quite feel she can "claim" Buddhism.

Manny often chooses to identify differently to Buddhists and non-Buddhists for fear of misunderstanding—"especially in a Western context where people have many associations about what a Buddhist 'is.'" He's more inclined to show (rather than talk about) what makes him a Buddhist.

"I think technically, officially I am a Buddhist, because I have a Buddhist name and a lineage paper. So I'm a card-carrying—well, I have a scroll, so actually I'm a scroll-carrying—Buddhist." Despite having sewed a *rakusu*, taken vows, and been given two Buddhist names (one in Korean and one in Sanskrit, from two different lineages), Manoj is hesitant to discuss his Buddhist identity. "I won't say that I identify myself as Buddhist; I would say I practice Buddhism." And if he must say he's Buddhist? "That doesn't completely prevent me from saying that I'm a Hindu as well."

Anthony considers himself a religious person, but he rarely describes himself as such, "since this can send the wrong message in a country like the United States, where 'religious' is often taken to mean 'conservative evangelical Christian.'" If asked directly about his religion, Anthony will say he is Buddhist. As for what kind of Buddhist he is—well, it's not an easy question to answer. "I am somewhat eclectic—I have had teachers from both Theravada and Mahayana lineages. I draw from both traditions in my practice and understanding of Buddhism, and find it difficult to situate myself as exclusively Mahayana or Theravada. I find a lot of the internecine polemics floating around on the English-language internet to be profoundly depressing, since I find so much value in both sets of teachings."

Vinod answers the "What kind of Buddhist are you?" question by saying he is nondenominational. Gabrielle has done the same.

Aaron Lee also called himself a nondenominational Buddhist, though he recognized the potential pitfalls of doing so. Reminiscing about his undergraduate days during our interview, Aaron told me about a meeting where the UCLA Buddhist Association was trying to decide the direction they wanted to go in.[6] The group was mostly students with a Theravada background. Aaron proposed that they think of themselves as nondenominational, at which point someone piped up: "You know, whenever someone says nondenominational, I think that just means Mahayana." Aaron had heard something similar for Christianity: "If you say you're nondenominational Christian, that's just means Protestant." Despite its shortcomings, Aaron figured the "nondenominational" label still signaled greater inclusivity than identifying with a specific Buddhist tradition.

Zoe wonders how she would have responded if the Pew Forum researchers had surveyed her for their report on Asian American religion. "I don't know if I would call myself a Buddhist, because I find labeling problematic and limiting sometimes, but I would say that there are Buddhist practices and beliefs that I incorporate into my life—where would I have fit in this study?"

Alyssa shares Zoe's skepticism. "If someone asks me, 'Are you a Buddhist?,' am I going to write that on a survey?"

Vince echoes their doubts about the Pew Forum's ability to accurately report on Asian American Buddhists. "One of the major problems is that they seem to use a Judeo-Christian lens for understanding religion. Is attending weekly services a good measure of religiosity? Buddhists don't have a sabbath every week. Should we ask how often Christians participate in retreats or observe Uposatha days to measure their religiosity? I also hope the researchers realize that Buddhists and Hindus have in-home altars for devotional activities. How are they measuring those sorts of religious activities outside of the temples? Context matters."

Although his Buddhist practice has primarily been in the Tibetan tradition, Altan takes an ecumenical approach to his adopted religion. "I don't consider myself married to any particular lineage or practice." He smiles. "Buddhism is sort of my secondary identity, and being human is my first." Altan is glad there is no such thing as "*the* Buddhist perspective," some kind of singular, sectarian view that trumps all others. "And that's the beauty of Buddhism," he concludes.

"There are a lot of young adult Buddhists like me who feel like they don't quite fit into a box," writes Gabrielle. "I have an interesting experience of, on the one hand, sitting zazen with my Japanese American *jichan* in a group of primarily older white male Buddhist practitioners, and on the other hand attending services at Shin Buddhist temples where Asian (and especially Japanese) Americans are the majority."

Gabrielle thinks such multifaceted experiences are becoming the norm within American Buddhism. "I am constantly straddling cultural, as well as spiritual, worlds.... I am sure as society continues to only become more racially diverse, there will be a lot more people straddling these different worlds."

In Anthony's view, the difficulty of fitting into a single box is not a liability but a boon. Indeed, he considers it a hallmark of his generation of American Buddhists.

My life is going to be very different than the life of a Japanese immigrant in the nineteenth century, or even a Beat poet in the 1950s. How exactly this affects my perspective on Buddhism is perhaps a little difficult to tease out, but I would suggest that because we are at a point when many different Dharma traditions are well established in this country, we younger Buddhists have more opportunities to learn about, and from, more schools of Buddhism than ever before.

Aware of the unique circumstances of being Buddhist in twenty-first century America, where "we have just about every tradition in one place," Anthony urges us to "take this amazing opportunity to learn from different schools." He certainly practices what he preaches. Anthony meditates in the Thai forest tradition; listens to Dharma talks by Thanissaro Bhikkhu; includes Master Sheng-yen, Buddhadasa Bhikkhu, and Kosho Uchiyama among his Buddhist influences; and models his ideal Buddhist community on a bilingual Chan Buddhist sangha run by Taiwanese nuns.

How do we categorize what type of Buddhist Anthony is? Maybe it's okay if we can't. Maybe it's okay to think outside the box.

I defer to these wise words from Holly's interview: "As a Buddhist, I know that the self is always inconstant and interdependent, so in a way my Buddhist practices help me be at peace in the midst of the tensions in multiplicity and diversity."

Speaking of alleviating tensions, there's a story from chapter 7 that I didn't finish telling. The young man who would become Bhikshu Jin Chuan was at an impasse, since his parents seemed to be thwarting his efforts to become a monk.

He asked a senior monk what to do—and was advised to listen to his mom more. This unexpected reply helped him realize how his approach to monasticism was damaging his family relationships, and he transferred the energy of preparing for monastic life into considering his parents' perspectives. As a result, he began to feel gratitude for all the ways they did support him.

I would see my mother tirelessly washing the dishes at night after every-one finished eating, or cooking special vegetarian dishes for me when everyone else was not vegetarian. Although my mom was not happy with my monastic aspirations, I saw how she was willing to still support it in quiet ways. The car I drove to the monastery came from them; the roof over my head came from them; and they were constantly trying to give me the best advice they could, hoping that I would live a happy and meaningful life.[7]

Over time, the entire family dynamic shifted.

The changes I made in my behavior changed my relationship with my family completely. My understanding of everyone deepened, and, as a result, so did my sense of well-being and groundedness. I wasn't a solitary person who had grown up in a secular family in a suburban town in California faced with the impossible task of trying to become a monastic. Now I felt like I was part of a group of people whom I cared about and who cared about me.

Ironically enough, reconnecting with my family roots provided me with the foundation I needed to "leave home." Before this I often felt like I was clenching tightly onto something ("I want to become a monk no matter what!"), but afterwards I was able to cultivate in a more open and relaxed way.[8]

It took thirteen years, but when Bhikshu Jin Chuan finally received full ordination, his parents attended the last day of the ceremony for the transmission of the Buddhist precepts.

"Each person creates their own identity labels to help make sense of their experience," Bhikshu Jin Chuan observes. "Sometimes it helps clarify something; sometimes it obfuscates."

I am reminded of my interview with Adam at a café in Long Beach. Adam's Filipino American mom is Catholic, his German American dad nonreligious. He grew up an Easter Catholic. As for his current religious

identity? "I can be a Christian sometimes, and I can be a Buddhist sometimes, and an atheist sometimes."

Adam isn't trying to be two-faced. He has studied Christianity, Buddhism, and atheism and still identities with aspects of each. He opts for
the label that will best connect him with the person he's talking to.

Bhikshu Jin Chuan also prioritizes relationality. Drawing on Buddhist
teachings of impermanence, not-self, and interconnectedness, he urges
American Buddhists of all backgrounds to consider that "we are all on the
same 'team.'"

"We all have the potential to become Buddhas," he explains. "If we
were to look past the surface—say, for instance, past lives, which I know is
not something generally believed in this modern scientific age—but even
just as a Buddhist theory—what that means is that we have all been family.
I might have been a European last life. They might have been Vietnamese.
Who is to say that he or she was not my mother?"

Some may interpret this viewpoint as an endorsement of race blindness,
since it appears to advocate for less attachment to one's racial identity. But
Bhikshu Jin Chuan is not asking us to ignore race and ethnicity. He is calling
for cooperation between Buddhists of different racial backgrounds—which is
only possible when our differences are fully acknowledged and understood.

When Vince is asked about his race or ethnicity, he'll say he's Asian
American or Chinese American or simply Chinese. "Sometimes these are
salient identities. Other times, they're identities that don't exist and arise
in the present moment."

In an article titled "Buddhism and bell hooks: Liberatory Aesthetics
and the Radical Subjectivity of No-Self," philosophy professor Leah Kalmanson argues that "to be nonattached is to be open to, and to care deeply
for, life in the present moment, while recognizing the futility of ever preserving, as if in stone, that for which one cares."[9] We can characterize
Vince and Bhikshu Jin Chuan's approach to identity as nonattached in the
sense Kalmanson describes. Caring for identity and recognizing identity's
limits thus become interdependent imperatives.

For Vince, knowledge about the history of Asian Americans and the
struggles they have faced (the internment of Japanese Americans, the

murder of Vincent Chin, to name just a few examples) are crucial "for understanding how others view you because of their perceptions of your racial and ethnic identity in American society." This knowledge informs his interactions with others and prepares him to respond to whatever misperceptions people may have: "I've been asked so many times in my life about my country of origin that it's almost expected, for better or worse."

"People will choose an identity for you and a story about you, even if you haven't chosen that identity or story for yourself," Vince argues.

All too true. Witness the "Stereotypology of Asian American Buddhists": The Oriental monk. The superstitious immigrant. The banana Buddhist. The Angry Asian Buddhist's satirical description of the "banana Buddhist" who just "happens to be Asian" ends on a sardonic note: "It really doesn't matter if she doesn't speak up because whatever she says isn't going to be any different from what the white Buddhists are saying."

Fortunately, there are a whole bunch of first-gen Asian American Buddhists who beg to differ.

With the study of Buddhism in the West, it's rare to find a scholar of Asian heritage, rarer still to find an academic article in which the author writes openly and vulnerably of their own Buddhist journey.

So you can imagine my astonishment upon reading Edwin Ng's journal article "The Autoethnographic Genre and Buddhist Studies: Reflections of a Postcolonial 'Western Buddhist' Convert."

I could see why Ed (whom I would meet several years later when he passed through Bangkok) put scare quotes around "Western Buddhist." As a third-generation Chinese migrant raised in Singapore who sees Buddhism as part of his cultural heritage, Ed considered himself Christian until his early twenties, when, having migrated to Australia, a personal crisis spurred him to find solace in the "rationalist interpretations" of "Western discourses on Buddhism."

In other words, his faith is complicated. Writing in a mix of first- and third-person poetry and prose, Ed reveals snippets of his religious journey: Kuanyin surrounded by fruit and rice cakes and smoldering incense on his grandmother's altar. The small amounts of money he accepted from his grandma "even though he had learned at the missionary school he attended that those things were superstitious practices of misguided beliefs." His grandmother's death, incomprehensible as the chants of the monks presiding over her wake.

Ed's article ends with questions—and an invitation:

> "Western, non-Western, both, or neither? Where do I fit in? Who do I speak as?" He remains uncertain…. There are yet more stories to discover.
>
> *I have written a story here, but I am not entirely sure it is "mine." Nevertheless, I would like to share it with you, and other stories too, if you would be interested. And if you are willing to share, I would like to read about yours. What is your story?*[10]

Here is one response, from someone else of Asian heritage in the West. Bhikshu Jin Chuan grew up on the opposite side of the world from Edwin Ng, yet he too had once found Buddhist chants opaque. Like many a first-gen Asian American Buddhist, he too is integrating multiple cultural spheres as he deepens Buddhism's roots halfway across the globe from the religion's historic homelands.

Going Home

Born on the East Coast
Grew up in the West
Asian descent—
American raised

Trained in science
Applied to studying religions
"Normal" suburban life—
Led to the monastery

Competitive and confused
Hungry for wisdom

Attached to my opinions—
Determined to get free

Narrow and self-serving
Mission to benefit all
A mix of dichotomies
Where can I find myself?

Still searching
Always learning
Aspiring to dedicate my life to
A worthy cause

PART 4

REFUGE-MAKERS

While we still need to articulate our principles, relay our stories, protest injustice, and cast our votes, we are most compelling when we are the very refuges we wish to see in this world.

—AARON

ANGER

Why I'm Angry

These three words appear on every page of the *Angry Asian Buddhist* blog. Clicking on the link leads us to a post explaining Arun's reasons for standing by his website's controversial title.

> *Anger is not a Buddhist virtue. More often than not, you'll hear Buddhists describe it as a mental defilement—and much worse. No surprise, then, that many visitors to this blog find themselves scratching their heads, "Why do you call yourself the Angry Asian Buddhist?"*
>
> *The title of this blog is an homage to a larger field of other "Angry Asian" Americans. Most notably the Angry Little Asian Girls and Angry Asian Man. These authors and artists address issues of race, culture, and privilege in American media and society. Likewise, I explore these issues in the American Buddhist community.*

For example, it's common parlance among English-speaking American Buddhists to use the term American Buddhist or Western Buddhist to refer to white people—or at the very least at the exclusion of American Buddhists of Asian heritage. I can certainly concede that the prototypical "American" in the media is a white American—but I hold the American Buddhist community to a higher standard. Especially since most American Buddhists are not white.

Furthermore, for all their self-proclaimed open-mindedness, the high-profile American Buddhist publications generally don't let in that many Asian American authors. Tricycle is the worst culprit. It's not as though we don't exist—it's just they don't care enough. I make it my job to point this out because, maybe, someday, it might lead to actual change rather than a privileged complacency.

There are plenty of other reasons that I blog here, but the main reason I maintain this site is because I'm encouraged by my readers. You may not see them leave comments, but I run into them all the time in the community. And, yes, they are angry—not writhing in conniptions, but seriously indignant. They are upset at a perceived injustice by predominantly white Buddhists of ignoring Asian Americans, who are the biggest part of Buddhist America.

They are angry when they hear people write about the history of Buddhism in America without reference to the hundreds of thousands of Buddhist Asian Americans who have been and who continue to be the greatest part of American Buddhism. Who will speak out for them when they're ignored? Who will stand up to let them know they're not alone?

That's why I'm the Angry Asian Buddhist.[1]

The five hundred-plus blog posts that arunlikhati/Arun wrote for *Dharma Folk* and *Angry Asian Buddhist* cover a gamut of topics. You'll find advocacy for *bhikkhuni* ordination and reflections on the author's personal meditation practice. Information about the plight of Buddhists in Asia, especially Burma, Bangladesh, Cambodia, and Vietnam. Celebrations of Buddhist holidays such as Rohatsu, Vesak, Ohigan, Ullambana, and Kathina, with the Lunar and Tibetan and Southeast Asian New Years thrown in for good measure. There's even a minor disquisition on rice weevils.

But the posts that garnered the most comments are the ones protesting the marginalization of Asian American Buddhists.

In a December 2008 post on *Dharma Folk* titled "Angry Asian Buddhist"—a harbinger of the blog he would start four months later—arunlikhati describes his reaction to a *Buddhadharma* article on "Next-Gen Buddhism: The Future of Buddhism in a Post-Baby Boomer World."[2] An image of Leela Lee's Angry Little Asian Girl, her indignant expression framed by blocky pigtails and zigzag bangs, accompanies his words.

> *It's insulting for a magazine like* Buddhadharma *to discuss the future of the Buddhist community in America without talking about Asian Americans. We're not some alien species in the Buddhist community— we brought Buddhism to America. We've been practicing Buddhism on American soil for well over a century. We speak English, we have youth groups, we go on retreats, and we do all the other crazy Buddhist stuff that white people do and more. Unfortunately, it seems we're just not white enough for even an honorable mention.*

After a few more paragraphs detailing his concerns, arunlikhati concludes: "So that's my rant. My fear is that white Buddhism is developing into a culture of oppression. My hope is that the next generation will overcome these divisions to build a stronger and tighter community." arunlikhati signs off with a Pali blessing for all beings to be kind to one another: *Sabbe satta abyapajjha hontu.*[3]

Much to his surprise, this relatively mild-mannered "rant" generated a firestorm of responses. Emotions run high in the fifty-three comments to the post. He had clearly hit a nerve.

Uncowed by his many detractors (and buoyed by a handful of encouragers), Aaron kept writing. He criticized how Asian Americans are both subtly and blatantly excluded from the categories of "American"[4] and "Western" Buddhism.[5] He objected to the way Asian American Buddhists are marked as "ethnic"[6] and "traditional."[7] He argued for their inclusion in the ranks of "convert" and "meditating" Buddhists.[8] He critiqued the term *cultural baggage* for implying the superiority of an "Asian-free Buddhism."[9] He advocated for the term *heritage Buddhist* over the infantilizing *cradle Buddhist.*[10]

These posts got me thinking: About the unfortunate tendency to equate "American" and "Western" with "white" in Buddhist spheres and elsewhere. About how frustrating it is when "Asians" are conflated with "Asian Americans." About the double standard that groups fifth-generation Japanese Americans among "ethnic" "immigrant" Buddhists while exempting first-generation Norwegian Americans or fourth-generation Jewish Americans from those foreignizing labels. About how entrenched the "two Buddhisms" narrative is, how polarizing its effects—it's hard to imagine "two Christianities" passing muster, though Martin Luther King Jr.'s lament that eleven o'clock on Sunday morning is America's most segregated hour rings sadly true more than half a century later.

arunlikhati began with the conviction that representation matters, starting with the very terminology we use when talking about American Buddhism. Not everyone shared that conviction. Some commenters insulted him for belaboring the "illusory" idea of race and sowing unnecessary "divisiveness." Others lambasted him and his supporters for being "antiwhite racists." We've (sadly) become inured to such views by now, but I can still remember my shock upon seeing that someone had lobbed an uncensored "f*** you" and signed off as "Angry Aryan Buddhist" in response to one of Aaron's posts.

Writing under a pseudonym offered Aaron a measure of protection from trolls, but that wasn't the only reason for his anonymity. As he explains in a 2012 interview with *Tricycle:*

> *I could be any Asian American. But often people come to assumptions of who I am and what my background is, based on what I write. And some have been extremely warm in their guesses, and some people extremely cold. Sometimes people use that guess to categorize who I am*

and to further categorize my writing. But I like to think that what I write about is true regardless of who I am. I could be a Black woman on the other side of the world—but my writing on the issues of Asians in Western Buddhism would still be true.[11]

Dolma certainly agrees. "I'm a loyal reader and big fan. It's definitely one of my favorite Buddhist blogs, and represents my political-religious perspectives well."

Born in Kathmandu—indeed the other side of the world from Aaron—Dolma grew up internationally before moving to America for college. Although she doesn't readily identify as Asian American—she didn't grow up here and doesn't consider herself culturally American—Dolma has found solidarity with the Asian-Pacific Islander activist community since moving to the United States.

Despite being an ambiguous fit for the category of "Asian American," Dolma happily completed an interview with me. Her willingness to participate was motivated in no small part by an anger akin to Arun's.

When I moved to the United States for college, I joined the Buddhist meditation group on campus. Meditation was not an active part of my practice previously, and I had always wanted to learn more. I remember being surprised that not only was I the only person of Asian descent, I was the only person of color, and the only person who was raised Buddhist in the group. While Buddhists are a religious minority in Nepal (the country is predominantly Hindu), I was used to a community where Buddhist resources (temples, community centers, classes) were easily available. It felt strange initially to take part in a Buddhist group where few identified as Buddhist, and everyone who did identify as Buddhist were recent converts. However, our sensei soon became my religious mentor, and I found home in studying with him immediately.

As a carless busy college student in Los Angeles, I didn't venture out in search of a Buddhist temple much. Any Nyingma temple I found was predominantly made up of wealthy, white, American converts. My experiences in these environments have been exhausting: I am either put on an exotified pedestal, or seen as having a "conservative and limited" view of Buddhism. Whenever I told people I was Buddhist, I got a variety of reactions. From ignorance ("Oh, but that's not an actual religion"), to immediate orientalization ("That's so crazy and exotic, you must be so Zen. Did I tell you I'm a yogi?"), to a compulsion to educate me on my own religion ("I'm in this Buddhist studies class, and we learned all about the eightfold path. Do you know what that is? That's what Buddhists believe in."). Since leaving college, these reactions haven't changed much.

I'm interested in this project because the way Buddhism is received and portrayed in the United States is infuriating. I am indeed an Angry Asian Female Buddhist, and I think our narrative is crucial to religious progression, rights, and reflection. I think the complete disregard for Buddhist cultural understanding is appropriative and disrespectful. I mean, why do acupuncture clinics have Buddha statues in their waiting rooms and restrooms? Why can you buy Buddha statues as garden ornaments? What is with om tattoos? Who is all that really for (not us) and who profits off of it (again, not us)?

Our dialogue isn't given airtime or respect, and I think projects like this flip that on its head.

From the May 2004 archives of *Angry Asian Man:* an online petition against Victoria's Secret's buddha- and bodhisattva-emblazoned swimwear.[12] From a January 2012 post on *Angry Asian Buddhist:* objections over a buddha image-decorated toilet brush holder from Bed Bath & Beyond.[13] In both cases, the companies quickly removed the offending merchandise.

From an October 2014 post on *Angry Asian Buddhist:* a critique of "Buddhy" (a.k.a. "The Mentor"), the long-running (long-sitting?) brand mascot of a San Francisco-based customer service start-up.

Buddhy is cultural appropriation at its most flagrant. Zendesk has taken Buddhist iconography, particularly that of Budai, and repackaged it as an integral component of their brand asset portfolio. What's worse is that when you flip through their social media stream, Zendesk employees repeatedly play on Oriental stereotypes and often put The Mentor in situations that many millions of Asian Buddhists would immediately perceive as blatant disrespect.[14]

Cristina also spoke out about the company's decision to use a headset-wearing, okay sign-flashing, fat laughing Buddha as their mascot: "I tweeted at their handle about the image they're using being racist and offensive, and the vice president of communications replied to me directly." But Buddhy's image remained draped across the front of the New York Stock Exchange.

When Zendesk finally changed their branding two years later because they felt Buddhy was too "limiting," an apology was hardly forthcoming. "The only problem we've had really are [people] offended on behalf of people who would be offended," said the company's chief creative officer[15]—a statement that neatly erases Cristina's indignation while absolving the company from responsibility.

Kim Tran raises another example of the reduction of Buddhism into something "'cool,' marketable, [and] consumable" in a 2016 article that opens with a scenario and a question: "Imagine this: you're a practicing Christian.... As you walk into the entrance of your workplace one day, you see a statue of a decapitated Jesus head sitting on the floor decorating the hallway. *How do you feel?*"[16] Tran goes on to explain that this is a real-life scenario—if we replace Christian with Buddhist and Jesus with Buddha.

Invisibility and marginalization. Orientalization and exotification. Appropriation and commodification. You could write a tome on any one of these topics; the Angry Asian Buddhist certainly wrote a trove of blog posts about them. Curious about the extent to which my interviewees shared Arun's anger, I decided to present them with an excerpt from Arun's August 2012 blog post "Why Is the Under 35 Project so White?"

> *This year* Shambhala SunSpace *has been posting weekly essays from the Under 35 Project, a laudable initiative to support and highlight the voices of the emerging generation of Buddhists and meditators. As usual, my naïveté never fails to let me down and I was once again shocked at the whiteness of the lineup. Not a single East or Southeast Asian among them.*[17]

The kicker, of course, was the accompanying collage showing nineteen apparently white faces and one South Asian.

As to be expected—after all, Asian American Buddhists are not a monolithic group—reactions varied. A few interviewees rebuke the blogger: "I don't think it's appropriate for him to be upset about it"; "I would invite him to meditate on his anger." Others try to justify the lack of Asian American representation: maybe the magazine is just appealing to its largely white readership; maybe Asian American Buddhists aren't being vocal enough. Several wonder whether the exclusion is accidental or deliberate.

For the most part, however, the young adults I interviewed can see where the Angry Asian Buddhist is coming from.

Supraja, for one, is indeed shocked by the whiteness of the lineup. "It's such a turn-off," she repeatedly exclaims, before presenting her reasons for why Shambhala is remiss.

> *I think if they're going to do something like this, they should invite people and not just take the people who are comfortable with always saying what their opinion is without being asked—because then white privilege comes into play.... I mean you should care to be diverse. It should creep them out to put up a picture like this themselves, right? Damn! That's just crazy.*

To be fair, *Shambhala Sun* did not post this photo collage themselves; Aaron created it from the profile photos of the weekly posts that Shambhala chose to publish. But the bottom line for Supraja is clear: "I don't want this to be my spiritual community: heavily white, only white. It should be diverse, and there should be Asians represented."

Dolma too is seriously indignant.

> *Honestly, I couldn't agree with Arun more on this one. I mean, really? Really? This is as bad as this* Huffington Post *piece on the "10 Buddhist Women Every Person Should Know."[18] The Buddha's stepmother is the only Asian, female Buddhist you could reference? That's just absurd!*

Cristina is also put off by the collage.

To be honest, the way some of these people come off in their photos—bowtie, hipster glasses, business headshots, making funny faces, meditating on the beach, of course!—makes it feel like someone could look at them and see being Buddhist as being "cool" or "alternative" in a superficial way.

Cristina was, in fact, one of the few Asian Americans published by the project. When she brought up the issue of diversity to the organizer, she was disappointed not to be able to get much out of him in terms of concrete solutions to attracting more writers of color.

As a hapa Buddhist practitioner, Luke is vexed by the collage. "This makes me upset because as someone who looks and identifies as Asian American, I feel excluded. But because I'm part European American, I also feel welcomed. It's an extremely confusing feeling. I feel like a half of me is missing."

Noel points out that the lack of Asian representation in American society is a systemic issue that includes but is hardly limited to Buddhism. He votes with his wallet when it comes to diversity in publishing: "I stopped buying *Shambhala* or *Tricycle* or *Vanity Fair* or *GQ* unless I see Asians in it."

I have to run interview number seven no differently than the others. When it comes time to gauge his reaction to his own collage, Aaron can only laugh.

"This feels like a trick question.... I know it's not!" Examining the printout next to the vegan cookies on my kitchen table, Aaron offers some of the back story. He had originally planned to write the post using a ratio (one out of twenty) or a percentage (5 percent). He considered a pie chart. Ultimately, he opted for the photo collage. He never expected it to provoke such strong reactions.

"I've looked at this in different ways." He points to the image. "This person is half-Black He's my friend.... These are good people, right?"

Aaron can sympathize with affronted readers. "A white American might say, 'Oh, these are just my friends. This is what my Facebook wall looks like.' And so you might be offended by me pointing out these are all white people. Or it's like, 'This is my family,' right? It's not racist if my family's white, that's my freaking family!"

Aaron didn't write the post to vilify people. But he did want to hold the American Buddhist media accountable to their promises of representing the full diversity of American Buddhism.

To balance out "Why Is the Under 35 Project So White?," I also presented interviewees with an excerpt from a 2012 *Secular Buddhist* podcast. Only a few people were able to correctly identify the speaker as Charles Prebish, the scholar who coined the term "two Buddhisms."

> *One of the blogs we're all familiar with is the one called* Angry Asian Buddhist, *and it seems that he only posts issues that refer to how much he seems to hate white Buddhists. And he never really gets out there and does something to counteract that.... Maybe the question isn't Why is American Buddhism so white, but Why are Asian American Buddhists so invisible?* "[19]

Once again, responses ranged widely. Some interviewees can see where the scholar is coming from: "Maybe Asian Americans choose to be more invisible?" "Most of the active and vocal Buddhists are white." "Angry Asian, maybe—but Angry Buddhist isn't right."

Others side with neither Prebish nor Arun: "It's childish to see a young Asian American arguing with an old Jewish American convert Buddhist about this." "I think the fact that we're having this argument is contrary to Buddhist teachings. One shouldn't care whether the followers of one's religion belongs to one race or another." "I don't feel like Asian American Buddhists are invisible, nor do I feel like white Buddhists are more recognized."

But most of the young adults I interviewed took umbrage with at least some part of Prebish's statement.

"Whoa. The remark, while a valid point, comes from a place of combativeness. I take it personally. I've been trying to engage this topic for months now, and the so-called invisibility of the Asian American Buddhist community does not come from lack of trying." Luke has had little success finding Asian Americans in the mostly white sanghas (Tibetan and Zen Buddhist) he attends, or in the American Buddhist media, for that matter.

Dolma's retort to the podcast quote is short and not so sweet. "Well, this is just seeping in white privilege, isn't it? There's a clear lack of acknowledgment of who controls and has access to the media, institutional racism, colonialism, I mean—I could go on and on."

When I read Prebish's words out loud during our interview, Andy literally jumps to Arun's defense. Leaping out of his chair, he shouts:

Angry Asian Buddhist is not there to represent all of Asian American Buddhism. He's just one guy. How are you going to expect him to both call out the oppressor and work with the oppressed? One, it's not his responsibility, so back off. And, two, at least he's doing something.... It's a lot easier to criticize than to create.

Vince also goes to bat for the Angry Asian Buddhist.

I don't think the Angry Asian Buddhist actually hates white Buddhists. He or she is raising an issue that's uncomfortable for most people to talk about in American Buddhist communities.

What's needed is serious intergroup dialogue. I see that as the first step before action and change can occur. We need open, honest exchange about race in American Buddhism before anything else can happen.

Zoe has a ready reply to the "Why are Asian American Buddhists so invisible?" question.

It's actually an effect of American Buddhism being so white. In other words, Asian Americans are not invisible but they are invisibilized by the whiteness of American Buddhism. In what's referred to as the "human

potential movement" of the 1960s and 1970s, privileged young adults
(mostly white, middle- to upper-middle class) from the suburbs traveled
to what's referred to and constructed by Orientalists as "the East" and
returned to the United States with a plethora of Eastern faiths to appropri-
ate, popularize, and claim. I understand many have good intentions, but
so much space is taken up by them while they make bank on others' faiths.

Like many of her fellow Asian American Buddhists, Lola speaks to the
structural issues underlying Prebish's statement.

This seems like yet another example of how many folks—of any color,
of any spirituality—get individual acts of discrimination confused with
systemic racism.... This is evidenced by the separation of these two ques-
tions as mutually exclusive. As if Asian American Buddhists are invisi-
ble because of our own being and doing. Not to mention the underlying
judgment that the Angry Asian Buddhist "never really gets out there
and does something to counteract that." Isn't the mere fact that this blog
exists an act of resistance and of "doing something?" This underlying
judgment is a very clear example of how Asian Americans, no matter
what they (we) do, are not seen. It's like we are ghosts or something! The
scholar has answered their own question by virtue of their own uncon-
scious bias that does not see the Angry Asian Buddhist as doing anything
worthwhile. Ironically, that is part of why "Asian American Buddhists
are so invisible." Like, duh! Breathing, breathing, breathing ...

Noel, meanwhile, refuses to be riled.

I've heard this in many arenas. Where are all the Asians in entertain-
ment or literature or politics or sports? Believe it or not, there are Asians
in all of these areas. They're all visible. However, media tends to pander
to its core audience, which tends to be white people.

That statement by the "scholar" showed what was exactly wrong with
society. Here you have Angry Asian Buddhist making himself known
and visible, and what's the response? Instead of encouragement, he gets
slammed. In a way, Angry Asian Buddhist is ruffling feathers, which is
a good thing.

Diversity takes work. This includes looking at one's own racism.

As for Aaron Lee's reaction to what one interviewee calls the "strong fighting words" of Charles Prebish? Suffice to say that we devoted a full twenty-five minutes of our conversation to parsing Prebish's perspective. (You can see why the vegan cookies were long gone by the end of interview number seven.)

Ever fond of analogies, Aaron asks me to imagine an ice cream shop where a long line of customers are waiting. All the employees are doing their jobs, but the handoffs between them aren't smooth.

"Who's responsible for the handoff? For pulling it all together? When you say it's everyone's responsibility, it means it's no one's responsibility." So too for ensuring racial diversity: when no one is held accountable—or if we say everyone is accountable without any concrete understanding of what this entails—the status quo doesn't change.

Aaron brings up another comparison from his graduate school work with computer science algorithms. "One of the important determiners of how things end up is how you start." Even if you run the same algorithm, your inputs strongly affect the range of outputs you get, he explains. "If American Buddhism is white right now, and we don't change anything, then it's going to turn out white."

Aaron takes another look at Prebish's opening salvo. "I heard him say that, and I have no idea what he meant by 'He never really gets out there and does something to counteract that' ... As for 'Why are Asian American Buddhists so invisible?'—I think it's a very astute question, but I think it's an important question to be asked in tandem with the other one: Why is American Buddhism so white?"

Contrary to what many of his critics believed, Aaron was always eager to brainstorm solutions. Part of Aaron's twenty-five-minute-long response to the podcast quote involved applying game theory to better understand the incentives and disincentives for editors of Buddhist magazines to reach out to Asian Americans, and for Asian Americans to submit their writing. (I guess this is what the first year of business school will do to you, he apologized with a sheepish smile.) I dare say Aaron was more proactive problem-solver than incorrigible complainer.

At times, Arun considered himself more "snarky" than angry.[20] At times, he was downright humble. He readily admitted that his views were more personal than academic (the Angry Asian Buddhist didn't have a degree in ethnic studies).[21] He posted apologies and corrections in response to reader comments.[22] He was transparent about when he changed his mind, modifying his blog posts by appending an "update" section or using strikethrough text (~~like this~~) so we could still see his original line of thinking.

I imagine Aaron making the slightest of emendations to Prebish's statement:

> *Maybe the question ~~isn't~~ Why is American Buddhism so white, ~~but~~ and Why are Asian American Buddhists so invisible?*

Amazing how a few minor edits can shift the tenor of the entire conversation.

"Sometimes we see white as a big blob," reflects Monica. "But there's also a lot of diversity within whiteness as a category." She ponders the Angry Asian Buddhist's Under 35 collage. "I think he—or she?—is starting a really interesting and provocative and necessary conversation."

As Monica points out, being willing to engage in nuanced discussions about race benefits all of us. She chuckles. "I suppose we should all become Angry Asian Buddhists."

"There is a stereotype, not just of Buddhists, but of Asians, that we are passive and we don't really act up," Aaron explains in his 2015 interview with Funie Hsu. "Just having this 'Angry Asian Buddhist' in the title challenges you to think about what it means to be Asian and Buddhist. And I think that's important, to have some sort of icon that can counter stereotypes."[23]

The icon certainly gave Kei reason for pause. "I am not familiar with this blog. It made me laugh, because it runs so contrary to what I've long believed—that Asian American Buddhists are fairly quiet, passive, unassuming, unpretentious, nonangry people."

But better to be associated with tolerance and peace than fanaticism and violence, right?[24]

Andy isn't so sure. "Buddhism is the model minority of religions because it causes no friction with Christianity or capitalism.... Asian Americans are perceived as the submissive model minority; Buddhism being the same exaggerates it." He thinks these stereotypes are likely to "come back and bite us."

Kumi felt that bite when a white male friend used romanticized stereotypes about Buddhism as a silencing tactic against her. "I was really upset. What he said was, 'You're a Buddhist, right? You should be calmer and control yourself.' But his comment made me *more* furious. I'm a human before I'm a Buddhist! Of course Buddhists get upset."

Shubha, for one, would love to see a corrective to the notion that all Buddhists are always calm and peaceful and never violent or angry.

I want Asian American Buddhists to talk about the realities of the culture—what is good and what isn't, in their experience. I think these voices will give some much-needed reality to the discourse. Sometimes I read these articles about sexual abuse in some Buddhist or Eastern traditions in Tricycle, *and people dealing with this shock as if they didn't realize that abuse of power happens everywhere, all the time. If Asian Americans were represented, I think the religion would take on more of the truth of every religion—people would have more stories, some positive, some negative, and Buddhism would take on less of this ideal view, less of a pedestal.*

When stereotypes are deployed as qualifications for identifying "real" Buddhists, entire groups of people can find themselves defined out of existence.

In "Military ≠ Buddhism?" the Angry Asian Buddhist pushes back against people who insist that Buddhists in the military should not be considered bona fide representatives of their religion.[25] You *can* be Buddhist and serve in the military, he insists.

Jeanette Shin, a Japanese American Shin Buddhist minister who was the first Buddhist chaplain in the U.S. military, sides with Arun.

Who are we to say who is and who is not following Right Livelihood?

There are many Buddhists who are willingly serving in the all-volunteer Armed Forces, and there are also Buddhist dependents of active-duty service members, some of whom are recent immigrants to this country. They may have signed up for various reasons, but each one has taken an oath to defend this country and its people. The Buddha allowed for a ruler of a country to provide for its defense, so where did these people come from? Can they not call themselves "Buddhists" because they are willing to sacrifice their safety or even their lives to protect their communities?[26]

In a follow-up post, Aaron spells out a number of reasons why joining the military does not make people "un-Buddhist." It's a topic that hits close to home. Aaron's great-grandfather, grandfather, father, and younger brother all took an oath to defend their country and its people. "I'm pretty sure that none of them sat down and wondered what the military means in terms of Buddhist precepts," Arun writes. "They joined for their country and also for the other benefits that come with service to help them move up in society. That sometimes happens when your country discriminates against you."[27]

Once again, Aaron wasn't going to let us ignore how racial and class privilege figure into the conversation. He wouldn't allow us to overlook the disproportionate numbers of poor and nonwhite folks in the American military. He wouldn't allow us to disregard the Japanese American soldiers who died for a country that put their families in concentration camps.

Aaron wasn't going to let us forget how the racialized stereotypes we traffic in are a disservice to all American Buddhists: white converts, Asian immigrants, and the many, many others who are left out of this woefully incomplete binary. Aaron knew we could never fully escape stereotyping. He knew stereotypes were the reason "Angry Asian Buddhist" sounds more absurd than Angry Black Buddhist or Angry Asian Muslim. So he harnessed the stereotype to provoke deeper conversations about race in American Buddhism.

I wish I could have held a forum with all my interviewees. I can imagine the chorus of voices and counterpoints that would result:

> *The whiteness of American Buddhism reflects our country's demographics, since Asian Americans only make up about 5 percent of the U.S. population. / Since Asian Americans make up two-thirds of Buddhists in America, they should be a lot better represented than they are now.*
>
> *Asian American Buddhists should step up and represent themselves—or just accept the status quo. / The onus is on the white-dominated mainstream Buddhist media to reach out to Asian Americans to contribute.*
>
> *Buddhist practices and teachings matter more than representation. / The representation of Buddhism affects the propagation of the religion.*
>
> *Insisting on Asian American Buddhist representation implies that you can't be Buddhist unless you're Asian. / Insisting on Asian American Buddhist representation is not at odds with believing that Buddhism can be practiced by people of all backgrounds.*

Sometimes these debates break out between loved ones. Dedunu admits to feeling conflicted about the value of anger as someone who aims "to bridge Buddhist principles with social justice values."

> *One of my family members and I often argue about how Buddhism can be used to address social and political situations.... A good example is when we discussed experiencing racial microaggressions. His response to this is "not letting yourself get angry about it" and "moving on," because it would be* creating *a problem. For me, I feel that acknowledging the feeling internally (whether good or bad) and bringing it*

up to the person (depending on the situation) in a constructive way is addressing *what I see already as the problem.*

Sometimes these debates flare up within a single individual. Holly muses:

I do sometimes find it comforting to read expressions of frustration at the hegemony of popular Buddhist representations, and so I feel some solidarity in reading the Angry Asian Buddhist *blog. Yet I also don't read the blog that often, because I don't want to fixate on my own anger. I think about ways I can help contribute to the situation, so that I'm less angry and more engaged via Gandhi's method of "being the change I want to see in the world."*

Anger is just one among many emotions that Holly feels in response to the invisibility of Asian American Buddhists:

When I read English-language articles and books on Buddhism, or see Buddhism depicted in various ways in the United States, I perceive a lack of voices from those with Asian backgrounds. I personally feel sad, frustrated, angry, weary and lonesome at times, seeing this lack of representation, because there are aspects of my Asian cultural heritage, and so many cultural heritages, that are not reflected adequately in popular American Buddhist dialogues. I see there are many types of suffering in life, and the more we learn about diverse experiences of sentient beings, the more skillful means we have to address suffering. As a Mahayana Buddhist interested in listening to the "cries of the world" compassionately, I feel motivated to listen to a diverse array of voices.

Although I feel shy talking about myself and also don't feel authoritative about American Buddhism, I want to participate in this project to do my part in contributing to dialogues that include more Asian-American and multicultural voices. I think American Dharma will be richer for hearing from more of us.

I am an anger-averse person. Okay, that is an understatement. During my yearlong chaplaincy residency, I would gladly sit with a grieving family in the ICU for hours, but give me one person yelling and I would be hightailing it out of there at the next available opportunity.

My chaplaincy supervisors, three African American Christian women, urged me to stay in the room. They told me: Anger is energy. Anger is information. It helps us protect what we hold dear. It helps us recognize injustice. (They'd had no shortage of practice in recognizing injustice.)

They gave me permission to be with anger—mine and others'—without apology, without shame, without fear. As an Asian American, as a woman, as a Buddhist, this is something radical.

Camilla assumed the Angry Asian Buddhist was a woman.

> *I am not familiar with the* Angry Asian Buddhist *blog, but to be quite honest I do see some possible reasons why she might be angry. There are many white Buddhists or Buddhist scholars who tend to appropriate Buddhism and marginalize the Asian population, misrepresenting them, twisting their words, and generally viewing them in a disparaging way.*

> *So, while I do think that anger is bad for one's body and mind, at the same time, I do agree with said blogger that righteous anger in this case is justified and even needed to bring about some degree of change.*

Would the civil rights movement have accomplished its purpose if everyone had just been gentle and nice when conveying their opinions? Camilla asks rhetorically. I think my chaplaincy supervisors would agree with Camilla: anger can be a skillful means.

Jeff Yang's description of the Angry Asian Man could well be applied to Aaron's writing: "It is occasionally 'angry,' but primarily better described as *open, passionate,* and *defiant* about the rights of Asian Americans to be included, the need for Asian American voices to be heard, and the responsibility of Asian Americans to participate."[28]

I think of the Angry Asian Buddhist as a controlled burn for preventing the devastating fires of racism and inequity that plague our societies.

Anger can be a trap, but it can also clear the way for freedom and growth.

One of my favorite comments to arunlikhati's December 2008 "Angry Asian Buddhist" post is written by a white ally.

Don't be fooled by the name of the blog. If he's hitting us with the Dharma stick, it's because he loves us enough to try and wake us up.

From the get-go, Arun knew the title of his blog would be contentious. But it also got the targets of his criticism to sit up and take notice. If he'd wanted to spark less ire, Aaron could have softened the name. But how would the Placid Asian Buddhist ignite any change?

PRIVILEGE

"Who do you think are the most famous Buddhist individuals in America?" The Dalai Lama and Thich Nhat Hanh are the first names to come up, of course.

"And what about Buddhists living *in* America?" Jack Kornfield, Robert Thurman, Steve Jobs, Sharon Salzberg, Joseph Goldstein, Richard Gere, Tina Turner, Pema Chodron, Joan Halifax ... A deluge of answers from the thirty-two people in the room.

"What about *Asian* American Buddhists?" Crickets.

Finally, someone mentions EBMC teachers Larry Yang and Anushka Fernandopulle, with the caveat that they might be better known to this crowd than Americans at large. We are, after all, sitting in the East Bay Meditation Center. EBMC is hosting the 2014 Buddhist Peace Fellowship National Gathering this Labor Day weekend, BPF's first such conference in eight years.

Someone adds Tiger Woods, whose Thai Buddhist mother raised him
in the religion. I suggest George Takei, surprising those in the room who
didn't know the *Star Trek* actor and LGBT rights activist is also a Shin
Buddhist.

Among the participants who stick around to talk with me after my
workshop is a Chinese American Unitarian Universalist raised with Buddhist influences. She tells me she doesn't know whether to laugh or cry.
She is happy and relieved to learn that her experiences and struggles are
shared by others. Yet she is saddened and angered by the underrepresentation and misrepresentation of Asian American Buddhists.[1]

She shakes her head. "It's like we're invisible not only to the mainstream
but also to each other."

When I ask Brian if he can think of any well-known Asian American Buddhists, his response is matter of fact. "The only ones I can think of are in
Asia or dead."

Luke has a similar answer. "I don't know, Shunryu Suzuki and D. T.
Suzuki? They aren't living, though!"

"Sadly I don't know of any prominent Asian American Buddhists."
Anthony can think of Asian Buddhists who are well-known and Ameri-
can Buddhists who are well-known, but no well-known Asian American
Buddhists.

Dedunu also draws a blank. "To be honest, I have absolutely no idea!
Even in my silly attempt to Google 'Asian American Buddhists,' I found no
one that poked my memory."

Andy can't hide his consternation. "Argh! It's such a shame that I
cannot answer this question! I don't know a single person.... That's a real
shame."

Even interviewees who *were* able to think of an answer weren't always
confident in their responses. "It's already kind of difficult thinking of
well-known Asian Americans; I'm not really sure which are Buddhist."
David ponders his Jodo Shinshu community. "There's George Takei and

Kristi Yamaguchi, but I don't think they are particularly known for being Buddhist."

Noel also thinks of George Takei—"he's broken down stereotypes on many levels"—before adding an Asian American Buddhist I hadn't heard of. "She may not be 'best-known,' but I think Angela Oh is rather noteworthy. I knew her from her work as an attorney, particularly during the civil unrest between Koreans and African Americans in the early 1990s. She became an ordained Zen priest."

Lola too couches her answer in a caveat. "I don't know if they are the 'best-known' Asian American Buddhists in the United States, but to me, they would be Larry Yang, Mushim Ikeda-Nash, Lee Mun Wah, and Ruth Ozeki."

In short, it was a lot easier to answer the question *Who do you think are the most famous Buddhist individuals in America?* if "Asian American" didn't enter the equation.[2]

Tiffany has noticed that many of her second-generation Asian American peers are reluctant to out themselves as Buddhist. "A lot of Asian Americans I know prefer not to talk too much about their Buddhist heritage because it isn't something that they grew up being proud of, but rather something that set them apart and made them even more different than everyone else around them."

After all, as Heather points out, "most of us aren't really walking around proudly wearing anything that identifies us as Buddhist."

Scholars Duncan Williams and Tomoe Moriya agree. "As long as Buddhists 'cover' (using David Yoshino's term)—for example, by not flaunting monastic robes or shaved heads—their presence in the Americas generally remains invisible to outsiders."[3]

Kei, one of my Shin Buddhist interviewees, relates a personal example of this phenomenon of hiding in plain sight. "I remember being surprised in high school when I found out that a friend of mine since seventh grade was also a Buddhist. It was a moment of, 'What? Me too!' as if we'd been keeping some sort of shared secret all those years."

The Angry Asian Buddhist conveys an anecdote like Kei's in an April 2015 tweet. He had just found out that a good friend who wrote for *The Economist* for many years was Buddhist: "a recurring secret among #Asians in the #West."

In other words, Asian American Buddhists generally aren't identifiable as such—unless they are vocal about their religion. Which can explain why they can be invisible even to each other.

Aaron Lee counted the number of Asian American writers in Buddhist magazines and anthologies—an exercise he dubbed the "Asian Meter"—and repeatedly came up with dismal percentages (often, zero).[4] He noticed the same pattern for speakers at Buddhist conferences and contributors to Buddhist blogs.[5] He wrote about his findings on *Dharma Folk* and *Angry Asian Buddhist*, earning him the moniker "community archivist of Asian American Buddhism" from a grateful Funie Hsu.[6]

In her contribution to "Making the Invisible Visible: Healing Racism in Our Buddhist Communities," Mushim Ikeda-Nash recalls "dropping the book as though it had burned me" upon realizing that none of the forty-five contributors to a 1991 anthology of contemporary American Buddhist poetry were Asian American.[7]

I know the feeling. In 2012, I eagerly purchased a newly published anthology featuring "pioneering voices in Buddhist chaplaincy" and proceeded to read it cover to cover.[8] A veritable wealth of essays—but something seemed to be missing. I went back and reviewed the three-page-long table of contents. Just as I feared, there wasn't a single Asian American among the thirty-two contributors.

The dominance of white convert Buddhists can be even more painful for Asian Americans when it manifests off the page in real-life communities. In his contribution to *Dharma, Color, and Culture: New Voices in Western Buddhism,* a collection that thankfully does include Asian American voices, Larry Yang writes:

As a person of color entering a retreat or meditation hall with all white folks, there are times that I have experienced deep distress and anguish. Even if my intentions are to feel interconnected, the sense of isolation and the experience of not seeing others like myself can trigger past feelings of injury or exclusion.[9]

T. Liên Shutt expresses similar feelings of alienation in predominantly white sanghas. Born in Saigon in the mid-1960s and raised by a single mother ("I still have vivid memories of my mother lighting long sticks of incense and bowing before an altar"), Shutt was adopted by Caucasian Americans at the age of eight. "As part of my 'Americanization,' I was baptized and raised as a Presbyterian," she explains in "Vietnamese American Thoughts on Being a Buddhist in America," her contribution to "Making the Invisible Visible."

For many Asian American Buddhists, Liên Shutt among them, finding a spiritual home is fraught with racialized tensions.

I remember talking about meditation with a friend in college in 1983, but the only meditators we saw in North Dakota were white ones. When I moved to San Francisco four years ago, I lived down the street from a Zen center, but once again, I was daunted because of its whiteness ...

On top of that, as a Vietnamese American, learning from white people teachings that I knew in my bones as having roots in my childhood in Vietnam, was hard to work through. Though there are strong Vietnamese Buddhist communities and many temples within the Bay Area, because I have lost my native Vietnamese, due to well-learned acculturation, I cannot attend these temples. This is ironic to me.

I would theorize that this is also true of many Asian-Pacifics and Asian-Pacific Americans. Therefore, my request is that the communities that call themselves "American Buddhists" make space for people like me.... By keeping sanghas and retreat centers most comfortable for and accessible to only or mostly European Americans or those who have best assimilated those values, "American Buddhism" remains, in my eyes, yet another act of appropriation, taken from Asian cultures and used to exclude Asian-Pacific Islander people.[10]

One of Liên Shutt's coessayists, the Japanese American Zen practitioner who writes candidly (and anonymously) about the racially charged moments she has struggled with in her sangha, recognizes "the tremendous work done by people of color and white ally sangha members"—but she remains concerned about what we are up against.

> *I do worry, though, that as certain American Buddhist institutions transform and adapt their forms and rituals from their current Asian encasings, they will replicate the cultural hegemony and oppressive dynamics that has occurred repeatedly in white-dominated institutions over the last four-hundred-plus years. I also worry that the currently middle- and upper-middle-class white-populated institutions will become defined as "the American Buddhism" and that the other Asian American, African American, and other Buddhist groups will be relegated to the margins or considered nonexistent.*[11]

This Zen practitioner, Larry Yang, and (now Rev.) Liên Shutt are older than my interviewees, but their concerns still resonate with a younger generation of Asian American Buddhists. Two decades after "Making the Invisible Visible," there is still work to be done. Consider, for example, Anthony's experience:

> *As a person with a multiethnic background and an ambiguous phenotype (I've been racially profiled several times by police who have completely mistaken my "race"), I've always been sensitive to issues surrounding racial identity.*

> *As a Buddhist, there are a number of trends in what I consider to be "mainstream American Dharma" that I find to be unsettling; in general, this has to do with what I consider to be a commodification of the Dharma and selling it to a particularly privileged subset of the population: a population that happens to be predominantly white. I find that I don't relate to the images of Dharma practitioners and the "Dharma lifestyle" peddled in publications like* Tricycle *and* Shambhala Sun, *or to the various "secular Buddhism" groups circulating on the internet, and that moreover I worry about American Buddhism turning into an "Upper Middle Class Way."*

I should add that for me this topic brings up issues of class as much as it does race; the two problems are, of course, deeply intertwined in American history and culture. I am just as alienated from "mainstream American Dharma" as an indebted member of the working class as I am as an Asian American, and for many of the same reasons.

In short, there's no escaping the effects of white privilege—and its entanglements with class privilege—in American Buddhism.

Kevin's response to Prebish's question (challenge?) of "Why are Asian American Buddhists so invisible?" is pragmatic.

I don't think Asian American Buddhists are unintentionally invisible. I think they are intentionally quiet and cautious so they don't arouse suspicion or misunderstanding, because Buddhism is still seen as foreign, and people are naturally afraid of the unknown. I recall opposition from residents when the first Burmese Buddhist monasteries opened in the United States. Even to this day, there's still this kind of resistance. A Taiwanese Buddhist temple in Rowland Heights [California] recently started construction after years of protests from residents and neighboring churches.

Eric has faced analogous opposition—merely for airing his Asian American Buddhist views.

When I have blogged about related issues on Dharma Folk, *such as the cultural appropriation of Buddhism by mainstream American culture, many people comment, criticizing me for "being too attached" to such trivial issues. Somehow, people become very defensive and reactionary (from my perspective, they are the ones who seem very attached to certain ideas and can't deal with criticism of those ideas) and can't accept that in the very real landscape of Buddhism in American society, Buddhism does not operate in a vacuum unaffected by the context and mechanisms by which the rest of American society operates under, such as issues of race, lack of opportunity, and lack of representation.*

White Buddhists may have the luxury of ignoring how racism and unequal representation actually do significantly affect the American Buddhist community. It's not a luxury that people like Eric can enjoy.

"It's so much harder for an Asian American person to get their voice heard in this society," Tiffany laments. "Speaking up is not a right but rather a risk for many."

Speaking up was a risk for C. N. Le. The sociologist fielded a barrage of insults over a July 2009 blog post in which he shared his observations about the racial dynamics at a multicultural and multiracial Buddhist retreat.[12] The overwhelming majority of the meditators who remained to clean up after the retreat were nonwhite, leading Le to critique the "White-privileged notion that service work should be left to people of color."

Speaking up was a risk for Liriel. In a June 2011 guest post on *Angry Asian Buddhist,* the second-generation Asian American Buddhist writes with unflinching honesty about her fear of being the target of white backlash. She had just witnessed a maelstrom of ad feminam attacks against fellow blogger Tassja, a young adult Sri Lankan Sinhalese woman whose decision "to reclaim the Buddhist identity I grew up with" is "a deeply personal act with political implications."[13] Liriel writes:

> *Every time I want to express my differing perspective, I'm silenced by the shitstorm I know is waiting to demean my person and mock my loved ones, rather than engage with the logic of my thesis.*
>
> *And so I take refuge in the nonwhite, non-English-speaking, immigrant sanghas I was raised in. And thus our bodies and our voices are absent from your conferences and self-congratulatory blogs. And consequently there are few to challenge your cocksure assertions of your own diversity and inclusiveness even as I stand here feeling alienated.[14]*

Unfortunately, Liriel's fears came to pass. She was indeed slammed by mocking comments: "It might be better to be a convert of Buddhism than to be born into it"; "Get over yourself."[15]

Speaking up was a risk for Funie Hsu. Vitriol flew her way after the publication of "We've Been Here All Along" in the winter 2016 issue of *Buddhadharma*. In a written response to these critics, *Buddhadharma* editor Tynette Deveaux notes that "we don't usually get much feedback from readers" and expresses her surprise at the tone of the letters: "Some were quite angry at Hsu and lodged personal attacks ('She should be grateful for what she has'; 'She ain't no Buddhist')."[16]

Who has the power to represent American Buddhism?

When I ask Dedunu who the best-known American Buddhists are, she can only think of Richard Gere. "His systemic privilege as a (well-recognized) white male has allowed him to promote the religion and appear coolly 'different' without the burden of being tokenized for it."

Lola thinks of Jack Kornfield and David Loy. "They're famous because they are white male elders, with the access and privilege to be 'seen.'" In the case of the Dalai Lama and Thich Nhat Hanh—who aren't technically American, but are certainly well known to Americans—"they are famous because white individuals have studied with them and took it upon themselves (made possible through their privileges) to translate and write books on their teachings."

Dolma concurs. "Individuals are more likely to pay attention to a white cisgender-heterosexual male celebrity's understanding of Buddhism than that of an Asian American's."

"When you mention American Buddhists," Wanwan confesses, "I think about the white blond woman on the cover of *Time* magazine who is the face of the 'Mindful Revolution' but is probably not Buddhist."[17]

Dedunu has become increasingly disturbed by how race, class, and gender privilege contribute to the marginalization of a huge swath of American Buddhists.

Recently, after years of internalizing my identity in many different ways, I have started to see how Buddhism has been both represented and, in other ways, ignored on many different levels. That is to say, I feel as though the face of Buddhism, including the recent trends in "mindfulness" practice within schools, has generally lacked Asian Americans in the conversation.

> *While I struggle in separating the cultural from the religious and phil-*
> *osophical ways in which I have experienced and perceive Buddhism,*
> *this gap in representation has left me feeling uneasy over the years....*
> *Most of the ways in which I have seen Buddhism as viewed through an*
> *"American" lens has been through its promotion by "hippy white folks,"*
> *as an exotified, "ancient," or "mystical" religion, or its representation as*
> *something practiced only by elder Asian American men (predominantly*
> *from East Asia) in culturally appropriated movies.*

When "ethnic" Buddhists are perceived as "fresh off the boat, mystical, exotic, living meekly, etc.," Dedunu adds, "I feel as though Asian American Buddhists are not 'American' enough according to white American standards."

A certain type of Asian Buddhist *is* widely represented in the American media: the Oriental monk. A wise and stoic figure, robed and bald-headed, shrouded in mystery. But being seen as exotic and mystical is preferable to being typecast as a superstitious immigrant, right?

Jane Iwamura argues otherwise. As she astutely points out in her book *Virtual Orientalism,* the most celebrated pupils of the "wise Asian sage" are his "Anglo pupils"—white students who rescue their masters' religions from "the Asian masses that fail to appreciate the value of their inherited tradition."[18] Ultimately, white converts are the best Buddhists of all within this storyline, since they are the ones who carry the torch of a new and improved, rational and modern, "enlightened" Western Buddhism.

"In our society we place a lot more faith and trust in something when it is helmed by a white or Caucasian American individual or group," Tiffany observes.

> *Even in terms of religion, when a lesser-known non-Christian religion*
> *suddenly gets a lot of white Caucasian followers, it adds a dimension of*
> *authenticity and puts that religion on a more mainstream path. Bud-*
> *dhism has been around for thousands of years, but people in America*

might not be very interested in what an Asian person has to say about it—yet when a Caucasian person says something about Buddhism, people really listen. We make assumptions that a Caucasian voice comes with a more educated background, a more liberal and open perspective.[19]

Soto Zen priest and former BPF executive director Alan Senauke can attest to this. He recognizes that though "most Buddhists even in America don't look like me," white people like him are disproportionately granted the power to speak for American Buddhism.

Recently I was invited to talk about Buddhism and race to a diverse group of teenagers doing an interfaith social action internship in San Francisco. I hope I did a good job talking to them, but it was curious to me that I was the organizers' first choice for a Buddhist speaker. The irony is that Buddhism in America gets defined as and by people who look like me, not by the far more numerous Asian and Asian-American practitioners.[20]

In another part of his essay "On Race and Buddhism," published in 2010 and reprinted on the *Angry Asian Buddhist* blog the following year, Rev. Senauke recognizes the ways white privilege prevents American Buddhism from being truly inclusive.

First, does one feel safe and seen in the community? Are the conditions of one's life acknowledged, welcomed, explored in the sangha? I suspect the answer is sometimes yes, and too often no. Thoughtless words can turn people from the temple and from the practice. I have seen this happen. An offhand comment is made about how we are all white and middle class here, with people of color and working-class friends sitting right there. When we unknowingly see through a lens of class and white supremacy, people are made to feel invisible and uncounted.

White supremacy is the cornerstone of racism, created out of blindness to one's (my) own privilege as a white man. It is at once personal and systemic. If one wants to see white supremacy, the practice of turning our light inward needs to be blended with dialogue with friends and sangha members who don't carry this very particular privilege.[21]

Holly, for one, knows what it feels like not to carry this privilege.

> *I feel intimidated and that I "don't belong" in conversations already dominated by Caucasian or primarily English-speaking contributors. I don't want to be the token "other" or have to symbolize a whole group of people.*

> *It's really true that cultural differences can be uncomfortable and cross-cultural conversations can be more awkward, conflictual, and prone to misunderstanding compared to conversations with people in the same cultural or language group. It takes a great deal of courage, patience, and compassion to participate in conversations outside of one's cultural comfort zones.*

Echoing Holly's advice, Rev. Senauke implores his fellow Buddhists to embrace the uncomfortable.

> *I try to uncover my own thought patterns. This is sometimes painful and embarrassing, but it is the essence of saving myself and all sentient beings. It is amazing to see the stories one can make up about other people, and how these stories are conditioned by race, or class, or privilege. Check it out for yourself....*

> *Then we can go farther into our extended communities. Ask your friends of color how they experience the practice and the community. This is entering the realm of not knowing, risky, but completely necessary. In the wider Buddhist community, it might mean making excursions and visits to Asian Buddhist temples. They are friendly places. The same Dharma resides there, though it may take some different forms.*

Like many of the young adults I interviewed, Dedunu doesn't need to be reminded to investigate issues of race, class, and privilege in American Buddhism—they are ever-present in her lived experience. As a matter of course, she listens to differing viewpoints and interrogates her own.

Consider, for example, Dedunu's complicated relationship with the issue of appropriation.

It's hard to find the balance of cultural appreciation and cultural appro-
priation, even as a person of color, and especially as someone born and
raised in the United States. There's a lot of conflicting opinions within
our own communities, and I often find it difficult to navigate these
conversations.

The issue raises difficult questions. What forms of appropriation merit censure? What forms count as uncontroversial adaptations of a religion entering a new cultural context? Does accusing white Buddhists of appropriation amount to racial chauvinism on the part of Asian Americans?

As someone who strives to bridge Buddhist principles with social justice values, Dedunu struggles to reconcile her personal, culturally informed connection to Buddhism with the political, sometimes violent implications of cultural chauvinism. On the one hand, she is uneasy about the rise of Sinhalese nationalist Buddhist monks in Sri Lanka; on the other hand, "watching the increasingly large, white convert Buddhist community take over narratives here also feels uncomfortable."

Dedunu also grapples with the tension between individualist and collectivist interpretations of Buddhist concepts when it comes to issues of appropriation and representation.

For instance, the concept of "karma," as I have learned it, empha-
sizes that the positive or negative thoughts and actions of a person
cyclically affects their past, present, and future lives. Does this place
all responsibility on the individual, without holding larger systems
accountable?

Correspondingly, if the notion of "anatta" refers to the illusion of self,
does representation of Buddhism matter? While I personally feel it still
does, I struggle with connecting these seemingly contradictory concepts
together.

There are no easy answers to these questions, but one thing is certain: Dedunu does not endorse the essentialist view that only people of Asian heritage can be the legitimate heirs of Buddhism. Like the Angry Asian Buddhist, she understands that an Asian Buddhist superiority complex is no less dangerous than a Western Buddhist superiority complex.[22]

#AsianBuddhistsMatter

So reads the subject line of a January 2015 email from Aaron Lee to me, Andy, Dolma, and Wanwan.

In chatting with Wanwan recently, Aaron had been contemplating the importance of including Asian American writing in Western Buddhist publications: "When we're absent, it feels as though the editors are saying we don't matter."

What did we think of the hashtag? Was it too sensitive? Andy responded the next day, urging Aaron to reconsider.

> *Hey friends,*
>
> *I understand where the sentiment comes from and I agree wholeheart-edly that the issue is white Buddhist publications not recognizing the importance of Asian American Buddhist voices. However, I do not believe it would be appropriate to use the hashtag #AsianBuddhistsMat-ter as it has no relation to the obvious reference #BlackLivesMatter.*
>
> *This hashtag does not do any service to the #BlackLivesMatter hashtag as it decenters the critique on anti-Black violence and shifts it toward Asian American Buddhists. While ... not our intention, that is what we are doing by appropriating the hashtag. And since we clearly are not aiming to take the spotlight from #BlackLivesMatter, we should come up with another hashtag.*

Dolma felt the same way. "I don't want to put my Asian/American Buddhism at odds with my solidarity with #BlackLivesMatter—especially when in my mind the two are very much aligned."

Aaron's swift reply:

> *Thank you so much for your response.*
>
> *I'm not going to use #AsianBuddhistsMatter. I really, really appreci-ate your thoughts—especially since I might have done something really inappropriate, insensitive, and misguided without really thinking through the implications of it.*

For Shubha, sensitivity to the issues of other POC Buddhists can actually inhibit them from telling their own story.

> *My sangha is very diverse but I often feel like the diversity is focused around the experience of Black people coming to the religion—which is important but different.... I don't want to take away from this POC space being about the struggles that Black people face on a daily basis, the way racism impacts them.*

I understand where Shubha is coming from. The black-white dichotomy that dominates discussions of race in America makes it hard to know where Asian Americans fit in. The model minority trope that renders Asian Americans white-adjacent can interfere with our desire to express solidarity with non-Asian people of color.

"I want to be able to tell the story of my experience and feel like it matters what I've experienced," Shubha writes. "I hope the ability to tell my story on paper and know that at least one person has read it will make me feel heard. I'm trying to embrace the idea that I can tell my story too."

Fortunately, this is not the Oppression Olympics. I think of the Black writers who have shaped my understanding of race in American Buddhism—Faith Adiele, bell hooks, Zenju Earthlyn Manuel, Charles Johnson, and Alice Walker, to name a few. I don't think their message is that the stories of Asian American Buddhists aren't also worth telling. If anything, their writing is an invitation for more of us to tell our stories. All of our voices are sorely needed in American Buddhist media, which, like the American media more generally, remains a bastion of white privilege.

For Holly, weighing the risks and merits of speaking up as an Asian American Buddhist woman presents a conundrum.

> *I know for myself that the reason people don't "hear" from me is that I don't want to be the center of attention. I find myself in a strange contradiction: How can I be myself in a more public way so as to help encourage the voices of other young, Asian American, and especially female Buddhists ... when my way of being myself is to be private? How does*

one step forward into more representation without being required to emulate the behavior of a dominant group?

"Why are Asian American Buddhists so invisible?" Perhaps Asian American Buddhists need to work to become more visible, while dominant groups need to learn to look and listen more closely.

Andy comes to a revelation about the second part of Holly's suggestion as we near the end of our three-hour-long interview. Throughout our conversation, he's been thinking out loud about the gaps and intersections between the Taiwanese American, Asian American, LGBT, and Buddhist communities he's a part of. (I'm not sure how this astronautical engineering major has time to sleep.) Andy hasn't found many people interested in talking with him about religion in the first three groups; he's been trying to create a space for the LGBT community in his Buddhist collegiate group. The Buddhist values he grew up with are an inspiration for these efforts:

I was raised in a Buddhist family. The way that I interpreted Buddhism as a child was, you do community service. You give yourself for the good of others.... The main premise that I understood was, there are other people worse off than you. They are suffering. You are in a position of privilege. You should use your privilege to help uplift those in suffering. So there was this virtue of compassion that was taught to me.

Andy is reexamining Prebish's podcast quote and explaining how his work in the LGBT community has challenged him to question what it means to be an ally when suddenly it all clicks.

A bodhisattva is an ally! A bodhisattva is someone who forsakes her enlightenment for those who cannot yet attain it. Like Guanshiyin Pusa would say: I'm not going to be enlightened until everyone is relieved from suffering....

Becoming an ally is understanding your privilege, and working against it. This person has not reached that point. He is not an ally. But he could be. He could be an ally. He's starting to ask the right questions.... It's his responsibility to take that white space, the space where white people get to talk about Buddhism, and turn it into an ally space!

Andy is also on board with the first part of Holly's suggestion about the need for Asian American Buddhists to become more visible.

Blogs are not enough. We need to have conferences. We need to have podcasts. We need to be at parades. We need to be talking to other faiths. That's what building a space is....

Which is also another thing I've realized. Space engineering is what I came to college for, and I've learned that I'm going to become a space engineer, but not in the building rockets sense.... I'm going to engineer community spaces!

Andy's realizations on privilege and allyship reoriented my thinking on Asian American Buddhists. We may be a group rendered invisible by white privilege—but we are also a group whose experiences of both strength and marginalization help us understand that privilege, like anger, is a kind of power: capable of helping or harming, depending on how we wield it.

Noel urges his fellow Asian American Buddhists not to be closeted about their religious lives. Speaking up is a form of empowerment, for ourselves and for others.

"Coming out" has been an important part of my life as a gay man. Declaring my identity as a Buddhist probably came from my history as an activist. Letting the world know who I am is quite liberating. I think some Asian Buddhists keep quiet about their religion because we're in a predominantly Abrahamic country. They don't want to deal with oppression. I learned that it's okay to be clear and vocal about who I am. People don't expect that from Asian people, actually, so I think it's wise to break that stereotype.

Noel might be heartened to hear how Kristie came to embrace her Taiwanese American Buddhist upbringing as a privilege rather than a problem:

When I was younger, I tried so hard to be "American"—I tried to hide all aspects of my "Asianness," including what I ate and what I believed, even though I grew up in a predominantly Asian town (Edison, New Jersey). It was difficult for me to truly adopt Buddhism with pride until recent years, and I'm still growing. I find, though, that I love it.... Once we realize how necessary Buddhism is (especially in American society), it releases a strength that I really don't think you can find elsewhere.

The Angry Asian Buddhist urged us not to ignore the ways white privilege undermines the inclusive vision of American Buddhism. He also reminded us that regardless of our race, it is a privilege to be followers of the Buddha, students of the Dharma, members of many a sangha. And, perhaps most fundamentally of all, he taught us that it is a privilege to be human, to be alive, to be able to care for others.

A couple days after the eight-year anniversary of his first *Angry Asian Buddhist* post, Aaron emailed me about his latest writing aspirations.

Recently I've been playing around with the notion of trying to write again on a new platform.... It's a fresh start on writing, going from Dharma Folk *to* Angry Asian Buddhist, *and now after a few months struggling with cancer, I'm leaning towards a new blog called* Be the Refuge ...

"Be the refuge" is something that I've thought about a lot since my diagnosis. When I was in pain, I used meditation as a refuge for my mind. In the hospital, I used my speech and actions as refuge for my family and caregivers—providing them with a space where they could feel calm, positive, and helpful. In organizing marrow drives, I try to create a refuge for my friends from the powerlessness of being able to "do nothing"—a space where they feel empowered to provide meaningful assistance toward finding my cure. And now after the [2016] election, I feel that the challenge to us is to create refuges of our own communities, to create spaces where people can find true comfort and well-being.

I'm not sure if I can align "Angry Asian Buddhist" with "Be the Refuge," but maybe one day ...[23]

A week later, Aaron emailed me again. "Somehow talking with you about your writing has inspired me to type up my own draft of something that I might actually post."[24]

Aaron thought the title might be the weakest part, but he felt ready to ask for feedback. Would I mind taking a look? Fighting back tears, I emailed him back twenty minutes later. I told him I wouldn't change a thing.

It was the last blog post he would ever write.

Be the Refuge

Dec 17, 2016

Turns out, I have cancer.

Back when I mistakenly thought I was healthy, I had paid repeated visits to various doctors with a basket of unexplainable symptoms. Joint aches. Headaches. Fevers. Night sweats. I was otherwise incredibly healthy, eating a mostly plant-based diet and getting a good night's sleep.

Always bewildered, the doctors ordered me dozens of blood tests, scans, and pain medications. By the time enough data had accumulated to warrant a hospital stay, the diagnosis had become grimly clear.

My cancer is a metastatic non-Hodgkin's lymphoma that has spread to my bone marrow, liver, kidneys, bones, central nervous system—not to mention dozens of lymph nodes throughout my body. It has been more painful than anything else I have endured in my short human life.

Worse yet, no matter how well I should respond to the six grueling rounds of chemotherapy my oncologists have scheduled for me, my hyperaggressive cancer is bound to relapse within a year. My only hope for a cure will come from a stem cell donor.

But there's a catch. Due to my diverse ancestry, my chances of finding a matching donor are unusually low. I often hear that my odds are about *one in a million*, which I've learned is the technical term for, "There's a chance. Just don't count on it."

So in the meantime, as I sit through my rounds of chemo and wait for that needle-in-a-haystack lifesaving stem cell donor to be found, I've decided that this is the time to get serious about my Buddhist practice.

.   .   .

Bundled up in excruciating pain on my hospital bed, the inevitability of my death brought an unexpected comfort. We all die, cancer or otherwise. Buddhism never fails to remind us that we are all subject to birth, aging, illness and death—and also gives us something to do about it.

I started by trying to recall various Buddhist teachings I'd imbibed in my short life, starting with the Four Noble Truths: life sucks, there's a reason why life sucks, life doesn't have to suck, and there's a path you can follow so your life doesn't suck. I figured it was time to start making some headway down that path, while I'm still able to do so.

I decided early on that now was not the time to struggle for enlightenment and a release from all suffering in this life. It seemed more prudent to focus on my unsurprisingly mundane priorities. I wanted to manage my pain. I wanted peace of mind. I wanted to ease the burden of my condition on my family and friends who had been with me through this whole ordeal. Anything was game, from meditation to chanting to readings.

During my first two weeks in the hospital, I tried playing around with different Buddhist practices to try to tease out which would work best for me. Unfortunately, I was hopelessly disorganized and found focus and consistency nearly impossible. I tried making a spreadsheet on my laptop, but never updated it. I brought a notebook, but would fall asleep before taking down notes.

One night, restless from a large dose of prednisone, I picked up my notebook and scribbled down the thoughts running around in my mind. What was I trying to achieve, if not ultimate liberation? Why was it important for me to delve into Buddhist practice? What would make it all worthwhile? And then I scribbled out one last line, closed my notebook, and went to sleep.

Be the refuge you wish to see in this world.

.   .   .

"Be the refuge" has become my strategy for engaging Buddhist practice in my battle with cancer. I'm okay with not reaching the fully liberating refuge of enlightenment in this lifetime. It would be enough if I could have somewhat of a refuge for myself from pain and anxiety, and then to try be a refuge for those around me.

When I was in my most intense pain, meditation became a refuge for my mind. Metta meditation was so effective at focusing my mind that, somehow, my intense pains would vanish for a time. I found myself taking refuge in my breath during my bone marrow biopsy and MRI scans, allowing my mind to dwell in a comfortable space during some rather uncomfortable procedures.

In the hospital, I found my speech and actions could become refuges for my family and caregivers—providing them with a space where they could feel calm, positive, and helpful. I try to be honest and let people help me when they can. I try to use the spirit of irony to take the edge off my complaints. Simple courtesies of thanks and asking nurses and aides how their days are going have gone a long way to making sure my care team knows that they can breathe easy around me.

As it became clear that my cure would depend on a stem cell or bone marrow donor, organizing marrow donor drives proved to be a refuge for my friends from the powerlessness of being able to "do nothing"—a space where they feel empowered to provide meaningful assistance toward finding my cure. It's amazing to see the faces of friends and family light up when they can see that they have the means to actually help save my life. In a world full of suffering, even complete strangers have shared with me how meaningful it is to learn they can do something simple to help save someone's life.

Even now after the election upset, I feel that the challenge is for us to create refuges of our own communities, to create spaces where people can find true comfort and well-being. Is our meditation center a place where newcomers can feel safe and secure? Do we feel supported by our communities? Are our spaces attentive to the needs of those of us marginalized by society?

There is a temptation to strive to change what's outside, rather than focus on ourselves and our own communities. While we still need to articulate our principles, relay our stories, protest injustice, and cast our votes, we are most compelling when we are the very refuges we wish to see in this world. When we can exist calmly in moments of suffering and confusion, others notice and are drawn to us. When our communities provide true and considered support, others notice and will attempt to recreate the same benefits for their own communities. The power of our refuges means others may even pay special attention to our work in community in ways they would never do otherwise. When our communities are welcoming to those in need of support and attentiveness, our communities will grow.

"Be the refuge" is a challenge. It is a challenge for me to recast my efforts and rethink the questions I use to focus my energies. For years I've wondered about how to create an op-ed project for Buddhists of color in order to encourage a greater diversity of writers. But when I now refocus the question—"How do I create a refuge for Buddhists of color?"—I find myself with a broader set of options to explore, not to mention more insightful ways to articulate my goals for increasing the diversity of Buddhist writers.

As I fling my body through successively brutal cycles of chemotherapy, my real challenge remains for me to be the refuge I wish to see in this world. My life has already been extended by months, and yet the end still seems so precariously near. I'm reminded every day to be thankful to be alive. May I strive for every day to be a refuge for myself and for all beings.[25]

SOLIDARITY

"It is hard to imagine an external force ... that could galvanize disparate Buddhist immigrant groups to forge a shared Asian-American and Buddhist identity," writes religious studies scholar Richard Seager in both the 1999 and 2012 editions of his book *Buddhism in America*.[1]

When I first read these words as an MA student at the Institute of Buddhist Studies, I wondered if I should abandon my fledgling idea of writing my thesis on Asian American Buddhists. Seager seemed to be saying that my topic wasn't viable, that I had better choose a specific ethnic group—Chinese or Japanese or Sri Lankan or Thai or Vietnamese American Buddhists.

But I was greedy. I wanted to think about all of these ethnicities (and then some) in a unified way. I wanted to explore the contours of a shared Asian American Buddhist identity, whatever that might mean. I know greed is not a Buddhist virtue. But in this case, I'm so glad I gave in. Had I abandoned my fledgling project idea, I think it would be fair to chide me for a failure of imagination.

What is your name and what does your name mean?

My name is George Masao Yamazawa, Jr., and people have been calling me "G" since middle school. *Masao* means "good husband," which
was my grandfather's name, and *Yamazawa* means "mountain valley."
George was the name my father gave himself when he arrived in America in the late '70s, and I'm proud to be a junior.

*What motivates you to contribute your stories and perspectives to this project
on Asian American Buddhists? What interests you most about this topic?*

First of all, I believe my story is valid, worthy, and important, just like
everybody else's. Secondly, I was born into the practice of Nichiren
Buddhism and the Soka Gakkai International community, but didn't
fully deepen my faith and understanding until I had to take responsibility of my own life and struggles.

This topic is interesting to me because I never viewed Buddhism in
terms of race. The SGI is an incredibly diverse community; from race,
to sexual orientation, to culture, to socioeconomic status, to age, to
educational background. Most of the pioneer members (senior citizens of faith) are Japanese immigrants who first began practicing back
home, and that's the only demographic of folks who are mostly Asian.
This topic is also interesting to me because it's the first time I'm forced
to deeply think about the cultural gap between Asian American and
non–Asian American Buddhists.

I was born into the SGI Buddhist practice, and learned how to chant
Nam myoho renge kyo from the moment I was first able to speak. Growing up in the Bible Belt, not believing in a God that created the uni-
verse, and being told I was going to hell for having a different form of
faith forced me to build a strong foundation for my own understanding
of religion and philosophy at a young age. I also began to notice that
the sect of Buddhism I practice was different from the ones they talk

about in schools; I'd never gone to any temples, never had any connections with priests, and never meditated in silence.

What racial or ethnic identities do you use to describe yourself? Do you identify as "Asian American"? Why or why not?

Definitely Asian American, head to toe. Specifically Japanese American, but I find particular solidarity with all people of immigrant and minority experiences.

In his 2003 article "Two Buddhisms Further Considered," Paul Numrich argues for "the validity of the basic two Buddhisms distinction" and offers the following anecdote to illustrate the "social chasm" that exists between "ethnic-Asian" and "white convert" Buddhists:

> *I recall the Asian-American Buddhist who thanked me for a talk I gave about ethnic-Asian Buddhism to a virtually all-white audience at the Smithsonian Institution in Washington, DC: "You described so well the Buddhism I was raised in," he said, with some emotion. For most of my audience that day, which included many Buddhist converts, the Asian American Buddhist experience was as foreign as Asia itself.[2]*

A note of caution from Chimamanda Adichie:

> *The single story creates stereotypes, and the problem with stereotypes is not that they are untrue but that they are incomplete. They make one story become the only story.*

What is your name and what does your name mean?

My name is Thao, and it means filial piety—a virtue of respect for one's parents and ancestors.

What would your ideal Buddhist community look like?

The following passage is my favorite quote regarding an ideal Buddhist community and spiritual friendships:

> *Ananda [the Buddha's cousin and later disciple] approaches the Buddha, intent on sharing a thought. Something—perhaps the cumulative effect of day-to-day association with the Buddha—has suddenly made him realize that such "lovely companionship" is far more crucial to spiritual progress than he had imagined. He enthusiastically declares, "Lord, this spiritual friendship, spiritual companionship, and spiritual intimacy is no less than half of the spiritual life." "Say not so, Ananda," the Buddha replies. "It is the whole, not the half of the spiritual life."*

> *Many of those Buddhists who are familiar with this concept of spiritual friendship or kalyana mitrata think of it in terms of a "teacher-disciple" relationship (or "vertical" friendship). As a result they pay little attention to a vital dimension of spiritual friendship that could be called "horizontal" friendship: that is, friendship with one's peers.[3]*

My ideal Buddhist community would consist of friendships described in the above passage—a community where we are able to learn from each other in "horizontal" friendship. We can relate based on sharing similar Buddhist values and principles. We are able to support each other through the good and bad times. We can bond over good conversation or shared interests.

American Buddhism, Peter Gregory argues, is a phenomenon "far too large for any one person to grasp in its totality."[4] Gregory likens our attempts to categorize and describe the complicated phenomenon of American Buddhism to the parable of the elephant and the blind men, each convinced their part (trunk, ear, torso, tusk, leg, tail) is the whole.

I used to believe that American Buddhism is an elephant divided: the white side on prominent display, the Asian side consigned to the shadows.

And then I started to listen to people like George and Thao. And what I heard were stories of interconnection overcoming conflict, solidarity healing division. What I heard were stories of spiritual friendship. Friendship that traverses boundaries of race and ethnicity, age and generation, sect and tradition, gender and sexuality, class and ability, language and nationality. These stories give me hope that American Buddhism is far more dynamic and diverse than any one of us can fully imagine.

In 2008, a group of friends banded together to start the blog *Dharma Folk*. They signed their blog posts arunlikhati, John, kudos, and Oz. The University Buddhist Association (UBA) had united them despite their different cultural backgrounds, though I wouldn't learn this until many years later.

That year, for the first time in his life, Aaron felt disconnected from the Buddhist community. Having graduated, he was no longer reaching out to different sanghas to bring speakers to campus, no longer arranging for his fellow students (Asian American and otherwise) to visit their local Sri Lankan, Chinese, Thai, and other temples. Aaron started browsing the Buddhist blogosphere. And that's when he noticed the lack of Asian Americans, a glaring contrast to his UBA experiences: "We weren't there. There was this absence."

Aaron wanted to do something about that absence, and he didn't want to do it alone. He thought about his friend John. "He's white ... but he's very deeply involved in the Buddhist community, so I felt John understood the world I grew up in."

Aaron ran an idea by John. "Hey, why don't we start a blog? We can just talk about the world that we're in, and we'd be adding something else to the discussion that no one else is adding."

With the help of Eric and Oz, that's exactly what they did.

"It's funny," Aaron muses, "because the Angry Asian part really spun out of that."[5]

Discrimination as a racial and religious minority. Confusion and anger at the appropriation of Buddhism. Conviction that her Buddhist faith and her belief in social justice are inseparable. Tassja writes about these topics and more in a June 2011 post on her blog *Womanist Musings*.

"I have plenty to be angry about in this world, and my anger at injustice does not make me a lesser Buddhist," she insists.

Of course there was backlash from white readers. But there was also a response from another young adult Asian American woman. Liriel is neither Sinhalese nor a Sri Lankan Buddhist, yet she finds many points of commonality with Tassja.

> *Thank you so much for writing this.*
>
> *I am constantly frustrated by the invalidation of my Buddhist experience by the mainstream American Buddhist powers as so much "cultural baggage" that "modern," "rational" Buddhism needs to be cleansed of. But every time I dip my toes into the waters of the U.S. mainstream to try to put forth another perspective, I am inundated with comments like, "The West has a lot to offer to the stagnate, codified Asian practices," and, "We in the West offer hope of rejuvenation," and perhaps my all-time favorite, by a well-respected white American convert Buddhist about feminism in Buddhism: "If we had not spoken up, the Buddhist women's movement, which started less than twenty years ago, would not even exist. Things might not have changed for another 2,500 years." And reading things like that, I don't know how I should open myself up to more abuse and silencing.*
>
> *I am hurt, and more than that, I am angry, but even more than that, I am tired. Nothing I say as a woman of color ever seems to be of any consequence to the all-knowing white Buddhist establishment, who remain determined as ever to tell me how I'm "doing Buddhism wrong."*
>
> *So I wanted to let you know that your words here were of consequence to this Buddhist woman of color. That your words spoke to a beaten-down, fatigued part of me and inspired me. Your words make me want to write my own Buddhism, out of solidarity rather than out of anger because you have reminded me that as white as Buddhism sometimes feels, my Buddhism is not monochromatic and I am not alone.*

Tassja's reply is equally heartfelt.

> @Liriel: I can't begin to tell you how much your words mean to me. I too often feel like I don't know "enough" about the "texts" and "history" of Buddhism when faced with the white Buddhist establishment. I'm so sorry you have had to endure the silencing and racism you described :(I have not interacted extensively with the white Buddhist community and so I have been spared some of the more painful realities of that in some ways.
>
> I used to think that I didn't know as much as they do about Buddhism, and then I realized, the history and context of Buddhism is written on my body, it's molded on my skin, it flows in my blood, it filled the air I breathed when I was born in Sri Lanka. We have everything we need, right here :)
>
> I hope you keep writing about your Buddhist experience as well. I would love for us to continue being in conversation.[6]

Witnessing the exchange between Tassja and Liriel, the Angry Asian Buddhist finds reason for optimism.

> Sometimes it feels as though I'm the only Asian American Buddhist blogger out there, but it's times like these that remind me I'm not alone. There are hundreds of thousands of Asian American Buddhists in this country, and we are ready to speak out and stand up for our inclusion, dignity and respect.[7]

What is your name and what does your name mean?

Defender of humankind.

What would your ideal Buddhist community look like?

The *dhamma* and social justice go together like peas in a pod, so an ideal community would elegantly fuse the two in all teachings. It would have guidelines around honoring our blessings, privileges, and oppressions. The ideal sangha would not engage in spiritual bypassing, but acknowledge the reality of the period in the world we live in, and have teachings specific to the societal context. It would be intentionally inclusive of people from every race, gender, class, age, sexuality, immigration status, and psychological, physical, and emotional ability.

How would you like to see Asian American Buddhists represented in the media?

It would be nice to see Asian American Buddhists of my generation represented at all. I'd like to see people from all sects of Buddhism, everyone from monastics to people like me whose spirituality is grounded in Buddhist beliefs and practices but who don't identify as a Buddhist. I'd like to see images of Asian American Buddhists that aren't rooted in Orientalist thinking. I would like to see Buddhists who do social justice work, not just people who want to get an out-of-body experience or reconcile the injustices they are perpetuating in the world.

Any final reflections on the unique challenges that young adult Asian American Buddhists face, and the religious and cultural strengths they can draw on?

Asian Americans are already marginalized in society and alienated as perpetual foreigners in their own country. I grew up with very little notion of my identity and ancestral history. Learning about the histories of resistance, struggle, and resilience of my ancestors has been incredibly empowering. A radical Buddhist meditation center like EBMC can help ground you in the teachings and practical aspects of Buddhism.... The center is where I can continually practice generosity, reflect on if my actions align with my beliefs, and challenge myself if I see conflict between them. The POC sangha is where I feel genuine solidarity with others who have been marginalized in Buddhist spaces.

From: Alyssa Cheung

Date: March 3, 2013

Subject: Thanks! And an article

Hi Chenxing,

I can't express how wonderful it was to speak with you yesterday. As much as it was an "interview" to help with your thesis, it was, in many ways, the first time that I was able to parse out a lot of the thoughts and reactions I've had floating around in my head, so thank you for listening and providing me with that opportunity. It's comforting and encouraging to meet others who have similar questions and concerns, and with whom I can talk about all these ideas.

I wanted to share with you an interview I found with Robert Sharf (whom I think you and Trent must know, as he's a professor at Berkeley in Buddhist Studies). Perhaps you've read it already.[8]

When I read it, I couldn't help but just smile real big and jump up and down saying "Yes! that's it!" Professor Sharf really eloquently touches upon so much of what I couldn't articulate yesterday (or any point up to now). About needing to understand Buddhism holistically—its origins and transformations—not merely for the sake of history or tradition, but because it is vital for engaging with the religion now and in the future as it continues to spread and root itself in new places. About Buddhism existing not so much as primarily a personal experience, but that it is grounded in and relies upon community and tradition to uphold teachings and values. ("So we must ask whether Buddhism, when practiced without the ties of community and tradition, instead of mitigating our tendency toward narcissism, actually feeds it.") And about so much more too ... but I'll let you read it.

And lastly, I was particularly struck by his idea of Buddhism as a conversation: "Rather, you are confronted with many answers that generate new sets of questions and perspectives. But it is important, I think, that we keep the conversation going here. It opens one up to dramatically different ways of understanding the world and our place in it. Through our participation we help shape the conversation, and the conversation, in turn, shapes us. To abandon it would be to lose something precious."

Which is why I am again so excited to hear what you're doing and that, perhaps, this can be the start of one of numerous dialogues within the communities we know and are a part of, and maybe even inspire many other conversations.

What is your name and what does your name mean?

I was born in Taiwan, and I have a two-character name, Su Zang. My parents went to their Buddhist teacher to ask for a name, because they respected him very much. (My sister got her name from him as well.) Apparently, it's a holy kind of name. Those two characters are quite common in religious texts. So whenever I tell people my name, they're like, whoa, that's a heavy name. I didn't realize it as a kid. But now I'm becoming more aware of what it really means.

When I was moving here to America, my parents recommended that I choose an English name. So I chose Andy, because at the time I liked the movie *Toy Story*.

What are your thoughts on the "net loss" of Asian American Buddhists?

What we need is a network, a community that says, "Hey, I was raised Buddhist, and I honestly don't have any idea what that means—can someone please tell me?" I struggled with that as a kid—and I'm still struggling with it. To have a network that says, "Hey, don't sweat it, kid, no one really understands what it means; we're all trying to figure it out"—that in and of itself would be reassuring.

I miss the way Aaron used to message me out of the blue.

March 13, 2014, 12:46 a.m.

I just used a Buddhist parable in a business school term paper. Check!

March 21, 2014, 11:10 p.m.

I can't believe "banana Buddhist" made it into your thesis!

March 21, 2014, 11:50 p.m.

This thesis is so great, it's better than packing!

March 22, 2014: 3:03 a.m.

I just finished. Your thesis is so great. I cried multiple times while reading it.... We'll talk more in about ten days!

My memory of that March 2014 trip to LA is a blur of impressions: A gentle earthquake welcome at my ninth-floor hotel room in Little Tokyo. Working alongside other students to help Professor Duncan Williams with a Buddhist bibliographic project at USC—the same project that made it possible for me to interview Adam, Andy, Brian, and Michael in SoCal the previous summer. Leaving Little Tokyo to meet up with Aaron, who had just arrived back from a trip to Hong Kong, and whose comfy living room couch I would be crashing on for my last couple nights in town.

I remember the warm smells of soothing vegan soup and invigorating espresso cookies in Aaron's immaculate kitchen. The loquat trees on University of the West campus, where I met with Jane Iwamura, who happily signed my copy of *Virtual Orientalism,* and Danny Fisher, who commented on how our mutual friend Aaron "has such a bodhisattva way about him."

I amassed ample evidence for Aaron's bodhisattva ways on that short trip. He offered to take the bus to his business school classes so I could borrow his car. My refusal utterly backfired; Aaron then insisted on chauffeuring me to UWest. He spent all his free time in those two days taking me to his favorite Buddhist communities and vegetarian restaurants.

I remember *shojin ryori* too beautiful to eat and too delicious not to eat. Warm greetings by members of all ages at Dharma Seal Temple. A

Friday evening meditation group with friends who called Aaron by his Vietnamese name, Phu. Meeting John and Larene and Nathan, not yet knowing their faces would become familiar to me through a yet-unfilmed documentary by Wanwan Lu.

We must have talked about TechnoBuddha 2014, which Aaron had managed to attend before jetting off to Hong Kong. Landon had invited his coworker, who was neither Japanese American nor Buddhist, to the previous year's conference. To everyone's delight, Drew volunteered to cochair TechnoBuddha 2014 with Landon. They chose the theme "Ichigo Ichie, Always Changing, Always Flowing."

I was sorry to have missed it, especially since it was Landon who first introduced me to the concept of ichi-go ichi-e during our interview in January 2013, back when I was still skeptical I'd find many Asian American Buddhists who'd be willing to talk to me.

What is your name and what does your name mean?

It's the name of a Tibetan Buddhist goddess, actually, one that traditionally is associated with music (not that I'm musical at all, lol!).

How would you like to see Asian American Buddhists represented?

I would like to just see them represented at all! And see them as community leaders, as teachers, mentors, people who are giving back ...

Happy Asian Pacific American Heritage Month!
May 18, 2014

If I had more time, I would celebrate Asian-Pacific American Heritage Month by writing a post about every Buddhist Asian American who has a great story to share. I would write about issues that affect the lives of Buddhist Asian Americans. I would essentially do all the things that I try to do every day on this blog.

So this year I did something different. I made a collage.

Beneath the colorful image of sixteen smiling faces, the Angry Asian Buddhist reflects on his own handiwork.

I was surprised. I'd never seen Buddhist Asian Americans presented like this before. Placed together are the portraits of the first sixteen Buddhist Asian Americans whose photos I could find with Google image search. Here you have writers, activists, politicians, consultants, professors, and dharma teachers. I could have gone on, but I need to rest before running the Bay to Breakers in a few hours.

In the past, I've caused a stir by making the exact same type of collage with photos of Buddhist Geeks conference speakers, the editors of *Shambhala Sun,* and the contributors to a magazine feature on women in Buddhism. Those collages demonstrate how American Buddhism's Asian majority are repeatedly marginalized from prominent discussions about Buddhism.

This image reminds me that there's still so much more to write about Buddhist Asian Americans. The portraits remind me that we cannot be described by the coarse stereotypes of Oriental monks, superstitious immigrants, or banana Buddhists. We have incredible stories to share with you—if only one takes the care to look for them.[9]

Individually, most of my interviewees could name only one or two of the faces in the collage. They fared better as group, successfully identifying fourteen of the sixteen Asian American Buddhists pictured.[10]

"It's interesting that the Angry Asian Buddhist wrote 'I'd never seen Asian American Buddhists presented like this before,'" Lan reflects. "In my mind, I'm thinking, 'I'd never seen Asian American Buddhists presented, ever!'"

Like many of the eighty-eight young adults I interviewed before him, Luke is heartened by the image. "My reaction is joy. I'm glad the Buddhist community has role models with Asian blood."

Noel is able to name five of the faces. "There are certainly more," he declares. "And I hope Filipinos will someday be among those Asian faces."

Other interviewees also notice that the collage falls short of reflecting the full diversity of Asian American Buddhists: "Why only one person of South Asian decent? I'd say I could be angry toward the Angry Asian Buddhist :)" writes Shubha. Vince points out that Southeast Asian Buddhist faces are altogether absent.

"I need to learn more about Asian American Buddhists!" exclaims another interviewee.

My feelings exactly. To my frustration, I couldn't figure out who everyone was, even after Aaron gave me a hint about the order of the photos (alphabetical by first name), even after I cheated and compiled all the names my interviewees came up with. Three months after Asian Pacific American Heritage Month, I was still stumped.

"Any chance you'd be willing to reveal the names to me?" I begged.

"I think one of the ones you've had trouble identifying is a reporter for the *Wall Street Journal*," Aaron wrote back.[11]

Four days later, he relented. Reading over the list, I realized just how many of these Asian American Buddhists had touched my life in some way.[12] I had listened to Dharma talks by Anushka Fernadopulle and Larry Yang and Mushim Ikeda-Nash at EBMC, heard Canyon Sam discuss her book *Sky Train* at a Stanford Friends of Tibet event, sought advice on my book project from Jane Iwamura at UWest, taken a class on Buddhist ritual with Harry Bridge at IBS.

I'd appreciated Duncan Williams's article in the *Journal of Global Buddhism* on his efforts to be "at ease in between" different identities, "to freely move between any position" as his Soto Zen teacher advised.[13] Apt advice for a person with a Buddhist Japanese mother and a British Christian father who would go on to become both a university professor and a Buddhist priest.

I'd resonated with Kenji Liu's Buddhist Peace Fellowship blog post on the stultifying effects of our hackneyed binaries of East-West, feminine-masculine, intuitive-logical, and so forth: "As an Asian American cultural critic and Buddhist practitioner, I have a finely tuned radar for phrases like 'East-West,' 'East meets West,' and other pithy phrases that set up a dichotomy between these two directions as if they were completely different, even complete opposites. To me, this is lazy thinking, though very much consistent with centuries of orientalist discourse."[14]

I'd related to Viveka Chen's essay in *The Buddha's Apprentices,* even if I didn't grow up in a white middle-class suburb of New Jersey or have ties to the Friends of the Western Buddhist Order (FWBO). A trip to China at the age of sixteen saved Viveka, a second-generation Chinese American, "from identity oblivion." In college, she set out to address her "ethnic amnesia" and stumbled across Buddhism in a class on Chinese philosophy. "Reading my first dharma book," she recalls, "I was again overtaken by a sense of remembering, as if I had long been a Buddhist." In a reflection that dovetails perfectly with Kenji's and Duncan's, Viveka writes about her appreciation of cultivating a Buddhist outlook that transcends dualities: "After all, I myself was neither East nor West, and was also both." Though FWBO's lack of diversity could feel stifling and tiresome, Viveka appreciates that "being in-between cultures all my life has provided some resiliency."[15]

And speaking of resiliency and being caught between cultures, I'd devoured Ruth Ozeki's *A Tale for the Time Being* in one breathless sitting, anxious to know the fate of sixteen-year-old Nao. The novel is full of curious convergences, and it led to an unexpected encounter in my own circuitous writing journey.

"Is this the book you showed me at your house? If it is, you should come to her talk!"

Quyen's excited email came on the heels of seeing me and Trent at our Berkeley apartment. Without our bibliophile friend, I would never have heard about Ruth Ozeki's January 2014 talk at the Stanford Humanities Center. At the book signing afterward, Ruth's warm smile and undivided attention dissolved my nervousness. When I asked if she had any advice for turning my master's thesis into a book, Ruth proposed that we talk over the phone when she got home in a couple weeks.

My notes from our conversation are like a well-worn mala. Beads of advice I would return to time and time again: "Your project is important," she declared, as if anticipating the many days in the future when I would doubt this. "Reach beyond an academic readership," she counseled, as if foreseeing the moment when I would decide to scrap the first completed draft, 463 footnotes and all. "Make it an account of your curiosity," she urged. "Put yourself in."

What is your name and what does your name mean?

My name is Brian, which means "strength" based on what I've read online. I do have a Laotian name, Bounnarath; it means "good fortune."

What are your thoughts on the Under 35 collage?

It feels incomplete.... By leaving out other ethnicities that practice Buddhism, you don't get the sense of understanding each other as well. To truly understand Buddhism, you have to connect with others. Especially in America, where Buddhism is still a minority, trying to connect with as many people as possible will probably bring the best results.

What inspired you to start a Buddhist club in high school and now college?

Growing up with people of different beliefs, I felt lonely. I realized it can't just be me; there's probably people out there who feel worse than me. So I want to build something for other like-minded people, to feel more comfortable.

Growing up, I experienced hardships being who I am, discrimination as an Asian American Buddhist. So I want to see if I can change that for other people in the future....

I mean, I don't want to be famous ... but I hope to make a difference.

In October 2014, Alyssa emailed to introduce me to a friend from college who was studying visual anthropology at USC and planning to make a short documentary on young adult Asian American Buddhists in LA.

During our Skype conversation the following week, I learned that Wanwan was an avid reader of *Angry Asian Buddhist*. She wondered if I could introduce her to the blog's author.

Aaron wrote back right away. "Thanks for making this connection. Also, how do you know Alyssa Cheung? I follow her on Twitter! I (= or someone) should make a list of Asian American Buddhists on Twitter!"[16]

I explained how Alyssa found out about my project online and reached out for an interview.

"Very cool," Aaron replied. "Let's keep this web of Asian American Buddhists growing!"

What is your name and what does your name mean?

Moon means culture—the original pictogram for this character would have looked like a man wearing a hat, which was garb reserved for those with education. Cristina reflects my father's formative years after migrating with his family from Korea to South America.

How would you like to see Asian American Buddhists represented?

As fearless leaders.

Any final reflections on the unique challenges that young adult Asian American Buddhists face, and the religious and cultural strengths they can draw on?

The biggest challenges that young Asian American Buddhists face are the same as those that all American Buddhists face—which is that American Buddhism is mostly conceptual, colonized, and white, and lacks places to effectively go deep. Asian Americans and others in Hawai'i have an advantage over folks on the continent in that they know what it's like to be connected to their cultural heritage and ancestry.

In one of my favorite parts of Wanwan's November 2014 film interview, Aaron riffs on why it drives him crazy when people think all Asian American Buddhists practice Buddhism in the same way.[17]

"It's the notion that if you go to Fa Yin Si, this temple in the San Gabriel Valley, everyone you talk to has the exact same idea and they do the exact same thing in terms of Buddhism. You wouldn't know that if you talk to different people there, they all have different reasons for being there."

Aaron brings up his friend Gary as an example.[18] Originally from Hong Kong, Gary volunteers every week at Dharma Seal Temple (Chinese name: Fa Yin Si), directing traffic. When he was unemployed, Gary had made a vow: if he were to get a certain job that he needed to support his family—it was a good blue-collar job—he would become a regular volunteer at the temple. He prayed—and he got the job.

"The reason why I bring this up is because I think on the one hand, people will see this and they'd be like, 'Oh, that's what Asian American Buddhists are…. They're those people who want material things, and they pray for it.'"

But Aaron urges us not to be so dismissive. For starters, who *isn't* inclined to take action to pursue what they want, whether through prayer or some other method? Furthermore, volunteering at the temple changed the way Gary practices Buddhism. Being at the temple all the time, he interacted frequently with the monks and nuns and developed a deeper understanding of Buddhism through their teachings.

"That's a really cool story. But a lot of people stop there at this notion of Asian American Buddhists are just immigrant superstitious Buddhists…. And I think it's true that if you go to a temple and you look for that, that's what you'll find."

Aaron compares this to going to Paris with a list of all the things you want to see—sure, you'll come home having met your expectations about the city. But if you go to the Chinese neighborhood where Aaron's uncle lives, you'll experience a completely different Paris than if you'd hit up all the tourist sites.

"Especially if you don't grow up around Asian American Buddhists, and all you know is what your mostly white Dharma center teaches you about what Buddhism in America is, you're just hearing these legends of these Asian Buddhists and their communities yonder."

Aaron isn't bringing all of this up to be divisive. "It's really sad that stereotypes prevent people from understanding American Buddhists for who we are. Simply because I like to think that if we were part of one community, we'd be greater together than we are apart."

In fact, Aaron's message is the exact opposite of separation. "I'd like to think the reason why diversity is so important is because each of us sees the world through a different lens. We only see a very narrow piece of the world. And so when you get all of our perspectives together, we have a better understanding of what the world is, and how things work. We have a better understanding as Buddhists of how people suffer, and how to alleviate suffering, and how to work together as a community, and support each other as a community."[19]

The inaugural issue of *Lion's Roar* hit newsstands as America's first Black president entered into the final year of his second term. "*Shambhala Sun* has changed its name to *Lion's Roar,*" the magazine staff explain in a January 2016 post on their website.

> *Over the past three decades, the* Shambhala Sun *has evolved from a community newspaper, to a small young magazine, to the largest-circulation Buddhist magazine in the English language. Much has changed within the pages of the magazine and on our website as we've worked to reflect the full range of Buddhist traditions and the diversity of practitioners today. As Buddhism in the West has grown, matured, and diversified, we have too.*[20]

The cover of the premier issue features a racially diverse group of fourteen Buddhist teachers along with the tagline "The New Face of Buddhism."

Later that month, five American Buddhists from diverse heritages (Taiwanese, Afro-Carribbean-Jewish, Sri Lankan Sinhalese, Honduran-white, and Toishanese-Ashkenazi) joined forces to discuss their reactions to this colorful cover. Their multivocal article on the BPF website is a powerful expression of POC–Asian American solidarity.[21]

Funie Hsu is relieved to see people of color represented. But she wonders: "Does the magazine's new face of Buddhism include the multilingual Asian and Asian American Buddhist communities as well? If so, we are not new. We've been here."

Katie Loncke also has mixed feelings. "Representation matters, and I appreciate that you've been thoughtful enough to avoid a glossy Buddhist print version of #OscarsSoWhite. But can we celebrate teachers we love without universalizing them? Proclaiming them '*The* Face of Buddhism'—whether new or old?"

Dedunu Sylvia is glad the cover affirms her "Dharma comrades of color," but she too has misgivings. "There is something unquestionably painful about labeling such representation as the 'new face' of Buddhism. What makes Asian Americans 'new' given the roots of Buddhism in South Asia?" Dedunu is also concerned that deeper structural issues remain unaddressed: "For far too long, the veil of diversity has whitewashed the realities of violence against Black and brown communities."

While grateful to be among the fourteen teachers included on the cover, Kate Johnson warns us that the magazine's efforts are no magic bullet.

> *Establishing equity and restoring wholeness will take much more than a facelift. Many of the people pictured in the cover photo are working to heal our wounded collective Body, have dedicated their lives to it, and there are many, many more doing this work who do not appear. However, we are still, overwhelmingly, the exception to the rule. Broader racial, ethnic, and gender representation in media is a great way to start addressing the systemic violence of racism and other forms of oppression that express themselves in our American Buddhist institutions, which are in this way a microcosm of America at large.*

In classic Angry Asian Buddhist style, Arun argues that *Lion's Roar* could go farther in promoting diversity.

The editors are still predominantly, if not all, white.... The faces on the magazine cover are not particularly new or young—Sylvia Boorstein is a pillar of the Buddhist publishing network and turns eighty this year. In a sense, this new face of Buddhism is mostly cosmetic.

But he balances his critique with a healthy dose of optimism too.

I still harbor hope that Lion's Roar *will be filled with the true diversity of Buddhist America. I certainly see this magazine cover as progress.... This cover told me that the editors care. The message I hear is that they're trying.*

What is your name and what does your name mean?

Dedunu means "rainbow" in the language of Sinhalese, which is mostly spoken in Sri Lanka. Sylvia comes from my maternal grandmother's name, and a time in which she and her family adopted English names during British colonization.

What motivates you to contribute your stories and perspectives to this project on Asian American Buddhists?

While I wholeheartedly believe that Buddhism, as with all other forms of religion and philosophy, is something that everyone can be engaged in, on another level I feel that acknowledging cultural roots is a critical part of that experience. As such, I was absolutely excited, curious, and, quite frankly, relieved that an Asian American-identified person was committed to bringing our stories to light....

I am truly mostly interested in simply hearing the stories of other Asian American Buddhists. Because I grew up in a community of predominantly Sri Lankan Sinhalese Buddhists, I have rarely found Buddhists of other Asian American backgrounds. I am excited to learn about others' experiences, and feel this is a most unique and necessary platform to hear the voices of a community whom I rarely see in Buddhist representation!

Thank Yous

March 11, 2016

The Angry Asian Buddhist's first blog post in over a year opens with an excerpt from his February 2015 interview with Funie Hsu. He admits he's not completely at ease with writing. There's a fear of being misinterpreted, and so much pressure to write clearly. Sometimes it's easier not to write. Arun knows he's not alone in feeling this way.

> There's a story I love, about a bunch of Thai American Buddhists who pulled together to save their temple, Wat Mongkolratanaram in Berkeley, California. The neighborhood of mostly non-Thai residents tried to get their temple food court shut down, and that would've cut off a major stream of revenue for the temple. But a bunch of young Thai American Buddhists banded together. I remember reading about it in the *Wall Street Journal*—and there was this *WSJ* video of them. One of the organizers, Pahole Sookkasikon, won *Hyphen* magazine's Mr. Hyphen award in 2009.[22] That was a really cool story—I wish that was in *Tricycle* magazine or *Shambhala Sun*. That's a really cool thing that young Buddhists did, getting together to save their parents' temple—saving *their* temple, their community's temple.

But when Aaron tried to interview the activists about their efforts, they demurred. He couldn't fault them for declining to talk with him.

> And it's funny because I feel like I'm the same way. When you insult my grandmother, then I'm going to write that flaming internet post. But when it's like, "I want you to talk about these ideas" ... I don't know what to talk about, I'm gonna make a fool out of myself.... *and* my community ... *and* my family.

Aaron knew there were so many stories yet to be told. And he knew firsthand how hard it could be to tell those stories.

> Talking about these issues has felt like a very lonely affair, but recently I've been getting some refreshing support. There are several Buddhist Asian Americans

(and Canadians) I've met over the past few years who have transformed my own view of what it means to be both Buddhist and Asian American.

How fortunate we are to have spiritual companions along the path. Aaron goes on to address these Asian American Buddhist writers directly in his blog post:

> Your writing and your encouragement is what compelled me to write more. You are the reason that I was willing to step back out of a very comfortable silence.[23]

I'm glad Aaron did the uncomfortable. I'm not sure if he ever fully realized how much he alleviated the loneliness of other Asian American Buddhists. How much he emboldened us to speak up.

What is your name and what does your name mean?

Even though I know the *hanja* (Chinese characters) for my Korean name, I'm not 100 percent sure how to translate this into English. Taken literally they might mean something like "talented life" or "bright world," but I wouldn't say either of those renderings is necessarily accurate.

How would you like to see Asian American Buddhists represented?

I would like to see us represented as we are: a part of the landscape of "American Buddhism." I think as more of us come together, we have the potential to add our narratives to the monocultural narrative of the mainstream and gain more exposure.

I hadn't expected the editors of *Buddhadharma* to ask me to write an article based on my research. I certainly didn't expect the warmhearted responses after "We're Not Who You Think We Are" came out in the summer 2016 issue of the quarterly magazine.

From: Luke

Date: July 3, 2016

Subject: Thank You

I wanted to email to reach out to you to express some deep gratitude for your article in *Buddhadharma*. It was incredibly timely and seems to reflect the social consciousness of what is happening in the greater American sangha these days.

I'm not exactly sure if my voice matters to you, but you ask on your website "Where are all the young adult Asian American Buddhists?" I've been wondering the same thing myself.

I'm fourth-generation mixed Japanese American and have been a part of a number of sanghas. If you're in need of another perspective, I would love starting a chat over email. I have many perspectives on the sangha that includes privilege, cultural appropriation, and transmission of the Dharma to a coming multiracial, multiethnic world.

I'd been so sure that interview #88, from a year and a half ago, would be the last. But of course Luke's voice mattered to me—and, I knew, not just me. And so he became my eighty-ninth interviewee.

Another letter came from Annie, a seventeen-year-old member of Buddha's Light International Association (BLIA), the youth organization of Fo Guang Shan.

> BLIA has established a Young Adult Subdivision with locations in over two hundred different places around the world, including North America. By being a part of my youth group and traveling to conferences around the country and world organized for young adult Buddhists, I've been able to meet many young adult Asian American Buddhists in these past few years.
>
> While it does seem like we are "invisible," as Buddhist young adults, we are proud to be extremely active volunteers in the community, and we have a wide network of friends around the country and world. As for me, I am happy to call myself a Buddhist even as many of my school friends are Christian, Jewish, or atheist. I like to be part of a diverse community.[24]

Readers from outside the United States also sent messages of appreciation. (Annie was right about how globally interconnected we all are.)
From New Zealand: a Thai Forest practitioner of Sri Lankan heritage told
me he'd been reflecting on the themes in my article for the past decade.
From Switzerland: a Korean-born meditator who'd been living in Europe
for fifteen years set up a Skype conversation with me to explore her anger
and deep hurt over the racism she'd encountered in Western Buddhist
sanghas.

I didn't just hear from Buddhists of Asian heritage. "I'm really grateful
to you and your work for helping to shift the whole landscape of conversation in these glossy Buddhist publications," wrote Katie Loncke. Later
that year, "as an Afro-Caribbean, Jewish, non-Asian codirector of the Buddhist Peace Fellowship," Katie would publish a blog post acknowledging
how she and others at BPF, "a historically white-majority organization
based in an Asian spiritual tradition," had contributed to the marginalization of Asian American Buddhists.[25]

"Thank you for raising this issue into the larger Buddhist consciousness here in North America," wrote Sumi Loundon Kim.[26] Sumi clarified
in her email that she is "a Euro-descended person" whose husband is of
Korean heritage; her Japanese first name came from her Zen meditating
parents in the 1970s.

I confessed to Sumi that I'd been meaning to write to her for a long
time—to let her know how *Blue Jean Buddha* and *The Buddha's Apprentices* had influenced my work, and to get Aaron to stop bugging me about
contacting her (he'd been at it for years). But I'd been too shy to do so.

From: Sumi Loundon Kim

Date: July 14, 2016

Subject: Research and writing

Dear Chenxing,

Oh, my goodness, please don't feel shy around me—or anyone else in the Buddhist
world, either ... the Dharma makes us all like family members to each other. The
older people actually enjoy having some contact with the younger generation....

I'm so sorry that you encounter stereotyping, and probably to some extent prejudice, in the predominantly white Buddhist and meditation communities. Some of the meditation communities are working hard to see and own that, and it's a little better in the Gen X contingent of teachers. My experience with university students today is that they are even more attuned, so there is hope. :-)

Sumi adds that she just met the new board president of the Insight Meditation Society in Barre, Massachusetts, a thirty-eight-year-old second-generation Korean American. She signs off on a note of solidarity.

Wishing you all the best in writing your book! I know how hard it is. It takes about three times longer than we expect.

Your sister in the Dharma,

Sumi

How right she is about the joy of intergenerational connections, the pain of stereotyping and prejudice, the hope in our collective efforts to end that pain. Though I disagree with Sumi on one point: I think three times longer is a bit of an underestimate.

What is your name and what does your name mean?

My Buddhist name is Dolma, which refers to an avatar of the goddess Tara.

Which Buddhist communities have you been a part of? Who, if anyone, do you consider to be your Buddhist teacher(s)?

When I was very young, my family didn't discuss religion much. It wasn't until I moved back home that I really embraced my Buddhist culture, and began engaging with the practice. My identification was very cultural, in that I honestly didn't think much about my Buddhist identity. My family was Buddhist, so of course I was as well. I went to temple because that's just what we did. When I moved from Nepal to America and joined a Buddhist meditation group in college, our sensei (a bishop in the Higashi Honganji sect) really encouraged us to ask questions and to learn more about Buddhism. I feel like studying with him is how I really came into my Nyingma Buddhist identity! I will always consider him my greatest Buddhist teacher. He introduced me to the works of Thich Nhat Hanh as well, which really resonated with me.

What would your ideal Buddhist community look like?

This is a beautiful question.

While I grew up in the Nyingma tradition, I have learned so much from other Buddhist traditions. We're all so different and have so much to offer each other. I would love to see a Buddhist community that embraces multiple traditions (with multiple shrines and altars, of course!) and applies the Dharma to modern-day issues. I envision a diverse and welcoming community that tackles challenging questions and strives to be culturally humble. A community that engages in the social and political reform necessary to create a kinder and healthier world.

How would you like to see Asian American Buddhists represented?

On the base level, I'd like to see Asian American Buddhists of all backgrounds be given the recognition and respect they deserve in the media, and for their work to be supported and uplifted (and yes, that also means funded!). And I'd like to see *lots* of us! Not one person on a panel with the impossible tokenizing task of representing "all of us." I want to see spaces created for us and by us.

On a rainy evening in October 2016, I was back at the East Bay Meditation Center in the very room where, two years earlier, no one had been able to name a single well-known Asian American Buddhist. Having arrived early to help set up, I had time to admire the colorful painting by Japanese American Buddhist artist and activist Mayumi Oda hanging on the wall above the altar.

Nearly two dozen people gathered that evening for a BPF-sponsored Asian, Asian American, Pacific Islander Buddhist Community-Building Dinner. The title was a mouthful, but it succeeded in calling forth people from a wide range of ethnic, Buddhist, and activist communities.

Funie, who dedicated many hours to organizing the event with the support of Buddhist Peace Fellowship codirectors Dawn Haney and Katie Loncke, sent us photos afterward. "Recovering our stories, resisting white supremacy, eating freshly steamed *momos* ... what a special space and moment in time we created together."[27]

It was a gathering that manifested, in real life, the answers to my interview question, "What would your ideal Buddhist community look like?" A gathering of people from different racial, ethnic, and religious backgrounds, a group involved in community service and social activism, a sangha committed to making American Buddhism diverse, inclusive, and accessible to all.

I'm sure Aaron would have joined us for the dinner if he could have. But his prognosis had become more grim. His type of lymphoma was very unique, very late stage, and very aggressive.

> *The good news is that there is a ray of hope—if I can manage to get a stem cell transplant.*
>
> *The catch is that I'm multiracial, and so my odds of finding a compatible match in the bone marrow registry are really small. I've heard it's as low as 1 in a million. If I were Caucasian, there'd be a 75 percent chance of finding a perfect match. If I were African American, that chance would be 19 percent. I've been told Asian Americans have as low as a 1 in 20,000 chance. I've read of multiracial patients who are told they have no chance.*

After many years of advocating for it through his writing, diversity had literally become a matter of life and death for Aaron. In collaboration with A3M (Asians for Miracle Marrow Matches) and AADP (Asian American

Donor Project), Aaron was working to diversify the national marrow registry. He implored his friends to help: "This is an important issue for people of color throughout the United States, who are significantly under-represented on the registry compared to Caucasian Americans."

Aaron encouraged us to register at Be the Match, host local bone-marrow drives, and help spread the word through our social networks: "If I have to go, I want to make sure I get as many people registered as possible to be matches for others."[28]

We've Been Here All Along
November 24, 2016

The penultimate post on *Angry Asian Buddhist* opens with a screenshot from @arunlikhati's Twitter account.

> Never in my life did I expect to see @buddhadharma publish a piece on #White-Supremacy in #AmericanBuddhism. Wow!

The tweet includes a photo of Aaron's copy of the magazine. The two-page spread features a black-and-white photo of the congregation of Bakersfield Buddhist Church. Aaron is not Japanese American. He is nearly a hundred years removed from that photo. Yet he finds in "We've Been Here All Along" a reflection of his life, his family, his Buddhism.

> There's a lot in Funie Hsu's article on the *Lion's Roar* website that strikes a chord with me. Even the title resonates with a point I find I'm compelled to make, again and again, that not only am I an American Buddhist, at least four generations of my family have been practicing Buddhism in America in uniquely *American* ways.[29]

But not everyone was thrilled with the article. A week later, Funie emailed a listserv of Buddhists of Asian heritage.

> *I received word from the* Buddhadharma *editor, who has been completely supportive and has put in a great effort to solicit pieces from*

Asian American Buddhists, that my article received some angry letters from white people. Buddhadharma *plans on posting a letter of support online sometime today.*

I'm hoping that anyone that is in support of Buddhadharma's *efforts to include voices from Asian and Asian American Buddhists and discussions of race in Buddhism might feel inclined to write a letter to the editor expressing this support so that they will continue to include perspectives from Asian and Asian American Buddhists.*

My concern is that the backlash might have a negative impact on the future possibility of Buddhadharma *and other publications publishing such perspectives. It's important to show clearly and strongly that there is a demand for such perspectives, especially in these times where white supremacy is so overt and dominating. There are other Asian American Buddhists writers whom we've yet to hear from, and I hope that there will be spaces for them to share their thoughts and to be taken seriously. It also means much to me that upcoming Asian and Asian American Buddhist youth know that an older generation is out there demanding our space and providing critiques of injustice, just as I've been inspired by writers like Mushim Ikeda-Nash, Larry Yang, Rev. Liên Shutt, Rev. Ryo Imamura, and others. As Rev. Imamura's letter to* Tricycle *demonstrates, it's been a long time coming.*

I would also like to recognize the longstanding public work of Arun Likhati for serving as what I often call the "community archivist of Asian American Buddhism." It was on his blog Angry Asian Buddhist *that I first learned of Rev. Imamura, his letter, and his connection to the Buddhist Peace Fellowship. Arun's blog helped me feel a sense of community in my early years of searching for other Asian American Buddhists.*

May we ensure that the voices of Asian American Buddhists continue to be heard.[30]

The weekend after giving the Institute of Buddhist Studies commencement speech in May 2017, I drove down to Santa Ana, California with

Trent to visit Aaron. We met at his apartment, immaculate by habit and now also necessity due to Aaron's immunocompromised state. He intro-duced us to his parents, who had come from Illinois to support their youngest son through his cancer treatment.

Trent and I would be heading back to Phnom Penh in June. We'd called the city home for a year and half, and would be staying on until October before heading back to the Bay Area for eleven months, after which we'd be moving to Bangkok. (Partnership with a scholar of Buddhist studies was proving to be quite the moveable feast.)

Before moving to Cambodia, I'd spent a year as a Buddhist chaplain on an oncology unit; I sensed that October would be too long to wait if I wanted to see Aaron one more time. I resolved to squeeze in one more visit. It just so happened that Funie would also be in SoCal that Tuesday at the end of June.

The three of us cooked together in Aaron's kitchen. As we savored our vegan meal, Funie insisted that we had to watch the *Chef's Table* episode about Ven. Jeong Kwan. According to a *New York Times* article about this Seon Buddhist monastic, "The most exquisite food in the world, say many celebrated chefs, is being made not in Copenhagen or New York, but in a remote temple complex south of Seoul by a fifty-nine-year-old Buddhist nun."[31]

Right after our visit, Aaron emailed the photo his dad took of us three. In it, Aaron is wearing a TechnoBuddha T-shirt and beaming his usual megawatt smile.

Send me your addresses. You will have surprise gifts coming your way!

Aaron wanted to make sure my gift would come to the right place.

When do you go back to Cambodia? Will you get the postcard if I mail it by Friday???

Aaron's next email, a minute later:

OH, CRAP, I GAVE AWAY THE SURPRISE

I laughed and told Aaron I was going back to Cambodia tomorrow, but the mail system there wasn't reliable. My parents would be happy to receive the postcard and email me a photo of it.

> Okay. I'll send it to your parents. They won't be offended if they get a card with "Angry Asian Buddhist" on it—will they?

The postcard arrived in my parents' mailbox a week later. On one side was a revamped logo for the *Angry Asian Buddhist* blog that Aaron had just designed. On the other was a handwritten message in his neat cursive: *"You have helped water the seeds of a community that never knew they existed."* He was never giving himself enough credit, I thought.

So far, Aaron had only sent the cards to me and Funie, but he planned to send more soon. Mushim would later show us the "Be the Refuge" card Aaron sent her.

Meanwhile, I borrowed access to a Netflix account and cried as Jeong Kwan explained how her cooking was an expression of gratitude for her parents, who had made it possible for her to pursue a life of true freedom as a Buddhist monastic. Kwan ordained in the Buddhist order at the age of seventeen after the sudden death of her mother. Many decades later, her seventy-year-old father spent a month living at the hermitage. One day during his stay, he got mad about the lack of meat in the temple food— how could anyone get enough energy from mere vegetables? What was the best food to be had here? Kwan made her father shiitake mushrooms with sesame oil and soy sauce and dispatched him to eat the delicacy quietly in the mountains. Her father came back transformed. "This is better than meat! You can indeed live without meat since you have this." At the end of his month at the temple, Kwan's father said to his daughter, "I am going back home without worries. Live well. They say even the king does three bows to a monk. Now I will bow to you." He bowed to her three times. A week later, he passed away in peace.[32]

Aaron was just as enamored with the *Chef's Table* episode.

> I watched it twice. Then I made shiitake mushrooms with sesame oil and soy sauce, and it was *incredible*. I want to eat that every day!

In a living room emptied of furniture in Phnom Penh, I received a text from Thao.

> Aaron passed surrounded by loved ones on October 21.

She texted again a few hours later.

> I cried for a while on my drive back to Ukiah thinking of Aaron. I am so grateful he connected the two of us. Safe travels and hope to see you when you're back in California.

When I landed in San Francisco, I learned that a memorial would be held in Southern California in a few days. I wanted to go, but I barely had my wits about me; my jetlag and nonfunctioning cellphone weren't helping.

Funie came to the rescue. She booked me a seat on the same flight as her. She borrowed a car and drove us to Hsi Lai Temple. She placed her flower next to mine on the mountain of marigolds at the altar. Aaron's father offered some words of comfort that seemed especially directed to those of us whose chanting during the service had been choked by sobs.

> *I believe we are a part of everyone we have met and every idea we have touched. We are so blessed that Aaron's presence and ideas are now a part of the many he touched.*

In an article commemorating his writing, activism, and community-building, *Lion's Roar* recognized Aaron Lee for helping to change the way Buddhism is represented in the West.[33] NPR's Code Switch honored Aaron in a list of ten notable people of color the world lost in 2017.[34] The TechnoBuddha community also mourned Aaron's death as a December 2017 *Wheel of Dharma* "In Memoriam" attests:

> *A little more than a year ago, we learned that the vibrant and always smiling Aaron had cancer and was seeking a stem cell donor. Because*

of his biracial heritage it was very difficult to find a match, but one was found. Aaron's friends rejoiced and were looking forward to seeing him again at another TechnoBuddha gathering. But it was not to be.

Something many people didn't know about Aaron was that he was the voice behind the blog site Angry Asian Buddhist. *Under the pen name "arunlikhati," he shared his feelings about the underrepresentation of Asian American Buddhists in the American Buddhist media. He also blogged about all aspects of our Asian American Buddhist sangha and was completely dedicated to serving our diverse American sangha....*[35]

Even though Aaron's life on this earth was but for a short thirty-four years, his smile, his dedication, his vibrancy, and his love of the Dharma were truly the blessings of a life well lived, a life grounded in compassion and gratitude. We wish to extend our sympathy and gratitude to Aaron's parents, family, and countless Dharma friends. Aaron is now a Buddha for all of us!

Na – mo – A – mi – da – butsu
Na – mo – A – mi – da – butsu
Na – mo – A – mi – da – butsu
Na – mo – A – a – mi – da – a – a – bu ...

We dedicated our chanting at the opening ceremony of TechnoBuddha 2018 to the memory of Aaron J. Lee.

This year's theme was "Sympathy and Empathy." I had interviewed the keynote speaker for my project four years prior; she was now a fully ordained Jodo Shinshu minister. I signed up to attend several of the weekend workshops—and, for the first time, presented one of my own. Many of the people in the group hadn't met Aaron, but they were drawn to the title: "In Memory of the Angry Asian Buddhist: A Collaborative Writing Workshop."

We talked about anger and grief and the ways we find refuge. And then we wrote. A free flow of words, stealing inspiration from our neighbors when needed.

Ding! Stopping at the sound of the bell, we passed our pages to our neighbors, relinquishing ownership of what we'd just written. Around the table the pages passed, gathering color with each trading of hands. Highlighting the phrases that spoke to us, we left our marks on each other's free-writes.

Our pages returned as rainbows. We turned them into poems. We read the poems out loud in pairs, alternating lines with our neighbor. A stereophonic sangha of interwoven voices.

In the eleven months after Aaron's memorial, before I moved to Thailand, Funie and I ran into each other on three separate occasions, though we lived forty miles apart at opposite corners of the Bay. It didn't quite feel like a coincidence. (Aaron, do I detect a gleam in your eye?)

At each of these chance meetings, our conversation invariably drifted to questions of how to continue Aaron's legacy. Concerned that *Angry Asian Buddhist* might go offline, we consulted with the person who first put me in touch with Aaron. Scott promised to help however he could, despite having his hands full as the new dean of IBS.

Funie and I could only laugh when we discovered we had been separately invited to join *Lion's Roar*'s monthly diversity meeting in January 2019. As luck would have it, though Trent and I had moved to Bangkok the previous October, we happened to be back in the Bay Area for a short visit. Had I still been in Southeast Asia, the time difference would have made it hard to join the videoconference.

In preparation for the *Lion's Roar* call, Funie started an email discussion with a group of other Buddhists of Asian heritage. She wanted to present more than just her own view on things.

With our different religious and ethnic backgrounds and our differing professional and political vantage points, the five of us on the email thread didn't always agree. Hearing my fellow Buddhists' perspectives, it dawned on me that solidarity is not groupthink, but rather a space for divergent views and healthy debate. We listened to each other with respect, widening our individual perspectives in the process.

It was Ed Ng who brought the offending article to our attention. The piece had just been posted to the *Lion's Roar* website, though it originally ran in the May 2016 issue of the magazine. The blurb beneath the title promises insights from two "leading Buddhist teachers," both of whom are white. A famous Asian Canadian American actor interviews the pair of insight meditation teachers about "the future of American Buddhism."

As I feared, "the future of American Buddhism" didn't seem to include much room for Asian Americans. The piece felt like a case study in the same faulty assumptions and tired metaphors that Aaron had spent years critiquing in his writing. For instance: the claim that "we were free to bring Buddhism into the twentieth century ... but in certain cultural forms Buddhism hadn't changed since the Middle Ages."[36]

I couldn't help but channel the Angry Asian Buddhist. Who exactly is the "we" that you're referring to here? Also, I'd really like to know which cultural forms of Buddhism haven't changed since the Middle Ages. Really, the *Middle Ages*? *No* change whatsoever? For a religion that holds impermanence as a central tenet, this beggars belief.

The Middle Ages comment is, alas, consistent with another opinion expressed by the same person the previous year, in a *Buddhadharma* forum with three other white meditation teachers:

> *If you really want to see watered-down Buddhism, travel to the beautiful Zen temples of Korea, a country where Buddhism is still alive and well, and you'll see all the ladies in temples working their malas, chatting about their kids, sometimes shucking peas; the temples are very much village and urban gathering places. How many people are deeply practicing?*[37]

Every time I read this, it feels like a punch in the gut. I think of Jeong Kwan, for whom "there is no difference between cooking and pursuing Buddha's way."[38] Why must shucking peas be separate from Buddhist practice? Why must stuck-in-the-Middle-Ages Asians play the foil to modern-and-enlightened white Buddhists?

The *Lion's Roar* staff wanted to know: "What voices are we lacking? How can we do better?" Borrowing an insight from Dawn Haney, Ed wondered if the editorial team would consider reflecting on their publications, much like the *Buddhadharma* editors did for Funie's "We've Been Here All Along" piece. We brainstormed together, building on and riffing off of each other's ideas.

Funie thanked us for taking the time to discuss these issues with her. Her intention—"to share these thoughts with metta, openness, and truthfulness, in the hope of moving forward in a way that's mutually beneficial and sincere"—was a reminder that we could channel our anger and hurt into constructive dialogue while remaining grounded in our Buddhist values.

At the meeting, *Lion's Roar* asked us about the voices they were lacking and the ways they could do better. We shared our thoughts. They listened.

From: Chenxing Han

To: Ed Ng and Zack Walsh

Date: March 8, 2019

Subject: Thank you for your "Making Refuge" paper

Greetings from Bangkok! I just wanted to send a quick email to say I really appreciated reading your paper in *Religions* journal.

There was so much in Ed and Zack's article that struck me. Their idea that making refuge means "making kin" of each other. Their encouragement not to limit making refuge to humans, but to consider it a "multispecies affair." Their suggestion that what the Angry Asian Buddhist was really doing was "asking whether we are truly listening."

emiko yoshikami didn't find out her father had been born in a concentration camp until her preteen years. In a review of *American Sutra*, she describes how Duncan Williams's book deepened her appreciation for her Asian American Buddhist ancestors.

> *Though Higashi Honganji Buddhism was foundational for my grandfather and grandmother, I knew nothing about this type of Buddhism growing up. Oddly, however, I was raised with the Dharma by my white mother in the form of vipassana meditation. In more recent years I've been heavily drawn to Mahayana Buddhism, and have started researching the Pure Land Buddhism of my ancestors. I don't know what my ancestors would make of this mixed-race, mixed-Buddhist of theirs—a queer, politically radical Buddhist who knows so little about them, but who indisputably feels the Dharma alive in her heart. Though I'm only just beginning to explore my relationship to my ancestors, Williams's book has helped me feel more connected to them and to the Dharma my grandparents helped keep alive through the war years.*[39]

Where does emiko fit within two Buddhisms?

When I ask Holly what her ideal Buddhist community looks like, her answer is not hypothetical.

> *What I helped create at University of the West was pretty ideal for me: a group of people from varied ages, countries, and primary languages all sharing contemplative practices and community-engaged projects together, as well as inviting advanced teachers to give Dharma talks and lead rituals.... I really felt free and confident there, so appreciative of the astounding cultural diversity at that school.*

Where does Holly's UWest community fit within two Buddhisms?

In Anthuan's view, "even if you just research within Asian American Buddhists, there's huge diversity.... We've moved beyond the immigrant versus convert categories."

As Joseph Cheah points out, the naming in the two Buddhisms typology "has been done almost exclusively by white American intellectuals."[40] Jan Nattier attests to this as a white American intellectual herself: "Some of us—perhaps most of us—are unwittingly engaged in the practice of defining large groups of our fellow Buddhists out of existence."[41] It's a phe-nomenon Jane Iwamura calls "Asian religions without Asians."[42] For all his support of two Buddhisms, even Paul Numrich recognizes that "we need creative new typologies."[43]

When I ask Holly how she would categorize American Buddhists, she brainstorms a list of Buddhist denominations with eight main groupings (including "hybrid North American Buddhisms") and twenty sub-groupings (Tendai, Seon, Dhammakaya, Bon, atheist or agnostic Buddhists, dual- or multiple-identity Buddhists, etc.). Holly is quick to add the caveat that her list is far from complete. Ideally, she would use much more specific catego-ries, as articulated by the practitioners themselves.

Other interviewees suggest categorizing by intensity of practice. Or by generation in Noel's sense (first-gen, second-gen, multi-gen American Buddhists). Or by generation in terms of historical period (baby boomer, Gen X, millennial).

In presenting their ideas for how to sort American Buddhists into dif-ferent categories, these young adults call forth a cornucopia of variables: Age. Race. Ethnicity. Gender. Class. Language. Way of practice: do they meditate, chant, bow, etc.? Degree of "out"-ness: secret or hidden versus vocal Buddhists. Way of relating to Buddhism: do they take a utilitarian, philosophical, academic, or religious approach; an individual or communal approach; a private, familial, or public approach? And so on and so forth.

Still others would sidestep categories altogether. "I didn't even know there were types," says Ratema. "I think of Buddhism as a whole."

As a group, these young adult Asian American Buddhists suggest that we must consider a constellation of factors. No single overlay will suf-fice. Race is one category of many—an important category, but one that shouldn't be taken to be determinative of others.

"I call myself an 'American Buddhist' because this is the country where I found Buddhism," writes Noel. "It is also a Buddhism, I feel, that is a mixture of different Buddhist philosophies. Even at UWest, I think the monastics are getting an American Buddhist education. A nun from Viet-nam is becoming familiar with Korean Zen, and I don't think she would have gotten that education in Vietnam."

In a sense, American Buddhists are one. But of course we are also many. Given our diversity and complexity, bifurcating American Buddhists into just two groups is a surefire way to exclude many—while simultaneously jeopardizing our aspirations of oneness.

As Anthony, Dedunu, George, Dolma, Zoe, and so many other young adults recognize, our Buddhist lives are multifaceted and ever influenced by race, class, gender, age, sexuality, ability, education, and so much more. We do not fit easily into two Buddhisms, because what we live is an intersectional Buddhism.

Two Buddhisms is part of the story of American Buddhism, but it is not the only story, and it is certainly not the whole story.

I first met Prumsodun Ok in September 2008 when he invited Trent to share the stage with him at a performance in San Francisco. Prum is a Cambodian American choreographer and dancer; Trent is a student of Cambodian Buddhist chant. The following year they performed together again, in Prum's hometown of Long Beach.

I had hoped to interview Prum in 2014 for my book project, but he was busy trailblazing a queer space in Khmer classical dance. Three years later, Trent and I watched a heart-wrenching performance by Cambodia's first all-male gay-identified dance company in Prumsodun Ok's candlelit living room in Phnom Penh.

Reflecting on his journey of founding Natyarasa in a 2019 interview for *Dance Magazine,* Prum writes:

> *There is a trope in American literature and culture of the minority torn between two cultures. A supposedly fast-paced American life is incompatible with the conservative values of the motherland. Somehow America always gets to play the force of liberation and freedom in this oversimplified scenario, with the places our parents come from being exoticized and flattened as backward. As a young person, I was trained to think this way.*
>
> *A big shift occurred when I recognized myself as a center. I am a being with the power to draw diverse forces together, am in, of, and between*

many different cultures, communities, histories, and approaches. Instead
of trying to place myself in a spectrum, I contained the spectrum inside
me. And, suddenly, my struggles became a richness.

I believe we are all situated as center.[44]

Religion is nowhere mentioned in this passage, and yet Prum perfectly encapsulates the experience of Asian American Buddhists. There is no need to place ourselves in a binary because we contain the binary—and so much beyond. Our struggles are a richness. Our experiences are central to American Buddhism.

Some may dismiss us as mere "cultural Buddhists," but we know that *all* Buddhists are cultural Buddhists. All of us have inherited cultural roots, all of us are being shaped by—and are always shaping—the cultures we live in.

The young adult Asian Americans I interviewed are not so much cultural Buddhists as they are *culturally engaged Buddhists.* They understand that the many manifestations of culture—race, ethnicity, gender, sexuality, and so on—are not a grime to be wiped off or a dross to be transcended, but phenomena that we must thoroughly explore and fully engage with if we are to realize a truly inclusive American Buddhism.

Best of all, you don't even have to be Asian American to be a culturally engaged Buddhist. Which means the possibilities for solidarity are truly boundless.

From: Scott Mitchell

Date: December 20, 2019

Subject: At long last the Angry Asian Buddhist has been reborn

It had taken almost two years for our aspiration to become a reality: Aaron's writing would stay online in perpetuity. The *Angry Asian Buddhist* archive was finally live.

It wouldn't have been possible without the dedicated individuals who donated their time, money, and technological expertise to the cause. Scott and Aaron's parents braved byzantine processes in their attempt to wrest control of Aaron's digital assets away from tech companies. Where they weren't able to succeed, an anonymous hacker friend came to the rescue.

Scott didn't begrudge for a minute the countless hours he spent over winter break painstakingly copying over the entire contents of Aaron's blog from the old site to the new one.

> Having gone through and looked at what Aaron accomplished, the wide range of topics he covered, the way he engaged and pushed back and held his own against the racists, is inspiring. I hope his work lives on, and I'm deeply honored to have been able to take on this project.

A few weeks later, I received a message from John Gill.

> You may not remember me: we met long ago at Aaron's funeral. I visited angry-asianbuddhist.com today and saw that you had worked with others to archive it. I too had backed up the site, ready if the registration ever lapsed, and was so glad to see you were so proactive. Thank you :)

I assured John that of course I remembered him; if I wasn't mistaken, we'd met briefly on my 2014 trip to LA. Then I asked him about something I'd been wondering for years. I knew the real identities of three of the four *Dharma Folk* writers, but I'd never been able to figure out the fourth.

"As for Oz, I don't think he (or anyone other than Aaron, actually) was writing intentionally anonymously," John explained as he gave me the full name of their other UBA friend. John offered to put us in touch.

But there was no need. Oz had already reached out and completed an interview for my project. I just hadn't associated his nickname with his real name. We were already connected.

What is your name and what does your name mean?

Chenxing, but it's not the *chen* people who know Chinese usually expect. (My parents took the last two characters of 日月星辰 and flipped them.)

In my dad's poetic rendering, my name means "eternal time" and "eternal star." "Morning star" is a simpler translation.

My mom briefly considered giving us all "American" names when we immigrated here. "Why didn't you?" I once asked. "Too lazy," she shrugged.

Up until my late twenties, I thought my name was like my upbringing: completely secular. But at the Buddhist college in Taiwan, multiple classmates said to me: "'辰星' is so Buddhist!" As if to remind me: don't believe everything you think. As if to remind me: a name, like a self, is not a static thing.

How would you like to see Asian American Buddhists represented?

More widely, more specifically, more boldly, more subtly, more accurately, more creatively, more heroically, more humanly. As everyday luminaries.

And more by Asian American Buddhists.

What would your ideal Buddhist community look like?

The voices in this book (and then some) come to life.

Trying and wondering and learning, in friendship and solidarity, how to build a refuge big enough for all of us.

BENEDICTION

Three years after we first met in Berkeley, as presenters at a Buddhist chaplaincy conference at IBS, I had a chance to spend a day with one of my interviewees.

We hadn't expected to reunite in the United Kingdom that summer of 2016. Monica's studies had taken her from one Cambridge to another. I was living in Cambodia with Trent, but a conference in Paris and my cousin in London gave us ample excuse to escape the heat of Phnom Penh.

As we strolled the leafy grounds of her university, Monica offered one of those reflections that lands softly and burrows deeply over time. "It's not just that you're working on the book—it's also working on you."

I was sure my next trip back to America would be doubly celebratory. I'd be finished with my book draft by then. I'd be going to Oregon for the wedding of one of my dearest friends.

I didn't finish the draft in time. I did get to attend the wedding, though under different circumstances than we all expected. I sat glued to my laptop screen at my writing desk in Phnom Penh, smiling and crying in equal measure as my friend married her beloved in the hospital room where she was recovering from a bone-marrow transplant.

Seven months after Aaron's diagnosis of lymphoma, six months after my dear friend's death from leukemia, I had my first phone conversation with Sumi Loundon Kim.

I'd finally finished the draft. I was thinking of submitting it to a Buddhist press. Sumi was all ears and encouragement. She was sure I would find the right publisher. She offered one of those reflections that lands mysteriously and unfurls slowly over time. "The book has its own karma."

It didn't work out with the Buddhist publisher. I tried again, this time with an academic press. They sent the manuscript on to peer review. I waited with bated breath, imagining the joyous email I would send to Aaron when I heard the good news.

But it was not to be. Three months after Funie and I visited him in Southern California, Aaron lost his fight with cancer. He died with twenty-one friends at his bedside.

It didn't work out with the academic publisher either. If you told me then that I would eventually consider this rejection a blessing, I'd have been hard-pressed to believe you through my anger and bitterness and grief. If you told me that I would come to see the rejections that followed as blessings too, I suspect my reply would have made even the Angry Asian Buddhist blush.

If you'd told me I would carry this book idea with me across seven years and eight apartments in four countries, if you'd told me that along the way I would need to throw out a 95,000-word draft and start anew, I might never have been foolhardy enough to start this project in the first place.

I'm embarrassed to admit how many times I almost gave up. But then I would think of that email from Aaron with the subject line "be the refuge."

In it, Aaron shows me some of the icons he's made for his new blog, *be* and *btr* in white brush lettering against a teal background.

> *Other than the graphic design, I'm working on a few essays, namely:*
>
> *How do you keep despair and complacency from drowning your resolve?*
>
> *What is it like to shift from planning for life to planning for death?*
>
> *How do you practice loving-kindness if you feel like it's a bunch of new-agey silliness?*
>
> *I need to work on the titles, but those are the big questions.*

Aaron tells me his rescue treatment has been mixed. He remains optimistic ("in the world of refractory lymphoma, I'm more than happy to take 'mixed'"), and he doesn't keep the focus on himself for long.

> *How are things going for you? I haven't had the chance to read but a few pages of the book draft, but I plan to do so later this week. I'd love to hear how your progress has been going …*
>
> *Whenever you may feel your energy flagging, know that somewhere I am quietly yet furiously cheering you on with a big smile :)*

Aaron's skepticism about loving-kindness always made me laugh, given his habit of signing his emails "Much metta"; given how, after telling me about his poor prognosis over the phone, the first thing he asked was "are *you* okay?"

Reading Aaron's "be the refuge" email, I would think about these mixed and metta-filled and too-brief lives of ours, and I would face the blank page and continue.

I started this project feeling very much alone, unsure if "Asian American Buddhist" even made sense as a category. Now I see that Asian American Buddhists are everywhere, even if we aren't a trending topic. I see how "Asian American Buddhist" is a meaningful category, even if we're all still trying to make sense of what it means.

I started this project feeling rather lost, unsure where I fit into the story of "two Buddhisms." My interviewees taught me that it's possible to center our stories without forcing ourselves into false dichotomies: traditional-modern, rational-devotional, meditating-chanting, immigrant-convert, and so on. They taught me to see our stories, with all their differences and resonances, as a ground for solidarity. They taught me there is still so much that we don't know about Asian American Buddhists, still so many stories untold.

The Angry Asian Buddhist invites us to rewrite the narrative of American Buddhism. He rejected both disparaging caricatures and romanticized archetypes of Asian American Buddhists, knowing neither would account for our complexity, our humanity. Trailblazers, bridge-builders, integrators, refuge-makers—these are my attempts at rewriting the stereotypes of the Oriental monk, the superstitious immigrant, the banana Buddhist. There are many other possibilities—I'm excited to hear your narratives.

It's up to us to author the rest of the blog that Aaron began at the end of his life. It's up to us to create refuge for ourselves and each other through our writing and stories—and, perhaps even more significantly, through our everyday thoughts and actions.

Up until the very last minute, I couldn't find the right title for this book. You could say I'm good at missing the obvious.

Writing this book has been a refuge for me. I hope reading it can be a refuge for you.

May this book cultivate the curiosity, generosity, goodwill, and interconnectedness that have shaped it into being.

May the voices in these pages inspire more of the stories we need to build truly inclusive sanghas.

May all beings abide in joy and compassion, peace and loving-kindness.

May we be the refuge, together.

APPENDIX 1
QUESTIONS FOR OTHER
ASIAN AMERICAN BUDDHISTS

"What questions would you like to ask other Asian American Buddhists?" I asked each of the young adults I interviewed. Below is a list of their responses, organized into sections and lightly edited for clarity.

BUDDHIST JOURNEY, PRACTICES, AND BELIEFS

- How did Buddhism become part of your life?
- What was your journey?
- Were you raised Buddhist? If so, what kind of household did you live in? How was the atmosphere, the relationships?
- What were some of the Buddhist traditions you grew up with?
- Will you still confidently call yourself a Buddhist five years from now?
- Do you feel just as curious but also nervous about how to delve into Buddhism as I feel?
- What kinds of practices do you do as a Buddhist?
- How does your practice impact your life and others around you?

- Do you go to temple every Sunday?
- What is your opinion of prayer in Buddhism?
- How do you meditate?
- Have you explored other forms of Buddhism? Have you explored other spiritual practices?
- How do you make Buddhism applicable to your daily life?
- How has Buddhism impacted your life?
- How does Buddhism help you?
- Have you found inner peace yet?
- What gives your life purpose?
- What does Buddhism mean to you?
- How do you feel about monasticism?
- Do you see Buddhism more as a philosophy or religion?
- What questions do you ask yourself about your religiosity or spirituality?
- What Buddhist precepts or concepts have resonated with you?

COMMUNITY

- What Buddhist communities are you a part of?
- Where do you find your spiritual community? Who is your sangha?
- What kind of Buddhist community would you like?
- What opportunities are available for young people to explore Buddhism within their school or youth groups?
- Are your Asian friends Buddhist?
- Do you prefer to practice in affinity groups? Which affinity?
- Do you feel alone as an Asian American Buddhist?
- How do we find each other?

- How can we connect better?

- What would it take for you to open up and contribute to Asian American Buddhist communities and general Buddhist communities alike?

- How does an Asian American Buddhist convert like me become more involved in an Asian Buddhist temple?

- What challenges do you face in sangha and practice today?

- How can we support the growth of conscientious, diverse sanghas all around the United States and put our values into everyday practice?

- Would you like to start an organization for Asian American Buddhists?

IDENTITY

- What does it mean to identify as Buddhist?

- What does it mean to be "Asian American Buddhist?"

- How do you define Asian American Buddhist versus Asian Buddhist? Is there a difference?

- Do you feel like a *good* Buddhist?

- Are you a "real" Buddhist?

- Have you ever been asked what kind of Buddhist you are?

- Have you ever felt an issue with you being Buddhist when the people around you weren't?

- Do you feel Buddhism is distinctly different from your race or just a component of it?

- Does your Asian American identity raise any anxiety around your "religious authenticity"?

- How has your ethnic or racial identity affected the ways in which you perceive, retain, or practice principles of Buddhism?

REPRESENTATION

- What are your thoughts on the representation of Buddhists today?
- How do you feel Asian Americans are represented in the American Buddhist community as a whole?
- What can we do to make our voices heard and to gain more visibility?
- What, if anything, prevents you from sharing your perspectives in public?
- How would you like to see Asian American Buddhists represented in the media?
- What are ways that Asian American Buddhists can be positively represented through the media?
- What makes you angry about how Buddhism is portrayed and received in the United States?
- Do you think that ethnic or racial representation matters when it comes to religion?

CULTURE

- How much do you connect Buddhism to your culture or heritage: is it something separate, or are these packaged together for you?
- How do you walk the line between tradition and modernity that is perhaps especially poignant for us as Asian Americans?
- How do we maintain Buddhism's relevance in the United States, and how do we adapt immigrant traditions into American life?
- How do you make sense of the differences in Western and Asian values?

FAMILY AND FRIENDS

- Would you want to raise your children as Buddhists?
- What is your parents' belief in Buddhism like?
- How is your relationship with your parents?
- Do you know your family history?
- Do you have good Buddhist friends?

OTHER SPIRITUAL AND RELIGIOUS TRADITIONS

- How do you view other religions?
- Do you believe in God, or a supreme being? If so, how do you define God?
- Have you ever considered another religion? If yes, which one and why? If no, why not?
- Are you agnostic?
- Do you think that Sunday temple-going is a practice that arose as a result of cross-cultural influence from Western (Christian) countries?
- What are your thoughts in stemming the tide of others who convert to Christianity or become nonreligious?
- What reflections do you have on the relationship between Asian American Christians and Asian American Buddhists?
- For those who grew up in mixed-faith families: Did you choose one path over the other? Was this even an issue because Buddhism is more open to syncretism? Or is Buddhism not as open to syncretism as people think it is?
- Are there parallels between what South Asian American Hindus think about yoga in America and what Asian and Asian American Buddhist communities think about Buddhism in America?

POLITICS AND SOCIAL JUSTICE

- Is there a relationship between Buddhism and social justice? If so, what is it?

- How do you think Asian American Buddhists should respond to the Buddhist violence in our homelands, if at all?

- Do you think that Buddhism supports individualist over collectivist ideals?

- Do you feel underprivileged as an Asian American Buddhist?

- Do you think it is possible to be politically engaged and still identify as Buddhist? If so, what political ideologies or movements most closely align with Buddhism?

RACE

- What do you think and how do you feel about the rise of non-Asian Buddhists in the West?

- What do Asian American Buddhists think of nonwhite American Buddhists? What do they think of Latino and Black Buddhists? Is there a unique connection that nonwhite Buddhists have with one another in communities that are largely white?

- What impact do interracial marriages have on the Asian American Buddhist community?

- What is your response to *Maybe the question isn't Why is American Buddhism so white, but Why are Asian American Buddhists so invisible?*

APPENDIX 2
INTERVIEW QUESTIONS

The young adults I interviewed via email answered the following set of questions. These questions are adapted from the more extensive protocol I used for in-person interviews.

INTRODUCTIONS

Please tell me a bit about yourself.

- What is your name and what does your name mean?
- Where do you currently live and who do you live with?
- What is your current occupation?
- Where were you born and where did you grow up?
- Where are your parents from? Who did you grow up with in your household?
- What language(s) did you speak growing up? What language(s) do you speak now?
- Where have you traveled to in Asia?

What motivates you to contribute your stories and perspectives to this project on Asian American Buddhists? What interests you most about this topic?

ON IDENTITY

When someone asks "Are you religious?" or "What religion are you?," how do you usually respond? If you identify as Buddhist, how do you respond to the question "What kind of Buddhist are you?"

What racial or ethnic identities do you use to describe yourself? Do you identify as "Asian American"? Why or why not?

Do you think of yourself as a young adult? How do you define young adult? What unique perspectives on Buddhism do you think young adults can offer compared to older Buddhists?

YOUR BUDDHIST JOURNEY

I invite you to tell the story of your journey to and through Buddhism and to reflect on the importance of Buddhism in your life. Some questions for inspiration: What Buddhist practices do you engage in, and how have your practices changed over time? Which Buddhist teachings or beliefs are most important to you? Which Buddhist communities have you been part of? Who, if anyone, do you consider to be your Buddhist teacher(s)?

REPRESENTATIONS

- Who do you think are the most famous Buddhist individuals in America and why?
- Who are the best-known *Asian American* Buddhists in the United States?
- What do you think are the best-known types of Buddhism and Buddhist organizations in America?

- If you had to categorize American Buddhists into different categories, which categories would you use?

- If you were to name three stereotypes about American Buddhists, what would they be? What about three stereotypes about Asian American Buddhists?

Four Viewpoints on Asian American Buddhists

In this section, I invite you to share your responses to four different viewpoints on Asian American Buddhists.

1. Pew Forum Report

A July 2012 Pew Forum Report about the religious life of Asian Americans says:

> Overall, Buddhism had the greatest net loss due to changes in religious affiliation within the Asian American community. One in ten Asian Americans (10 percent) were raised Buddhist and have left the faith, while 2 percent of Asian Americans have become Buddhist after being raised in a different faith (or no faith), resulting in a net loss of eight percentage points due to religious switching.

What are your thoughts and feelings about this? Note that Asian Americans in all other religious groups are holding steady or, in the case of Asian American Christians, growing in number. What reflections do you have on the relationship between Asian American Christians and Asian American Buddhists?

2. Convert Buddhism

> The introduction to a book by a Buddhist studies scholar defines North American convert Buddhism as "the Buddhism of Americans who are not of Asian descent."

What are your thoughts and feelings about this? What are your reflections on the role of "conversion" in Buddhism?

3. *Angry Asian Buddhist*

An August 2012 blog post on *Angry Asian Buddhist* has the title, "Why Is the Under 35 Project So White?" The Angry Asian Buddhist writes:

> *This year* Shambhala SunSpace *has been posting weekly essays from the Under 35 Project, a laudable initiative to support and highlight the voices of the emerging generation of Buddhists and meditators. As usual, my naïveté never fails to let me down and I was once again shocked at the whiteness of the lineup. Not a single East or Southeast Asian among them.*

The blog post includes this picture: https://tinyurl.com/ulvq6sg. What are your thoughts and feelings about this? Are you familiar with the *Angry Asian Buddhist* blog?

4. *The Secular Buddhist Podcast*

Finally, in a podcast called *The Secular Buddhist,* a scholar of Buddhism in America says:

> *One of the blogs we're all familiar with is the one called* Angry Asian Buddhist, *and it seems that he only posts issues that refer to how much he seems to hate white Buddhists. And he never really gets out there and does something to counteract that.... Maybe the question isn't Why is American Buddhism so white, but Why are Asian American Buddhists so invisible?*

What are your thoughts and feelings about this?

VISIONS AND NEXT STEPS

- What would your ideal Buddhist community look like?
- How would you like to see Asian American Buddhists represented in the media?
- What questions would you like to ask other Asian American Buddhists?

- Is there any group or individual you would recommend that I connect with for this project?
- Any final reflections on the unique challenges that young adult Asian American Buddhists face, and the religious and cultural strengths they can draw on?

HOUSEKEEPING

Age:

Ethnicity:

Gender:

Your anonymity preferences for the information in this interview*:

*(1) You may use my first name. (2) You may use my full name. (3) Please keep my responses anonymous; use a pseudonym instead of my real name. (4) Please keep my responses confidential; do not share information that someone could use to potentially identify me.

EXTRA CREDIT

Can you identify these Asian American Buddhists? For Asian–Pacific American Heritage month, the Angry Asian Buddhist posted the following collage: https://tinyurl.com/vtnl6tj. The Angry Asian Buddhist writes, in part:

> I was surprised. I'd never seen Buddhist Asian Americans presented like this before. Placed together are the portraits of the first sixteen Buddhist Asian Americans whose photos I could find with Google image search. Here you have writers, activists, politicians, consultants, professors, and dharma teachers.

- How many of these faces do you recognize?
- What is your reaction to this collage?

APPENDIX 3
LIST OF INTERVIEWS

The eighty-nine individuals I interviewed for this project are listed below in alphabetical order. Some interviewees gave permission for their full name to be used; others asked that only their first name be used; still others opted for a pseudonym. These preferences are respected here, with asterisks marking pseudonyms.

1. Aaron Huang, email and Skype interview, May 6, 2014

2. Aaron Lee, in-person interview, Berkeley, California, March 8, 2013

3. Abby, email interview, June 12, 2014

4. Adam, in-person interview, Long Beach, California, June 27, 2013

5. *Altan, in-person interview, Berkeley, California, June 18, 2013

6. Alyssa Cheung, in-person interview, Berkeley, California, March 1, 2013

7. Andy Su, in-person interview, Los Angeles, June 28, 2013

8. *Anthony, email interview, May 3, 2014

9. Anthuan, in-person interview, Hillsborough, California, December 28, 2012

10. Bhikshu Jin Chuan, email interview, June 5, 2014

11. Brian Chansy, in-person interview, Los Angeles, June 28, 2013

12. *Camilla, email interview, May 13, 2014

13. *Catherine, email interview, May 12, 2014

14. *Claire, in-person interview, Berkeley, California, June 21, 2013

15. Connie Chow, email interview, July 18, 2014

16. *Craig, in-person interview, Stanford, California, June 22, 2013

17. Cristina Moon, email interview, June 27, 2014; revised March 21, 2020

18. Dan Huynh, email interview, May 21, 2014

19. David, email interview, May 27, 2014

20. *Dawa, email interview, June 14, 2014

21. Dedunu Sylvia, email interview, June 21, 2014

22. *Diep, email interview, June 2, 2014

23. Dolma, email interview, July 2, 2014

24. *Eileen, in-person interview, Stanford, California, July 6, 2013

25. Emily Wang, email interview, June 25, 2014

26. Eric Ku, email interview, May 18, 2014

27. *Felix, email interview, May 25, 2014

28. Farrah, email interview, June 14, 2014

29. Forest Jiang, email interview, July 2, 2014

30. Gabrielle Nomura, email interview, May 4, 2014

31. George Yamazawa, email interview, July 31, 2014

32. *Heather, in-person interview, Berkeley, California, June 16, 2013

33. Holly Hisamoto, email interview, May 16, 2014

34. *Huyen, email interview, June 29, 2014

35. Kaila, email interview, May 21, 2014

36. Katrina Dene, email interview, June 29, 2014

37. Kei, email interview, May 17, 2014

38. *Kevin, email interview, May 13, 2014

39. Khoi Tran, email interview, June 16, 2014

40. Kiet Truong, in-person interview, San Jose, California, July 7, 2013

41. Kirthi, email and Skype interview, May 7, 2014

42. Kiyonobu Kuwahara, email interview, June 9, 2014

43. Kojo Kakihara, email interview, June 27, 2014

44. Kristie Kuo, email interview, June 13, 2014

45. Krystal, email interview, July 1, 2014

46. *Kumi, in-person interview, Berkeley, California, September 15, 2013

47. Lan, in-person interview, Stanford, California, June 10, 2013

48. Landon Yamaoka, in-person interview, Palo Alto, California, January 26, 2013

49. Larene Woo, email interview, May 18, 2014

50. Leslie Teng, email interview, June 11, 2014

51. Lola, email interview, June 16, 2014

52. *Luke, email interview, July 18, 2016

53. Manny, email interview, June 10, 2014

54. Manoj, in-person interview, San Francisco, March 24, 2013

55. *Mari, in-person interview, Berkeley, California, July 11, 2013

56. Martin, in-person interview, Stanford, California, June 11, 2013

57. Mary, email interview, July 7, 2014

58. *Matthew, email interview, May 4, 2014

59. Michael, in-person interview, Monterey Park, California, June 27, 2013

60. Minh Do, email interview, May 11, 2014

61. *Monica, in-person interview, Berkeley, California, June 26, 2013

62. Nathan, email interview, May 11, 2014

63. Noel Alumit, email interview, June 23, 2014

64. *Nora, in-person interview, Berkeley, California, January 28, 2013

65. Ratema, in-person interview, Berkeley, California, February 28, 2013

66. Rebecca Nie, email interview, May 24, 2014

67. *Sam, email interview, June 3, 2014

68. *Sarah, in-person interview, Berkeley, California, July 2, 2013

69. Sarong Vit-Kory, email interview, May 20, 2014

70. Shubha Bala, email interview, May 21, 2014

71. Steve, email interview, June 25, 2014

72. Steve, email interview, July 11, 2014

73. Supraja, in-person interview, Sunnyvale, California, July 27, 2013

74. Tenzin Chagzoetsang, email interview, June 7, 2014

75. Thao Phi, email interview, May 29, 2014

76. *Tiffany, email interview, June 10, 2014

77. Toby, email interview, June 25, 2014

78. Vince Lim, email interview, May 26, 2014

79. *Vinod, email interview, May 25, 2014

80. Vita, in-person interview, Berkeley, California, July 19, 2013

81. *Wanisa, email interview, November 5, 2014

82. Wanwan Lu, email interview, May 21, 2014

83. Wenli Jen, email interview, May 17, 2014

84. Wesley Koo, email interview, June 1, 2014

85. *Xiao, email interview, June 27, 2014

86. Yeeshen Tien, email interview, May 14, 2014

87. *Yima, in-person interview, Hillsborough, California, December 2, 2012

88. Youmin Bhikshu, email interview, June 13, 2014

89. *Zoe, email interview, July 19, 2014

APPENDIX 4
INTERVIEWEE ETHNICITIES

Below is the list of all eighty-nine interviewees' stated ethnicities. For clarification, I have added ethnic identifiers in square brackets based on interview data in some cases. Since the categories I have chosen encompass specific ethnic groups (Chinese, Taiwanese, Vietnamese, Japanese, Korean, and Tibetan), larger geographic regions (Southeast Asian, South Asian, Central and West Asian), as well as mixed-heritage individuals, there is potential for overlap. For example, though the "Chinese Indonesian," "Chinese from Malaysia," and "Burmese Chinese" interviewees could be categorized under "Chinese," I have placed them under the "Southeast Asian" category to highlight their connections to the region.

Chinese (23)

    "Asian" (2)

    "Asian-American"

    "Chinese" (12)

    "Chinese-American"

    "Chinese American" (6)

    "Chinese Han"

Mixed heritage (14)

    "Asian American" [half Filipina, quarter Japanese]

    "Asian American (Chinese/Japanese)"

"Asian/Caucasian" [half Filipino]

"Chinese/Ashkenazi"

"Chinese-Vietnamese"

"Filipina, Japanese, Chinese, Spanish"

"Half Asian" [half Korean]

"Japanese, English, Irish, Danish"

"Mixed (Iranian-Mexican)"

"Mixed-ethnicity" [Japanese, Jewish]

"Multiracial: half Japanese, quarter French, quarter German"

"Nepali and Belarusian-American"

"Taiwanese-Mexican American"

"Two or More Races, Hapa, Korean, Asian"

Taiwanese (11)

"Asian American"

"Han Chinese (Taiwanese-American)"

"Taiwanese" (3)

"Taiwanese American" (3)

"Taiwanese (Han Chinese)"

"Taiwanese/Chinese" (2)

Vietnamese (10)

"Asian"

"Vietnamese" (9)

Japanese (9)

"Japanese" (5)

"Japanese-American"

"Japanese American" (3)

Southeast Asian (10)

"Asian" [Burmese Chinese]

"Burmese Chinese"

"Cambodian" (2)

"Chinese" [Malaysian]

"Chinese Indonesian"

"Filipino"

"Laotian American"

"Thai"

"Thai/Thai American"

South Asian (6)

"Indian"

"Indian-American"

"South Asian" [Indian]

"South Asian American" [Indian]

"South Indian" [Tamil], "Hindu, Canadian"

"Sri Lankan" [of Sinhalese ethnicity]

Central and West Asian (2)

"Iranian"

"Turkmen"

Korean (2)

"Korean American" (2)

Tibetan (2)

"Asian"

"Tibetan"

APPENDIX 5
A DIVERSE GROUP

ETHNICITY

The eighty-nine interviewees for this project gave forty-six distinct responses when listing their ethnicities (see appendix 4 for the full list).

These young adult Buddhists trace their Asian heritages to East, Central, South, Southeast, and West Asia. A plurality of them are of Chinese heritage. The next largest subset are those of mixed heritage: these thirteen individuals describe their ethnicity in thirteen different ways, including "Chinese/Ashkenazi," "Filipina, Japanese, Chinese, Spanish," "Nepali and Belarusian-American," and "Taiwanese-Mexican American." Other interviewees are of Burmese, Cambodian, Filipino, Indian, Iranian, Japanese, Laotian, Sri Lankan, Taiwanese, Thai, Turkmen, and Vietnamese heritage.

However wide-ranging these ethnic labels are, they lack the descriptiveness revealed through more nuanced discussions. For example, Kevin, who lists his ethnicity as "Burmese Chinese," explains: "I usually describe myself as an American of Burmese Chinese descent. Both sides of my family have some indigenous Burman (Bamar) ancestors, but they identify as being overseas Chinese and ultimately trace their ancestry to Fujian Province. But, of course, Burmese-born Chinese have specific cultural differences from Chinese in Chinese-speaking countries."

My interviewees' relationships to the broader racial category of "Asian American" vary. Kevin writes: "I do identify as an Asian American because I believe there are some collective similarities and cultural nuances shared within the community." By contrast, Kaila, a Jodo Shinshu Buddhist, prefers the label "Japanese American" to "Asian American" because the latter "takes away from the individual histories of each ethnic group."

AGE

Most of my interviewees were in their twenties and thirties. They ranged in age from eighteen to forty-six, with an average age of twenty-eight and a median age of twenty-six. Some identified unequivocally as young adults, while others expressed confusion, ambivalence, or nonchalance toward adopting the label. Those who gave a numerical age for young adulthood proposed ranges as narrow as eighteen to twenty-four and as wide as eighteen to forty. A few know of young adult Buddhist groups with members in their forties who still felt young in the context of their majority-fifty-plus sanghas.

Others posited a more subjective definition for young adulthood based on life stage. Anthony, my first email interviewee, offers this reflection:

I am a member of the so-called "millennial" generation, and while I am approaching thirty years of age—arguably the ending of "young" adulthood—I think the unique socioeconomic challenges of people in my age group (what some sociological writers have termed "waithood") mean that even the oldest of us count as "young adults." Most people in my age group that I know are either living at home with their parents, or struggling to make ends meet, or taking on more education (and more debt)—in other words, they are deferring those things that traditionally mark the beginning of "adulthood" proper in our society, i.e. starting a career, getting married, buying a home, having children, etc. Adults who haven't embarked on these pursuits yet are still "young adults" in my book.

By Anthony's reckoning, the vast majority of my interviewees qualified as young adults. Most were unmarried and childless at the time of the interview: only ten of the eighty-nine participants mentioned a spouse, and only three of these ten (one woman and two men in their mid- to late thirties) had children. Some interviewees lived with their parents or extended family, while others shared apartments, houses, co-ops, and dorm rooms with classmates, friends, partners, pets, or—more rarely—lived alone.

GENDER AND SEXUALITY

Gender and sexuality were not a central focus of my project; I hope future research will illuminate the experiences of Asian American Buddhists through these important lenses. When invited to write their gender on a demographic form at the time of the interview, forty-two interviewees wrote "male," forty-five wrote "female" or a related variation (specifically: "woman," "woman (female)," "woman or preferred gender pronouns she/her/they," and "cis-female"), one interviewee wrote "female nonconforming," and one interviewee wrote "genderqueer." I did not ask questions about interviewees' sexual orientation.

LANGUAGE

About two-thirds of my twenty-six in-person interviewees know one or more languages in addition to English: eighteen of the twenty-six use an Asian language to communicate with family and (less frequently) for work purposes; of the remaining eight, several are learning the language of their heritage or have basic proficiency in that language. A few who came to America in their teen years or later feel more comfortable in their native Asian language than English. A large percentage of my email interviewees are also bilingual or multilingual: only a few of them are monolingual English speakers, and many communicate in one or more Asian languages at home with varying degrees of fluency.

GENERATION

The young adults I interviewed run the gamut from first- to fifth-generation Asian American. Not all Asian Americans self-identify with a generational label; indeed, some may actively resist one. Katrina writes: "Being half Asian, I'm not as connected to specific generation categorizations that apply specifically to the Japanese American community. I identify more with the fact that I am hapa."

Generation labels are not always clear-cut. Kaila explains, "I identify as yonsei [fourth-generation], though I am technically a 'yo-go.' If I am counting from my mom's side I am a yonsei, and from my dad's side I am a gosei [fifth-generation]."

Kaila is one of six fourth- or fifth-generation Japanese American Jodo Shinshu Buddhists I interviewed. While most of my interviewees of full or partial Japanese heritage are fourth- or fifth-generation Americans, only two interviewees not of Japanese heritage identify as such: one is of mixed Chinese (Toishanese) and Jewish heritage, the other is of mixed Korean and Irish-Scottish heritage.

Most of my interviewees are second-generation Asian Americans, the children of parents who are part of the post-1965 wave of Asian immigrants to America. Some may identify as 1.5- or 1.75-generation, having emigrated from Asia to America anytime between their anytime between their toddler to teenage years.

The young adults I spoke to also included first-generation immigrants who moved to America after they turned eighteen. Some might argue that this group is simply "Asian." Rather than quibble over labels, I consider their perspectives as people of Asian heritage who have spent significant amounts of time in the United States and—with the exception of two interviewees who returned to Asia after pursuing graduate education in Buddhist studies in America—have chosen to settle there.

Adopting Noel's idea of using generational categories to describe where the induction of Buddhism falls in one's life (described in chapter

8), the young adults I interviewed range from "first-gen" to "multi-gen" American Buddhists. Finally, to bring up yet another definition of *generation,* my interviewees are a mix of older millennials and younger generation Xers.

GEOGRAPHIC LOCATION

The twenty-six young adults I interviewed in person in California have lived in many places outside the Golden State, including Georgia, Hawaiʻi, Massachusetts, Minnesota, Texas, and New York as well as China, France, Indonesia, and Japan. The sixty-three email interviewees only added to this geographic diversity: about half were living in California, while the other half wrote to me from eleven different states; Washington, DC; and five countries outside the United States. Including the places these sixty-three young adults were born and raised would add at least another ten states and seven countries to an already extensive list of locales.

RELIGIOUS PRACTICE AND BELIEF

When I asked Holly, an interviewee of mixed Japanese American and Jewish American heritage who practices Vajrayana Buddhism, how she might categorize American Buddhists, her detailed answer—which she emphasizes is far from a comprehensive list—demonstrates a keen awareness of the vast diversity of American Buddhism:

Chinese, Taiwanese-American Buddhisms

Chan

Pure Land

Vajrayana

Mixed-Mahayana sects, such as Fo Guang Shan

Japanese

   Zen

   Tendai

   Rissho Kosei-kai

   Shingon

   Nichiren

Korean

   Seon

Vietnamese

   Mahayana

   Thich Nhat Hanh's Zen

Thai

   Thai Forest/Dhammayut

   Dhammakaya

Sri Lankan, Indian, Burmese

   Theravada

   Mahayana

Tibetan, Nepalese

   Vajrayana

   Bon

Hybrid North American Buddhisms

   Atheist or agnostic Buddhists (such as Stephen Batchelor)

   Dual- or multiple-identity Buddhists, such as Jewish-Buddhists, Christian-Buddhists, etc.

The eighty-nine young adults I interviewed have practiced in all eight of the main categories—and most of the subcategories—on Holly's list. Many practice in more than one tradition.

OCCUPATION AND SOCIOECONOMIC STATUS

More than a quarter of my interviewees were students (seven undergraduates and eighteen graduate students), while the remainder already held postsecondary degrees. This reflects a high level of educational attainment, though their socioeconomic backgrounds vary. Lumping all Asian Americans into "the best-educated, highest-income, fastest-growing race group in the country" problematically "obscures sharp disparities within a highly diverse population," as Jane Iwamura points out.[1]

Although I did not explicitly ask questions about socioeconomic status, some interviewees mentioned facing economic hardships as the children of immigrant and refugee parents and as young adults getting established in their careers.

The career interests of these eighty-nine Asian American Buddhists encompass a plethora of fields: education, art, journalism, health care, engineering, marketing, law, finance, and others. About a sixth of the group were engaged full-time in Buddhism-related pursuits, including seven graduate students in Buddhist studies (among them two female Jodo Shinshu ministers or ministers-in-training and one Mahayana Buddhist monk), six young adults serving at Buddhist temples or organizations (two male Jodo Shinshu ministers, two Mahayana monks, one woman teaching English at a Buddhist monastery in China, and one man working for a Buddhist charity), and one lay female Buddhist chaplain working in an interfaith setting. Almost all of my interviewees are lay Buddhists rather than monastics.

PUSHING THE BOUNDARIES

Some of my interviewees would seem to test the boundaries of the classification "young adult Asian American Buddhist."

A few are in their forties, too old to be "young adults" by some standards—though not by others, as Anthony points out.

Several interviewees are less connected to the "American" aspect of "Asian American," having grown up in Asia. These interviewees typically moved to America for high school, college, grad school, or work.

A few are connected to *North* America, having grown up in Canada, though they now live in the United States.

Some feel less connected to the "Asian" aspect of Asian American: perhaps because they are multiracial and have limited exposure to their Asian heritage, or because they are of South, Central, or West Asian heritage and tend to associate "Asian American" with East and Southeast Asians.

Still others do not self-identify as Buddhist, though their interview responses evince a strong interest in Buddhism.

Over the course of getting to know this remarkably diverse group of eighty-nine interviewees, I have come to understand this book as a collective project of *thinking into being young adult Asian American Buddhists.* The double entendre behind "thinking into being" is deliberate. There is "thinking into" in the sense of "thinking about." There is also "thinking *into being*": the process of thinking as an act of creation. "Young adult Asian American Buddhists" is in many ways a nebulous category—but that need not be a liability. The difficulty of defining us is itself a powerful catalyst for creativity and connection.

NOTES

Introduction

1. In general, I refer to the blogger as "arunlikhati" when citing *Dharma Folk* posts and "Arun" when citing *Angry Asian Buddhist* blog posts, though I sometimes use the pseudonyms interchangeably since they ultimately refer to the same person.

2. Emma Varvaloucas, "Who Is the Angry Asian Buddhist? An Interview with arunlikhati." *Tricycle: The Buddhist Review,* May 21, 2012. https://tinyurl.com/w76cfz4.

3. Andrew Bowen, "Interview with Buddhist Author, Sumi Loundon Kim," *Project Conversion* (blog), May 2011. https://tinyurl.com/vujd35p.

4. Wendy Cadge, *Heartwood: The First Generation of Theravada Buddhism in America* (Chicago: University of Chicago Press, 2005), 15; Sharon A. Suh, *Being Buddhist in a Christian World: Gender and Community in a Korean American Temple* (Seattle: University of Washington Press, 2004), 53–56; Carolyn Chen, *Getting Saved in America: Taiwanese Immigration and Religious Experience* (Princeton, NJ: Princeton University Press, 2008).

5. arunlikhati, "Asian American Buddhists," http://dharmafolk.wordpress.com.

6. arunlikhati, "Buddhist Youth Conferences."

7. Pew Research Center, "U.S. Religious Landscape Survey," Washington, DC, February 2008, 53. https://tinyurl.com/rat3c67.

8. arunlikhati, "Pew Study Doesn't Add Up"; "Estimates of Asian American Buddhists"; "Finding Those Missing Hawaiian Buddhists"; "So How Many Asian American Buddhists Are There?"; Arun, "Stop Using the Pew Study,"

www.angryasianbuddhist.com; "Why Shouldn't Buddhists Use the Pew Study?"; "The Pew Study Marginalizes Asian Americans"; "Please Double Check Your Asian Counts."

9. arunlikhati, "Estimates of Asian American Buddhists."

10. The 2008 survey was conducted only in English and Spanish, on landlines, in the forty-eight continental states. By contrast, the 2012 survey was conducted in English and seven Asian languages, on landlines and cell phones, in all fifty states.

11. Pew Research Center, "Asian Americans: A Mosaic of Faiths," Washington, DC, July 19, 2012, 33, https://tinyurl.com/rd7kun6.

12. Michelle Boorstein, "A Political Awakening for Buddhists? 125 U.S. Buddhist Leaders to Meet at the White House," *Washington Post,* May 12, 2015, https://tinyurl.com/kww6dv8.

13. Pew Research Center, "Asian Americans," 51.

14. Academic literature on the "two Buddhisms" typology abounds. For a recent overview of this scholarship, see Ann Gleig, *American Dharma: Buddhism Beyond Modernity* (New Haven, CT: Yale University Press, 2019), 35–36, 45.

15. Kenneth K. Tanaka, "Epilogue: The Colors and Contours of American Buddhism," in *The Faces of Buddhism in America,* ed. Charles S. Prebish and Kenneth K. Tanaka, 287–98 (Berkeley, CA: University of California Press, 1998), 287.

16. Though Charles Prebish's 1979 coining of the term "two Buddhisms" was meant to differentiate between "two completely distinct lines of development in American Buddhism" based on organizational stability (or lack thereof), the heuristic has become, to the scholar's surprise, strongly racialized. Charles S. Prebish, "Two Buddhisms Reconsidered," *Buddhist Studies Review* 10:2 (1993), 187.

17. Arun, "Stereotypology of Asian American Buddhists."

18. bell hooks, "Waking up to Racism," *Tricycle: The Buddhist Review,* Fall 1994, 43.

19. Jan Nattier, "Visible & Invisible: The Politics of Representation in Buddhist America," *Tricycle: The Buddhist Review,* Fall 1995, 42. https://tricycle.org /magazine/visible-invisible/.

20. Natalie E. Quli, "Western Self, Asian Other: Modernity, Authenticity, and Nostalgia for 'Tradition' in Buddhist Studies," *Journal of Buddhist Ethics* 16 (2009): 1–38.

21. Arun, "Stereotypology of Asian American Buddhists."

22. In other words, they could be "Buddhist sympathizers," to borrow a term from Thomas A. Tweed, "Night-Stand Buddhists and Other Creatures," in *American Buddhism: Methods and Findings in Recent Scholarship,* ed. Duncan Ryuken Williams and Christopher S. Queen, 71–90 (Richmond, UK: Curzon Press, 1999).

23. Aaron Lee, personal email communication, August 30, 2012.

24. In accordance with his wishes, Aaron's anonymity was lifted only after his death.

25. About half the group took the initiative to contact me for an interview after hearing about my project online or through word of mouth. The other half agreed to my request to interview them. I was granted permission to voice record all twenty-six interviews and transcribed the seventy-plus hours of conversation from the resulting audio files. For more details about my research methods, see Chenxing Han, "Diverse Practices and Flexible Beliefs among Young Adult Asian American Buddhists," *Journal of Global Buddhism* 18 (2017): 1–24, https://tinyurl.com/rlbbwm2.

26. See appendix 1 for a list of questions that my interviewees wanted to ask to other Asian American Buddhists.

27. See appendix 2 for my email interview questions and appendix 3 for the full list of interviews. Two people completed their interviews on Skype; I recorded and transcribed both conversations. For the sake of simplicity, I categorize these two individuals with the other email interviewees since they answered the same set of questions. When quoting email and in-person interviewees, I hew as closely as possible to the original, though I have edited out fillers such as "um" and "like" and made minor corrections and grammatical changes without the use of square brackets for ease of reading. I follow the same conventions when quoting from blog posts and films. Throughout the book, I use interviewees' actual names or pseudonyms depending on their stated preferences.

28. See appendix 4 for a list of my interviewees' stated ethnicities and appendix 5 for a discussion about the diversity of this group of interviewees.

1. Erasure

1. Helen Tworkov, "Many Is More," *Tricycle: The Buddhist Review,* Winter 1991, https://tricycle.org/magazine/many-more/.

2. An excerpt of Rev. Imamura's letter was published in Prebish, "Two Buddhisms Reconsidered," 190–91. The full text of the letter was first published

in Funie Hsu, "Lineage of Resistance: When Asian American Buddhists Confront White Supremacy," Buddhist Peace Fellowship, May 8, 2017, https://tinyurl.com/u2ntwkm.

3. Buddhist Churches of America, "Jodo Shinshu Center," n.d., https://tinyurl .com/teacqzh; Palo Alto Buddhist Temple, "Jodo Shinshu Center," n.d., https://tinyurl.com/wg9pmqs.

4. Mark Unno, "The Original Buddhist Rebel," *Tricycle: The Buddhist Review,* Winter 2017, https://tinyurl.com/t42h352.

5. Historical information about Japanese American Buddhism in this chapter comes from Duncan Ryuken Williams, *American Sutra: A Story of Faith and Freedom in the Second World War* (Cambridge, MA: Harvard University Press, 2019); Michael K. Masatsugu, "'Beyond This World of Transiency and Impermanence': Japanese Americans, Dharma Bums, and the Making of American Buddhism during the Early Cold War Years," *Pacific Historical Review* 77:3 (2008), 423–51; and Jeff Wilson, "'All Beings Are Equally Embraced by Amida Buddha': Jodo Shinshu Buddhism and Same-Sex Marriage in the United States," *Journal of Global Buddhism* 13 (2012): 31–59, https://tinyurl.com/s3pwvcr.

6. Tricycle, "They Teach the Buddhist Faith," *Tricycle: The Buddhist Review,* Summer 1996, https://tinyurl.com/skes46q.

7. Though nowadays, "BCA-affiliated sanghas are alternately labeled churches, temples, and *betsuin,* and for all intents and purposes, there is little substantive difference between these types of institutions." Scott A. Mitchell, "Locally Translocal American Shin Buddhism," *Pacific World,* Third Series, no. 12 (Fall 2010), 111, www.shin-ibs.edu/documents/pwj3-12/04Mitchell.pdf.

8. Information about the Imamuras in this chapter comes from Densho Digital Depository, "Ryo Imamura," August 3, 1999, https://ddr.densho.org/narrators/31/; Damin Esper, "Friends, Family Remember Jane Imamura, 91, Longtime Berkeley Resident," *The Mercury News,* February 2, 2012, https://tinyurl.com/yx4cwpaa; Jon Kawamoto, "Remembering the Remarkable Life of Jane Imamura," [Albany, CA] *Patch,* January 25, 2012, https://tinyurl.com/sm5cnaq; "Jane Imamura Remembered for Her Contributions to Buddhism," *The Rafu Shimpo,* February 2, 2012, https://tinyurl.com /vsnl3um; and Rev Imamura, personal email communication, March 19, 2019. Throughout this book, I use the term "concentration camps" for the War Relocation Authority–run confinement sites where Japanese Americans (most of whom were U.S. citizens) were sent during World War II, as distinct from the "internment camps" run by the Army and the Department

of Justice for Japanese, German, and Italian nationals who were deemed "enemy aliens." Special thanks to Duncan Ryuken Williams for clarifying these naming conventions.

9. Arun, "Why Is the Under 35 Project So White?"

10. See the comments section in arunlikhati, "Angry Asian Buddhist," https://tinyurl.com/y7pm8byj.

11. Louise H. Hunter, *Buddhism in Hawaii: Its Impact on a Yankee Community* (Honolulu: University of Hawaiʻi Press, 1971), cited in Paul David Numrich, "Two Buddhisms Further Considered," *Contemporary Buddhism* 4:1 (2003), 56.

12. Gary Y. Okihiro, "Religion and Resistance in America's Concentration Camps," *Phylon* 45:3 (1984), 221.

13. Furthermore, this statement overlooks Japanese American Shin Buddhists' efforts to resist Christian conversion (Duncan Ryuken Williams, "Complex Loyalties: Issei Buddhist Ministers during the Wartime Incarceration," *Pacific World*, Third Series, no. 5 [Fall 2003], 255–74, https://tinyurl.com/snzsroa; Lori Pierce, "Buddha Loves Me This I Know: Nisei Buddhists in Christian America, 1889–1942," in *American Buddhism as a Way of Life*, ed. Gary Storhoff and John Whalen-Bridge, 167–82 [Albany, NY: State University of New York Press, 2010]). It also ignores the pains that Shin Buddhists have taken to differentiate their religion from Christianity (Masatsugu, "'Beyond This World,'" 446). Tara Koda argues that Shin Buddhism "was not diluting its message, but rather strengthening its position" with these Christianizing adaptations (Tara K. Koda, "Aloha with Gassho: Buddhism in the Hawaiian Plantations," *Pacific World*, Third Series, no. 5 [Fall 2003], 249, https://tinyurl.com/t67f66p).

14. Joseph Cheah, *Race and Religion in American Buddhism: White Supremacy and Immigrant Adaptation* (New York: Oxford University Press, 2011), 75.

15. Jane Naomi Iwamura, *Virtual Orientalism: Asian Religions and American Popular Culture* (New York: Oxford University Press, 2011), 22.

16. James Atlas, "Buddhists' Delight," *New York Times*, June 16, 2012, https://tinyurl.com/7wfzkjv.

2. Belonging

1. Quoted in Arun, "The Emerging Face of Buddhism."

2. Ann Gleig, "From Buddhist Hippies to Buddhist Geeks: The Emergence of Buddhist Postmodernism?" *Journal of Global Buddhism* 15 (2014), 20, https://tinyurl.com/stbnhpp.

3. Buddhist Geeks, "A Brief History of Buddhist Geeks," n.d., https://tinyurl.com/uxoclkj. For an in-depth look at the storied history of Buddhist Geeks, from its launch as an online media company in 2007 to its dismantlement in 2016 to the revival of its podcast in 2017, see chapter 6 in Gleig, *American Dharma*.

4. Joanne Yuasa, "TechnoBuddha Conference 2011: The Journey," *Wheel of Dharma* 37:4 (April 2011), 6, https://tinyurl.com/s5emuut.

5. Steven Tamekuni, "TechnoBuddha Conference 2012: Who Am I? The Search for Spiritual Self in the Digital Age." *Wheel of Dharma* 38:4 (April 2012), 5, https://tinyurl.com/tn44etn.

6. David K. Yoo, *Growing Up Nisei: Race, Generation, and Culture among Japanese Americans of California, 1924–49.* (Champaign, IL: University of Illinois Press, 2000), 40.

7. Mark Unno, "The Voice of Sacred Texts in the Ocean of Compassion: The Case of Shin Buddhism in America," *Pacific World,* Third Series, no. 5 (Fall 2003), 299, https://tinyurl.com/wgn8834.

8. Japanese Americans have among the highest rates of intermarriage for any Asian American group, with nearly two-thirds of newlyweds between 2008 and 2010 marrying a non-Asian (55 percent) or other Asian American (9 percent) (Pew Research Center, "The Rise of Asian Americans," Washington, DC, April 4, 2013, 106, https://tinyurl.com/7dnpkpt). Thai Americans have the highest rates of intermarriage among Asian Americans (Todd LeRoy Perreira, "The Gender of Practice: Some Findings among Thai Buddhist Women in Northern California," in *Emerging Voices: Experiences of Underrepresented Asian Americans,* ed. Huping Ling [New Brunswick, NJ: Rutgers University Press, 2008], 164).

9. As two sociologists of religion put it, "there is less social pressure in America to adhere to a particular religion, or any religion at all—alternatives to one's traditional religion are many and easily accessible" (Fenggang Yang and Rose Ebaugh, "Transformations in New Immigrant Religions and Their Global Implications," *American Sociological Review* 66:2 [April 2001], 273).

10. Pew Research Center, "Millennials in Adulthood: Detached from Institutions, Networked with Friends." Washington, DC, March 7, 2014, 4, https://tinyurl.com/pbpw3tv; Beth Downing Chee, "The Least Religious Generation," San Diego State University News Center, May 27, 2015, https://tinyurl.com/nmgngga.

11. Tetsuden Kashima, "The Buddhist Churches of America: Challenges for Change in the Twenty-First Century," in *Shin Buddhism: Historical, Textual,*

and *Interpretive Studies,* ed. Richard K. Payne, 321–40 (Berkeley, CA: Institute of Buddhist Studies and Numata Center for Buddhist Translation and Research, 2007), 338.

12. Patricia Kanaya Usuki, "American Women in Jodo Shin Buddhism Today: Tradition and Transition," *Pacific World,* Third Series, no. 7 (Fall 2005), 164. https://tinyurl.com/w2npokw.

13. Kashima, "Buddhist Churches of America," 36–39.

14. Only Asian American Hindus are less likely to think of themselves as typical Americans, at 27 percent (Pew Research Center, "Asian Americans," 7).

15. Ibid., 30.

16. This mission statement appears on the BCA website, www.buddhist-churchesofamerica.org.

17. David K. Yoo, "Enlightened Identities: Buddhism and Japanese Americans of California, 1924–1941," *The Western Historical Quarterly* 27:3 (Autumn 1996), 292.

18. Kenneth K. Tanaka, "Right Action, Buddhism, and Our Participation in the World," in *Dharma, Color, and Culture: New Voices in Western Buddhism,* ed. Hilda Gutiérrez Baldoquin, 169–78 (Berkeley, CA: Parallax Press, 2004), 171.

3. Lineage

1. Aaron Lee, "TechnoBuddha Conference 2013: Striving for Happiness, Floating with Change," *Wheel of Dharma* 39:4 (April 2013), 4, 6, https://tinyurl.com/w6yy2f5.

2. Patti Nakai, "'Thank Buddha': Asian American Community Leaders," *Taste of Chicago Buddhism,* February 8, 2016.

3. Wilson, "'All Beings Are Equally Embraced,'" 47–48.

4. Cited in Lilly Greenblatt, "Buddhist Churches of America Shares Statement on Executive Order Temporarily Banning Refugees from Entry to U.S.," *Lion's Roar,* February 2, 2017, https://tinyurl.com/stpzvgb.

5. Alyssa Cheung, personal email communication, April 6, 2017. The podcast about Manzanar's history is available at https://tinyurl.com/ya86jjyg. The Densho Archives are available at https://tinyurl.com/y983a7ow.

6. Caitlin Yoshiko Kandil, "Pilgrimage to an Ugly Past at Manzanar," [Orange County, CA] *Daily Pilot,* May 23, 2016, https://tinyurl.com/yagmcjvf.

7. Williams, *American Sutra,* 11–14.

8. Duncan Ryuken Williams, "Masatoshi Nagatomi Remembered," *Tricycle: The Buddhist Review,* Fall 2001, https://tinyurl.com/van65ul.

9. Williams, *American Sutra,* 10.

10. Tricycle, "Q&A with Lt. Jeanette Shin, U.S. Military's First Buddhist Chaplain," *Tricycle: The Buddhist Review,* October 4, 2011, https://tinyurl.com/t94jpcs.

11. Funie Hsu, email to Radical Asian and Asian American Diaspora listserv, November 30, 2016.

12. Funie Hsu, "BPF and the Angry Asian Buddhist," Buddhist Peace Fellowship, February 22, 2015, https://tinyurl.com/thdqr77.

13. Funie Hsu, "We've Been Here All Along," *Buddhadharma: The Practitioner's Quarterly,* Winter 2016, 24–31, www.lionsroar.com/weve-been-here-all-along/.

14. Tynette Deveaux and Ajahn Amaro, "A Response to Critics of 'We've Been Here All Along,' from the Winter 2016 *Buddhadharma,*" *Lion's Roar,* December 1, 2016, https://tinyurl.com/wh33zlx.

15. Williams, *American Sutra,* 13.

16. Reuben Micu, "Kogetsu-Do: Home of Over 100 Years Old Japanese Confection Recipes," *Fresno Foodways,* April 25, 2018, https://tinyurl.com/u5y9kfe; "Hidden Gem: Japanese Bakery Kogetsu-Do in Fresno's Chinatown" *The Fresno Bee,* n.d., https://tinyurl.com/sbspubp.

17. Nancy Ukai, "Jerome and Rohwer Revisited," *Pacific Citizen: The National Newspaper of the JACL,* May 18, 2018, https://tinyurl.com/y945pkty.

18. Funie Hsu, personal text messages, March 14, 2019.

19. Duncan Ryuken Williams, "Buddhist Protest of Inhumane Treatment of Migrant Children," video, YouTube, August 11, 2019, www.youtube.com/watch?v=i3GbRteuoLM; Duncan Ryuken Williams, "Fort Sill and the Incarceration of Japanese 'Enemy Aliens' during World War II," 2019, https://tinyurl.com/uj88wr2.

20. Emphasis in original.

21. Burton Watson, trans., *The Complete Works of Chuang Tzu* (New York: Columbia University Press, 2013).

22. Rev. Ryo Imamura, personal email communication, April 27, 2019.

4. Gaps

1. Todd M. Kerstetter, *Inspiration and Innovation: Religion in the American West* (Hoboken, NJ: Wiley-Blackwell, 2015), 221.

2. Laura Paisley, "Students Meet the Many Faces of Buddhism in Los Angeles," *USC News*, July 14, 2014, https://tinyurl.com/urhjk2b.

3. Rohan Gunatillake, "Second Generation Practitioners ... Where Are You?" *Legacy 21awake Blog,* February 12, 2009, https://tinyurl.com/uo49wbg. Gunatillake would go on to design the meditation app Buddhify and become an influential member of Buddhist Geeks (Gleig, "From Buddhist Hippies," 18, 22).

4. Mihiri Uthpala Tillakaratne, "Multiculturalism, Ethnicity, Religious Identity and the 1.5 and Second Generation in Two Los Angeles-Area Sri Lankan Buddhist Temples" (master's thesis, University of California Los Angeles, 2012), 108.

5. Charles S. Prebish, *Luminous Passage: The Practice and Study of Buddhism in America* (Berkeley, CA: University of California Press, 1999), 63.

6. A clarification on the meaning of BOCA, from John Gill, personal email communication, February 16, 2020: "BOCA is actually the name of the association for Dharma Seal Temple that the youth group is part of. It stands for Buddhist Ortho-Creed Association, which is actually an old-fashioned 1970s-style translation of 佛教正信會. A more contemporary translation would be something like 'Buddhist Right Faith Association.' If the name sounds a little familiar, it does have a history: Ven. Yinhai (印海), the temple's founder, named it after one of the more prominent lay Buddhist associations created by Ven. Taixu (太虛) in China. From my understanding, there's no direct or organizational connection, just that Ven. Yinhai chose the name for this nascent Buddhist association in Los Angeles to connect it to the Buddhist reform movement that he grew up in. The name has actually been a touchpoint ('Have you ever wondered what the 'ortho creed' on our shirts means?') in the past to talk to youth group members about the temple's connection to folks like Vens. Taixu, Yinshun (印順), and Cihang (慈航)."

7. Jane Naomi Iwamura, Haeyoung Yoon, Leng Leroy Lim, David Kyuman Kim, Rita Nakashima Brock, and Rudy V. Busto, "Critical Reflections on Asian American Religious Identity," *Amerasia Journal* 22:1 (1996), 180.

8. This insight comes from Larene's email interview. Unless mentioned in the context of the *Youth Group* film, quotes from Larene are from her email interview.

9. Jane Naomi Iwamura, "Homage to Ancestors: Exploring the Horizons of Asian American Religious Identity," *Amerasia Journal* 22:1 (1996), 162.

10. Jane Naomi Iwamura, "Altared States: Exploring the Legacy of Japanese American *Butsudan* Practice," *Pacific World,* Third Series, no. 5 (Fall 2003), 286, https://tinyurl.com/rbg3owd.

11. Heather L. Weaver, "Buddhist Student, Religious Liberty Prevail in Louisiana," American Civil Liberties Union, March 14, 2014, https://tinyurl.com/wsoq96y.

5. Reclamation

1. Cadge, *Heartwood,* 157; Wendy Cadge and Elaine Howard Ecklund, "Immigration and Religion," *Annual Review of Sociology* 33:1 (2007), 363–64.
2. This viewpoint shows up in academic literature as well: "In many Buddhist groups the teachings and practices are, if anything, attractive to the people who participate in them because of their flexibility and nonexclusivity" (Robert Wuthnow and Wendy Cadge, "Buddhists and Buddhism in the United States: The Scope of Influence," *Journal for the Scientific Study of Religion* 43:3 [2004], 366).
3. Iwamura et al., "Critical Reflections," 171.

6. Compassion

1. Thich Nhat Hanh, "The Nobility of Suffering," in *Dharma, Color, and Culture: New Voices in Western Buddhism,* ed. Hilda Gutiérrez Baldoquin (Berkeley, CA: Parallax Press, 2004), 69.
2. arunlikhati, "White Buddhist for Asians."
3. For a discussion of community service and other Buddhist practices among my in-person interviewees, see, Han, "Diverse Practices."
4. Chenxing Han, "Young Adult Asian American Identities," in *A Thousand Hands: A Guidebook to Caring for Your Buddhist Community,* ed. Nathan Jishin Michon and Danny Clarkson Fisher, 277–85 (Toronto: Sumeru Press, 2016).

7. Tension

1. Pew Research Center, "Asian Americans," 8.
2. Sheridan Adams, Mushim Ikeda-Nash, Jeff Kitzes, Margarita Loinaz, Choyin Rangdrol, Jessica Tan, and Larry Yang, "Making the Invisible Visible: Healing Racism in Our Buddhist Communities," Buddhist Teachers in the West Conference, June 2000, Woodacre, CA, 49–53, https://tinyurl.com/szof522.
3. Arun, "Stereotypology of Asian American Buddhists."
4. Numrich, "Two Buddhisms Further Considered," 69.

5. Paul David Numrich, *Old Wisdom in the New World: Americanization in Two Immigrant Theravada Buddhist Temples* (Knoxville, TN: University of Tennessee Press, 1996).

6. Ibid., 63.

7. Kristian Petersen, "Jane Iwamura, *Virtual Orientalism: Religion and Popular Culture in the U.S.*," New Books Network, August 22, 2013, https://tinyurl.com/rx4oogv.

8. Robert H. Sharf, "Introduction: Prolegomenon to the Study of Medieval Chinese Buddhist Literature," in *Coming to Terms with Chinese Buddhism: A Reading of the Treasure Store Treatise* (Honolulu: University of Hawai'i Press, 2002), 23.

9. While the second-generation Buddhists I interviewed also represent a wide range of ethnicities, only about 5 percent of them identify as multiracial or multiethnic.

10. Rick Fields, "Divided Dharma: White Buddhists, Ethnic Buddhists, and Racism," in *The Faces of Buddhism in America*, ed. Charles S. Prebish and Kenneth K. Tanaka, 196–206 (Berkeley, CA: University of California Press, 1998), 200. An earlier version appears in Rick Fields, "Confessions of a White Buddhist," *Tricycle: The Buddhist Review*, Fall 1994, 55.

11. Bhikshu Jin Chuan, *Dharmas*, http://blog.drbu.edu. Written between October 2011 and October 2013, the blog posts, in chronological order, are "A Journey to Monkhood"; "Heroes"; "What is Success?"; A Christian Heart with a Buddhist Mind"; "Repaying the Kindness of my Parents?"; "How to be a Good Son?"; and "Connecting to my Family Roots."

12. Second-generation Asian American Buddhists don't necessarily find support for their monastic aspirations either: two sociologists observe that observe that "most Thai parents [in America] report not wanting their children to become monks" (Wendy Cadge and Sidhorn Sangdhanoo, "Thai Buddhism in America: An Historical and Contemporary Overview," *Contemporary Buddhism* 6:1 [2005], 26).

13. Shubha Bala, "Meditation and Diversity," *Ganesha's Scarf* (blog), n.d.

14. Adams et al., "Making the Invisible Visible," 6.

8. Affinity

1. Pew Research Center, "Asian Americans," 51.

2. For a reflection on the limits of applying Christian notions of conversion to Buddhist contexts, see Anne C. Spencer, "A Response to *The Oxford*

Handbook of Religious Conversion from Two Perspectives," *Pastoral Psychology* 67:2 (2016), 219–26.

3. Peter N. Gregory, "Describing the Elephant: Buddhism in America," *Religion and American Culture* 11:2 (2001), 242.

4. For one version of the story about how the Buddha taught loving-kindness to a group of five hundred monks when their rains retreat was disturbed by frightening forest spirits, see Marcia Rose, "The Power of Metta: A Buddhist Story," The Mountain Hermitage, n.d., https://tinyurl.com/yxx5ooeq.

5. For an analysis that supports Dolma's critique, see Jane Naomi Iwamura, Khyati Y. Joshi, Sharon Suh, and Janelle Wong, "Reflections on the Pew Forum on Religious and Public Life's *Asian Americans: A Mosaic of Faiths* Data and Report," *Amerasia Journal* 40:1 (2014), 1–16.

9. Roots

1. For one formulation of the Five Remembrances, see Thich Nhat Hanh, ed. *Plum Village Chanting and Recitation Book* (Berkeley, CA: Parallax Press, 2000), 35.

2. arunlikhati, "Running in the Family."

3. Numrich, "Two Buddhisms Further Considered," 69.

4. Wakoh Shannon Hickey, "Two Buddhisms, Three Buddhisms, and Racism," *Journal of Global Buddhism* 11 (2010): 7, https://tinyurl.com/yx3nht2j.

5. This is a different Nathan than the one featured in the *Youth Group* documentary.

6. All mentions of "Aaron" after this point in the book refer to Aaron Lee rather than Aaron Huang.

7. Bhikshu Jin Chuan, "How to be a Good Son?"

8. Bhikshu Jin Chuan, "Connecting to my Family Roots."

9. Leah Kalmanson, "Buddhism and bell hooks: Liberatory Aesthetics and the Radical Subjectivity of No-Self," *Hypatia* 27:4 (2012), 821.

10. Edwin Ng, "The Autoethnographic Genre and Buddhist Studies: Reflections of a Postcolonial 'Western Buddhist' Convert," *Australian Religion Studies Review* 25:2 (2012), 181.

10. Anger

1. Arun, "Why I'm Angry."

2. Diana Winston, "Forum: Next-Gen Buddhism," *Lion's Roar,* December 1, 2008, originally published in *Buddhadharma: The Practitioner's Quarterly,* www.lionsroar.com/forum-next-gen-buddhism/.

3. arunlikhati, "Angry Asian Buddhist."

4. arunlikhati, "Who Are Those American Buddhists?"; Arun, "Will the Real American Buddhists Please Stand Up?"

5. arunlikhati, "I Am a Western Buddhist"; Arun, "What Western Buddhism Shouldn't Be"; arunlikhati, "Is Western Buddhism White?"

6. Arun, "Who Are Non-Ethnic Asian Westerners?"; "American Buddhism's 'Ethnic' Problem."

7. Arun, "Becoming Chinese Buddhists in the West."

8. arunlikhati, "Insufferable Meditators"; "Asians Meditate Too."

9. Arun, "Asian-Free Buddhism."

10. Arun, "From Cradle to ...?"

11. Varvaloucas, "Who Is the Angry Asian Buddhist?"

12. Phil Yu, "Archived Posts: May 2004," *Angry Asian Man,* May 2004, https://tinyurl.com/s5r6t7o.

13. Arun, "Buddha Toilet Brush Holder."

14. Arun, "The Buddha Is the New Face of Customer Service."

15. Mark Wilson, "Zendesk Unveils a Dynamic New Brand Inspired by Classic Danish Design," *Fast Company,* October 26, 2016, https://tinyurl.com/r7huc5s.

16. Kim Tran, "4 Signs You're Culturally Appropriating Buddhism—and Why It's Important Not To," *Everyday Feminism,* July 21, 2016, https://tinyurl.com/u2qr423. Italics in original.

17. Arun, "Why Is the Under 35 Project So White?"

18. Zesho Susan O'Connell, "10 Buddhist Women Every Person Should Know," *The Huffington Post,* March 30, 2012, https://tinyurl.com/wx9mgql.

19. Ted Meissner, "Charles Prebish, Sarah Haynes, Justin Whitaker, Danny Fisher: Two Buddhisms Today," *The Secular Buddhist,* September 22, 2012, https://tinyurl.com/rm9966f.

20. Arun, "Take Two."

21. arunlikhati, "A White Buddhist on Race."

22. arunlikhati, "Just Stand up and Complain"; Arun, "Apologia"; "Sometimes I Get It Wrong."

23. Hsu, "BPF and the Angry Asian Buddhist."

24. A 2004 survey on the scope of Buddhism's influence in America finds that public opinion about Buddhists is generally favorable: "Relatively small proportions of the American public thought negative words, such as violent (12 percent) and fanatical (23 percent) applied to the Buddhist religion, while a majority thought this about positive words such as tolerant (56 percent) and peace-loving (63 percent)," according to Wuthnow and Cadge, "Buddhists and Buddhism," 365.

25. Arun, "Military ≠ Buddhism?"
26. See the comments section in Arun, "Military ≠ Buddhism?," https://tinyurl
.com/vdxv7by.
27. arunlikhati, "Engaging in Un-Buddhist Activities."
28. Jeff Yang, "Angry vs. Angry and Why All of Us Lose," *Medium,* February 19,
2015, https://tinyurl.com/la8l2ss. Italics in original.

11. Privilege

1. I am reminded of a 2001 PBS *Religion and Ethics Newsweekly* video titled
"Tensions in American Buddhism" (https://tinyurl.com/rohlaut) in which
Kim Lawton reports: "Despite their numbers, many Asian Americans say
they don't feel sufficiently acknowledged in this country's Buddhist landscape.
Hollywood and the media have perpetuated the impression that the American
Buddhist community consists of mostly white practitioners who follow charis-
matic Asian leaders such as Thich Nhat Hanh or the Dalai Lama."
2. The Dalai Lama and Thich Nhat Hanh were by far the most common answers
to this question among my eighty-nine interviewees. Excluding Buddhists
based outside America, the most common answer was Richard Gere, followed by Jack Kornfield, Pema Chödrön, and Steve Jobs. Of the nineteen
American Buddhists considered famous by at least two interviewees, sixteen are white, only five are female (Pema Chödrön, Sharon Salzberg, Tina
Turner, Joanna Macy, and Joan Halifax), and just two are of Asian heritage
(George Takei and Tiger Woods). Of the more than twenty other names
named by just one interviewee, white males are similarly overrepresented—
only one Asian American made the list, again a celebrity (Keanu Reeves).
3. Duncan Ryuken Williams and Tomoe Moriya, eds. *Issei Buddhism in the
Americas* (Urbana, IL: University of Illinois Press, 2010), 41–42.
4. See, for example, arunlikhati, "An Asian American Misunderstood"; "Tri-
cycle by Numbers"; "Asian Watch"; "Buddhadharma on the Asian Meter";
"Asian Meter"; "Wisdom Anthology Meets the Asian Meter"; "*Shambhala
Sun* Again Tops the Asian Meter"; and "Asian Meter with R"; as well as Arun,
"Tricycle and Its Token Minorities"; "Asian Meter 2009"; "Best Buddhist
Writing 2010"; "On White Women and Buddhism"; "Beneath a Single Moon";
"Best Buddhist Writing 2011"; and "Best Buddhist Writing Back to Normal."
5. See, for example, Arun, "Angry Asian Buddhist"; "A Bit More Than a
Smattering?"; "The White Face of Buddhism: Now at Patheos"; "Why

Is American Buddhism So White?"; "On the Newtown Shootings"; and "Making Our Way without Asians."

6. Funie Hsu, email to Radical Asian and Asian American Diaspora listserv, November 30, 2016.

7. Adams et al., "Making the Invisible Visible," 14.

8. Cheryl A. Giles and Willa B. Miller, eds., *The Arts of Contemplative Care: Pioneering Voices in Buddhist Chaplaincy and Pastoral Work* (Boston: Wisdom Publications, 2012).

9. Larry Yang, "Staying on Your Seat: The Practice of Right Concentration," in *Dharma, Color, and Culture: New Voices in Western Buddhism,* ed. Hilda Gutiérrez Baldoquin, 157–63 (Berkeley, CA: Parallax Press, 2004), 159.

10. Adams et al., "Making the Invisible Visible," 24–25.

11. Ibid., 52.

12. C. N. Le, "Reflections on a Multicultural Buddhist Retreat," Asian-Nation (website), July 15, 2009, https://tinyurl.com/u8lyklp; arunlikhati, "Exegesis of a White-Privileged Nation."

13. Tassja, "The Unbearable Whiteness of Being, Part III: A Brown Buddhist and a Handful of Mustard Seeds," *Irresistible Revolution,* June 21, 2011, https://tinyurl.com/yx8xzj79.

14. Liriel, "It's Not about Richard Gere," *Angry Asian Buddhist,* June 28, 2011, https://tinyurl.com/vawgung.

15. See the comments section in Liriel, "It's Not about Richard Gere"; and Arun, "What Marginalization"?

16. Deveaux and Amaro, "Response to Critics."

17. The image is available online at Kate Pickert, "The Mindful Revolution: Finding Peace in a Stressed-Out, Digitally Dependent Culture May Just Be a Matter of Thinking Differently," *Time,* February 3, 2014, https://tinyurl.com/syw828f.

18. Iwamura, *Virtual Orientalism,* 161.

19. For example, in the 2009 media response to news of Tiger Woods's extramarital affairs, the go-to source for information on the professional golfer's Thai Theravada Buddhist background were white male scholars rather than Asian American or other nonwhite Buddhists (Scott A. Mitchell, "'Christianity Is for Rubes; Buddhism Is for Actors': U.S. Media Representations of Buddhism in the Wake of the Tiger Woods Scandal," *Journal of Global Buddhism* 13 (2012): 61–79, https://tinyurl.com/wngys2o). This phenomenon of assigning white people the authority to speak for Asian Americans isn't

limited to Buddhist spheres. Two sociologists of religion observe that "the few white converts at our Buddhist, Hindu, and Muslim sites are often designated as spokespersons for the religion when dealing with the larger society" (Yang and Ebaugh, "Transformations," 283).

20. Arun, "Alan Senauke: On Race & Buddhism."

21. Ibid.

22. I borrow these terms from Arun, "A Western Buddhist Superiority Complex"; "An Asian Buddhist Superiority Complex."

23. Aaron Lee, personal email communication, December 9, 2016.

24. Aaron Lee, personal email communication, December 17, 2017.

25. arunlikhati, "Be the Refuge," is the first and only post on Aaron's new blog. The description for *Be the Refuge* reads: "An exploration of Buddhism in daily life by an Asian American cancer patient."

12. Solidarity

1. Richard Hughes Seager, *Buddhism in America,* 1st ed. (New York: Columbia University Press, 1999), 239; Richard Hughes Seager, *Buddhism in America,* rev. and expanded ed. (New York: Columbia University Press, 2012), 271.

2. Numrich, "Two Buddhisms Further Considered," 69.

3. Good Company: Friendship in the Spiritual Community," Urban Dharma n.d., https://tinyurl.com/2ajwfdd.

4. Gregory, "Describing the Elephant," 240.

5. Quotes in this section are from Wanwan Lu, "Interview with Aaron Lee," unpublished video, 2014.

6. Quotes in this section are from Tassja, "Unbearable Whiteness of Being." Liriel's response is reprinted in Arun, "A Brown Buddhist and a Handful of Mustard Seeds."

7. Arun, "A Brown Buddhist and a Handful of Mustard Seeds."

8. Tricycle, "Losing Our Religion," *Tricycle: The Buddhist Review,* Summer 2007, 44–49, https://tinyurl.com/y7s45ape.

9. Arun, "Happy Asian Pacific American Heritage Month!"

10. After "Happy Asian Pacific American Heritage Month!" was published, I added an "extra credit" section to my email interviews to ask interviewees how many of the faces they could name and what their reactions to the collage were. I also emailed this extra section to those who had already completed interviews, thus giving all interviewees (except Aaron Lee, since he created the collage) a chance to weigh in. Of the sixty-one interviewees who responded, eleven couldn't

identify any of the faces in the collage, twenty-two could name one, eleven recognized two people, nine spotted three familiar faces, and the remaining eight could identify four to eight of the Asian American Buddhists pictured.

11. Aaron Lee, personal email communication, August 29, 2014.

12. The full list: Anushka Fernandopulle, Barbara Chai, Canyon Sam, Colleen Hanabusa, Duncan Williams, George Takei, Harry Bridge, Ira Sukungru-ang, Jakusho Kwong, Jane Iwamura, Kenji Liu, Larry Yang, Mazie Hirono, Mushim Ikeda-Nash, Ruth Ozeki, and Viveka Chen.

13. Duncan Ryuken Williams, "At Ease in Between: The Middle Position of a Scholar-Practitioner," *Journal of Global Buddhism* 9 (2008): 155–63, https://tinyurl.com/y8ap6eeg.

14. Kenji Liu, "The Influence of Orientalism on U.S. Buddhism," Buddhist Peace Fellowship, June 7, 2013, https://tinyurl.com/me2gesw.

15. Viveka Chen, "The Dharma of Identity," in *The Buddha's Apprentices: More Voices of Young Buddhists,* ed. Sumi Loundon, 49–53 (Boston: Wisdom Publications, 2006).

16. Aaron Lee, personal email communication, October 20, 2014.

17. Lu, "Interview with Aaron Lee."

18. "Gary" is a pseudonym.

19. Quotes in this section are from Lu, "Interview with Aaron Lee."

20. *Lion's Roar* Staff, "Inside the First Issue of *Lion's Roar* Magazine," *Lion's Roar,* January 13, 2016, https://tinyurl.com/y8jblplk.

21. Funie Hsu, Arun, Kate Johnson, Katie Loncke, and Dedunu Sylvia, "5 Responses to the Awkwardly Titled 'New Face of Buddhism,'" Buddhist Peace Fellowship, January 27, 2016, https://tinyurl.com/yaebo6xs.

22. An overview of these efforts, including a photograph of the Thai American youth involved, can be found in Jonathan H. X. Lee, "Acting Out: Thai American Buddhists Encounters with White Privilege and White Supremacy," in *Southeast Asian Diaspora in the United States: Memories and Visions, Yesterday, Today, and Tomorrow,* 120–42 (Newcastle upon Tyne, UK: Cambridge Scholars Publishing, 2014).

23. Arun, "Thank Yous."

24. Annie, personal email communication, December 29, 2016.

25. Katie Loncke, "'We've Been Here All Along'—Love for Asian American Buddhists," Buddhist Peace Fellowship, December 7, 2016, https://tinyurl.com/y7r2nyzf.

26. Sumi Loundon Kim, personal email communication, July 6, 2016.

27. Funie Hsu, personal email communication, October 19, 2016.

28. Quotes in this section are from Aaron lee, personal email communication, October 19, 2016.

29. Arun, "We've Been Here All Along."

30. Funie Hsu, email to Radical Asian and Asian American Diaspora listserv, November 30, 2016.

31. Jeff Gordinier, "Jeong Kwan, the Philosopher Chef," *New York Times,* October 16, 2015, https://tinyurl.com/hrplelg.

32. David Gelb, dir., *Chef's Table,* season 3, "Jeong Kwan," Netflix, February 17, 2017.

33. Sam Littlefair, "Aaron Lee, the 'Angry Asian Buddhist,' Has Died, Age 34," *Lion's Roar,* October 25, 2017, https://tinyurl.com/y7arc7o6.

34. Karen Grigsby Bates, "The Year in Race: Saying Goodbye," NPR, December 27, 2017, https://tinyurl.com/yb6vt6zo.

35. "In Memoriam: Aaron Lee," *Wheel of Dharma* 39:12 (December 2017), 5, https://tinyurl.com/y77ex38p.

36. Jack Kornfield and Trudy Goodman, "Sandra Oh, Jack Kornfield, and Trudy Goodman on the Future of Buddhism," *Lion's Roar,* January 4, 2019, originally published May 2016, https://tinyurl.com/vhfo8dz.

37. Trudy Goodman, quoted in *Lion's Roar* Staff, "Forum: What Does Mindfulness Mean for Buddhism?" May 5, 2015, https://tinyurl.com/ybr7ra83; also quoted in Edwin Ng and Zach Walsh, "Vulnerability, Response-Ability, and the Promise of Making Refuge," *Religions* 10:2 (2019), 9, doi:10.3390/rel10020080.

38. Gelb, "Jeong Kwan."

39. emiko yoshikami, "Review: Reading My History through 'American Sutra.'" Buddhist Peace Fellowship, October 22, 2019, https://tinyurl.com/yc2s25wc.

40. Cheah, *Race and Religion,* 75.

41. Nattier, "Visible & Invisible," 42.

42. Jane Iwamura, "On Asian Religions without Asians," *Hyphen Magazine,* March 25, 2011, https://tinyurl.com/ycr7xebm.

43. Numrich, "Two Buddhisms Further Considered," 71.

44. Courtney Escoyne, "Why Prumsodun Ok Founded Cambodia's First Gay Dance Company in His Living Room," *Dance Magazine,* June 27, 2019, https://tinyurl.com/uy3tngo.

Appendix 5

1. Jane Iwamura, "Re-Modeling Reporting on 'The Model Minority,'" USC Annenberg School Trans/Missions, June 26, 2012.

BIBLIOGRAPHY

DHARMA FOLK BLOG POSTS
BY ARUNLIKHATI (AARON LEE)

"Angry Asian Buddhist." December 3, 2008. https://dharmafolk.wordpress.com
/2008/12/03/angry-asian-buddhist/.

"Asian American Buddhists." May 5, 2008. http://dharmafolk.wordpress.com
/2008/05/05/asian-american-buddhists/.

"An Asian American Misunderstood." December 11, 2008. https://dharmafolk
.wordpress.com/2008/12/11/an-asian-american-misunderstood/.

"Asian Meter: Best Buddhist Writing." March 19, 2009. https://dharmafolk
.wordpress.com/2009/03/19/asian-meter-best-buddhist-writing/.

"Asian Meter with R." June 4, 2009. www.dharmafolk.wordpress.com/2009
/06/04/asian-meter-with-r/.

"Asians Meditate Too." March 13, 2009. https://dharmafolk.wordpress.com
/2009/03/13/asians-meditate-too/.

"Asian Watch." February 12, 2009. https://dharmafolk.wordpress.com
/2009/02/12/asian-watch/.

"Buddhadharma on the Asian Meter." March 15, 2009. https://dharmafolk
.wordpress.com/2009/03/15/buddhadharma-on-the-asian-meter/.

"Buddhist Youth Conferences." April 18, 2008. https://dharmafolk.wordpress
.com/2008/04/18/buddhist-youth-conferences/.

"Engaging in Un-Buddhist Activities." June 30, 2009. https://dharmafolk
.wordpress.com/2009/06/30/engaging-in-un-buddhist-activities/.

"Estimates of Asian American Buddhists." March 27, 2009. https://dharmafolk
.wordpress.com/2009/03/27/estimates-of-asian-american-buddhists/.

"Exegesis of a White-Privileged Nation." July 24, 2009. https://dharmafolk
.wordpress.com/2009/07/24/exegesis-of-a-white-privileged-notion/.

"Finding Those Missing Hawaiian Buddhists." April 5, 2009. https://dharmafolk
.wordpress.com/2009/04/05/finding-those-missing-hawaiian-buddhists/.

"I Am a Western Buddhist." May 29, 2009. https://dharmafolk.wordpress.com
/2009/05/29/i-am-a-western-buddhist/.

"Insufferable Meditators." March 5, 2009. https://dharmafolk.wordpress.com
/2009/03/05/insufferable-meditators/.

"Is Western Buddhism White?" October 16, 2009. https://dharmafolk.wordpress
.com/2009/10/16/is-western-buddhism-white/.

"Just Stand Up and Complain." August 25, 2008. https://dharmafolk.wordpress
.com/2008/08/25/just-stand-up-and-complain/.

"Pew Study Doesn't Add Up." March 21, 2009. https://dharmafolk.wordpress
.com/2009/03/21/pew-study-doesnt-add-up/.

"Running in the Family." May 18, 2008. https://dharmafolk.wordpress.com
/2008/05/18/running-in-the-family/.

"*Shambhala Sun* Again Tops the Asian Meter." April 25, 2009. https://dharmafolk
.wordpress.com/2009/04/25/shambhala-sun-again-tops-the-asian-meter/.

"So How Many Asian American Buddhists Are There?" April 24, 2009. https://
dharmafolk.wordpress.com/2009/04/24/so-how-many-asian-american
-buddhists-are-there/.

"*Tricycle* by Numbers." December 21, 2008. https://dharmafolk.wordpress
.com/2008/12/21/tricycle-by-numbers/.

"A White Buddhist on Race." March 11, 2009. https://dharmafolk.wordpress
.com/2009/03/11/a-white-buddhist-on-race/.

"Who Are Those American Buddhists?" March 24, 2009. https://dharmafolk
.wordpress.com/2009/03/24/who-are-those-american-buddhists/.

"Wisdom Anthology Meets the Asian Meter." April 18, 2009. https://dharmafolk.
wordpress.com/2009/04/18/wisdom-anthology-meets-the-asian-meter/.

ANGRY ASIAN BUDDHIST
BLOG POSTS BY ARUN (AARON LEE)

"Alan Senauke: On Race & Buddhism." August 26, 2011. www.angryasianbuddhist
.com/2011/08/alan-senauke-on-race-buddhism/.

"American Buddhism's 'Ethnic' Problem." May 2, 2012. www.angryasianbuddhist
.com/2012/05/american-buddhisms-ethnic-problem/.

"Apologia." Angry Asian Buddhist, November 12, 2009. www.angryasianbuddhist .com/2009/11/apologia/.

"An Asian Buddhist Superiority Complex." July 9, 2009. www.angryasianbuddhist .com/2009/07/an-asian-buddhist-superiority-complex/.

"Asian-Free Buddhism." September 17, 2009. www.angryasianbuddhist.com/2009 /09/asian-free-buddhism/.

"Asian Meter 2009." December 31, 2009. www.angryasianbuddhist.com/2009 /12/asian-meter-2009/.

"Becoming Chinese Buddhists in the West." June 20, 2009. www.angryasianbuddhist .com/2009/06/becoming-chinese-buddhist-in-the-west/.

"Beneath a Single Moon." January 11, 2011. www.angryasianbuddhist.com /2011/01/beneath-a-single-moon/.

"Best Buddhist Writing 2010." November 27, 2010. www.angryasianbuddhist.com /2010/11/best-buddhist-writing-2010/.

"Best Buddhist Writing 2011." August 22, 2011. www.angryasianbuddhist.com/2011 /08/best-buddhist-writing-2011/.

"Best Buddhist Writing Back to Normal." December 18, 2012. www .angryasianbuddhist.com/2012/12/best-buddhist-writing-back-to-normal/.

"A Bit More Than a Smattering?" June 12, 2011. www.angryasianbuddhist.com /2011/06/a-bit-more-than-a-smattering/.

"A Brown Buddhist and a Handful of Mustard Seeds." June 24, 2011. www .angryasianbuddhist.com/2011/06/a-brown-buddhist-and-a-handful-of -mustard-seeds/.

"The Buddha Is the New Face of Customer Service." October 28, 2014. www .angryasianbuddhist.com/2014/10/the-buddha-is-the-new-face-of -customer-service/.

"Buddha Toilet Brush Holder." January 31, 2012. www.angryasianbuddhist.com /2012/01/buddha-toilet-brush-holder/.

"The Emerging Face of Buddhism." April 6, 2011. www.angryasianbuddhist.com /2011/04/the-emerging-face-of-buddhism/.

"From Cradle To ...?" March 27, 2010. www.angryasianbuddhist.com/2010/03 /from-cradle-to/.

"Happy Asian Pacific American Heritage Month!" May 18, 2014. www.angryasianbuddhist.com/2014/05/happy-asian-pacific-american- heritage-month-2/.

"Making Our Way without Asians." February 9, 2015. www.angryasianbuddhist .com/2015/02/making-our-way-without-asians/.

"Military ≠ Buddhism?" June 28, 2009. www.angryasianbuddhist.com/2009/06 /military-%e2%89%a0-buddhism/.

"On the Newtown Shootings." December 30, 2012. www.angryasianbuddhist
.com/2012/12/on-the-newtown-shootings/.

"On White Women and Buddhism." December 11, 2010.
www.angryasianbuddhist.com/2010/12/on-white-women-and-buddhism/..

"The Pew Study Marginalizes Asian Americans." November 21, 2011. www
.angryasianbuddhist.com/2011/11/the-pew-study-marginalizes-asian
-americans/.

"Please Double Check Your Asian Counts." November 18, 2012. www
.angryasianbuddhist.com/2012/11/please-double-check-your-asian-counts/.

"Sometimes I Get It Wrong." August 26, 2010. www.angryasianbuddhist.com
/2010/08/sometimes-i-get-it-wrong/.

"Stereotypology of Asian American Buddhists." April 30, 2014. www
.angryasianbuddhist.com/2014/04/stereotypology-of-asian-american
-buddhists/.

"Stop Using the Pew Study." April 29, 2010. www.angryasianbuddhist.com/2010
/04/stop-using-the-pew-study/.

"Take Two." April 5, 2009. www.angryasianbuddhist.com/2009/04/take-two/.

"Thank Yous." March 11, 2016. www.angryasianbuddhist.com/2016/03
/thank-yous/.

"*Tricycle* and Its Token Minorities." May 3, 2009. www.angryasianbuddhist.com
/2009/05/tricycle-and-its-token-minorities/.

"A Western Buddhist Superiority Complex." July 8, 2009. www.angryasianbuddhist
.com/2009/07/a-western-buddhist-superiority-complex/.

"We've Been Here All Along." November 24, 2016. www.angryasianbuddhist.com
/2016/11/weve-been-here-all-along/.

"What Marginalization?" October 31, 2011. www.angryasianbuddhist.com/2011
/10/what-marginalization/.

"What Western Buddhism Shouldn't Be." July 11, 2009. www
.angryasianbuddhist.com/2009/07/what-western-buddhism-shouldnt-be/.

"White Buddhist for Asians." August 12, 2010. www.angryasianbuddhist.com
/2010/08/white-buddhist-for-asians/.

"The White Face of Buddhism: Now at Patheos." November 29, 2011. www
.angryasianbuddhist.com/2011/11/
the-white-face-of-buddhism-now-at-patheos/.

"Who Are Non-Ethnic Asian Westerners?" March 21, 2014. www
.angryasianbuddhist.com/2014/03/who-are-non-ethnic-asian-westerners/.

"Why I'm Angry." May 8, 2010. www.angryasianbuddhist.com/why-im-angry/.

"Why Is American Buddhism So White?" December 19, 2011. www
.angryasianbuddhist.com/2011/12/why-is-american-buddhism-so-white/.

"Why Is the Under 35 Project So White?" August 17, 2012. www
.angryasianbuddhist.com/2012/08/why-is-the-under-35-project-so-white/.
"Why Shouldn't Buddhists Use the Pew Study?" November 15, 2011. www
.angryasianbuddhist.com/2011/11/why-shouldnt-buddhists-use-the
-pew-study/.
"Will the Real American Buddhists Please Stand Up?" April 7, 2011. www
.angryasianbuddhist.com/2011/04/will-the-real-american-buddhists
-please-stand-up/.

OTHER CITATIONS

Adams, Sheridan, Mushim Ikeda-Nash, Jeff Kitzes, Margarita Loinaz, Choyin
Rangdrol, Jessica Tan, and Larry Yang. "Making the Invisible Visible: Heal-
ing Racism in Our Buddhist Communities." Buddhist Teachers in the West
Conference, June 2000, Woodacre, CA. https://tinyurl.com/szof522.
Adichie, Chimamanda Ngozi. "The Danger of a Single Story." Video. TED Talks,
July 2009. https://tinyurl.com/yau52d8p.
arunlikhati. "Be the Refuge." Medum, December 17, 2016. https://tinyurl.com
/y3ltw88b.
Atlas, James. "Buddhists' Delight." New York Times, June 16, 2012. https://
tinyurl.com/7wfzkjv.
Bala, Shubha. "Meditation and Diversity." Ganesha's Scarf (blog), n.d.
Bates, Karen Grigsby. "The Year in Race: Saying Goodbye." NPR, December 27,
2017. https://tinyurl.com/yb6vt6zo.
Boorstein, Michelle. "A Political Awakening for Buddhists? 125 U.S. Buddhist
Leaders to Meet at the White House." The Washington Post, May 12, 2015.
https://tinyurl.com/kww6dv8.
Bowen, Andrew. "Interview with Buddhist Author, Sumi Loundon Kim." Project
Conversion (blog), May 2011. https://tinyurl.com/vujd35p.
Buddhist Churches of America. "Jodo Shinshu Center." n.d. https://tinyurl.com
/teacqzh.
Buddhist Geeks. "A Brief History of Buddhist Geeks." n.d. https://tinyurl.com
/uxoclkj.
Cadge, Wendy. Heartwood: The First Generation of Theravada Buddhism in
America. Chicago: University of Chicago Press, 2005.
Cadge, Wendy, and Elaine Howard Ecklund. "Immigration and Religion."
Annual Review of Sociology 33:1 (2007), 359–79.

Cadge, Wendy, and Sidhorn Sangdhanoo. "Thai Buddhism in America: An Historical and Contemporary Overview." *Contemporary Buddhism* 6:1 (2005), 7–35.

Cheah, Joseph. *Race and Religion in American Buddhism: White Supremacy and Immigrant Adaptation.* New York: Oxford University Press, 2011.

Chee, Beth Downing. "The Least Religious Generation." San Diego State University News Center, May 27, 2015. https://tinyurl.com/nmgngga.

Chen, Carolyn. *Getting Saved in America: Taiwanese Immigration and Religious Experience.* Princeton, NJ: Princeton University Press, 2008.

Chen, Viveka. "The Dharma of Identity." In *The Buddha's Apprentices: More Voices of Young Buddhists,* edited by Sumi Loundon, 49–53. Boston: Wisdom Publications, 2006.

Densho Digital Repository. "Ryo Imamura." August 3, 1999. https://ddr.densho.org/narrators/31/.

Deveaux, Tynette, and Ajahn Amaro. "A Response to Critics of 'We've Been Here All Along,' from the Winter 2016 *Buddhadharma.*" *Lion's Roar,* December 1, 2016. https://tinyurl.com/wh33zlx.

Escoyne, Courtney. "Why Prumsodun Ok Founded Cambodia's First Gay Dance Company in His Living Room." *Dance Magazine,* June 27, 2019. https://tinyurl.com/uy3tngo.

Esper, Damin. "Friends, Family Remember Jane Imamura, 91, Longtime Berkeley Resident." *The Mercury News,* February 2, 2012. https://tinyurl.com/yx4cwpaa.

Fields, Rick. "Confessions of a White Buddhist." *Tricycle: The Buddhist Review,* Fall 1994.

Fields, Rick. "Divided Dharma: White Buddhists, Ethnic Buddhists, and Racism." In *The Faces of Buddhism in America,* edited by Charles S. Prebish and Kenneth K. Tanaka, 196–206. Berkeley, CA: University of California Press, 1998.

Gelb, David, dir. *Chef's Table,* season 3, "Jeong Kwan," Netflix, February 17, 2017.

Giles, Cheryl A., and Willa B. Miller, eds. *The Arts of Contemplative Care: Pioneering Voices in Buddhist Chaplaincy and Pastoral Work.* Boston: Wisdom Publications, 2012.

Gleig, Ann. *American Dharma: Buddhism Beyond Modernity.* New Haven, CT: Yale University Press, 2019.

Gleig, Ann. "From Buddhist Hippies to Buddhist Geeks: The Emergence of Buddhist Postmodernism?" *Journal of Global Buddhism* 15 (2014): 15–33. https://tinyurl.com/stbnhpp.

Good Company: Friendship in the Spiritual Community." Urban Dharma, n.d. https://tinyurl.com/2ajwfdd.

Gordinier, Jeff. "Jeong Kwan, the Philosopher Chef." *New York Times,* October 16, 2015. https://tinyurl.com/hrplelg.

Greenblatt, Lilly. "Buddhist Churches of America Shares Statement on Executive Order Temporarily Banning Refugees from Entry to U.S." *Lion's Roar,* February 2, 2017. https://tinyurl.com/stpzvgb.

Gregory, Peter N. "Describing the Elephant: Buddhism in America." *Religion and American Culture* 11:2 (2001), 233–63.

Gunatillake, Rohan. "Second Generation Practitioners ... Where Are You?" *Legacy 21awake Blog,* February 12, 2009. https://tinyurl.com/uo49wbg.

Han, Chenxing. "Diverse Practices and Flexible Beliefs among Young Adult Asian American Buddhists." *Journal of Global Buddhism* 18 (2017): 1–24. https://tinyurl.com/rlbbwm2.

Han, Chenxing. "Young Adult Asian American Identities." In *A Thousand Hands: A Guidebook to Caring for Your Buddhist Community,* edited by Nathan Jishin Michon and Danny Clarkson Fisher, 277–85. Toronto: Sumeru Press, 2016.

Hickey, Wakoh Shannon. "Two Buddhisms, Three Buddhisms, and Racism." *Journal of Global Buddhism* 11 (2010): 1–25. https://tinyurl.com/yx3nht2j.

"Hidden Gem: Japanese Bakery Kogetsu-Do in Fresno's Chinatown." *The Fresno Bee,* n.d. https://tinyurl.com/sbspubp.

hooks, bell. "Waking up to Racism." *Tricycle: The Buddhist Review,* Fall 1994.

Hsu, Funie. "BPF and the Angry Asian Buddhist." Buddhist Peace Fellowship, February 22, 2015. https://tinyurl.com/thdqr77.

Hsu, Funie. "Lineage of Resistance: When Asian American Buddhists Confront White Supremacy." Buddhist Peace Fellowship, May 8, 2017. https://tinyurl.com/u2ntwkm.

Hsu, Funie. "We've Been Here All Along." *Buddhadharma: The Practitioner's Quarterly,* Winter 2016, 24–31. www.lionsroar.com/weve-been-here-all-along/.

Hsu, Funie, Arun, Kate Johnson, Katie Loncke, and Dedunu Sylvia. "5 Responses to the Awkwardly Titled 'New Face of Buddhism.'" Buddhist Peace Fellowship, January 27, 2016. https://tinyurl.com/yaebo6xs.

"In Memoriam: Aaron Lee." *Wheel of Dharma* 39:12 (December 2017), 5, https://tinyurl.com/y77ex38p.

Iwamura, Jane. "On Asian Religions without Asians." *Hyphen Magazine,* March 25, 2011. https://tinyurl.com/ycr7xebm.

Iwamura, Jane Naomi. "Altared States: Exploring the Legacy of Japanese American *Butsudan* Practice." *Pacific World,* Third Series, no. 5 (Fall 2003): 275–91. https://tinyurl.com/rbg3owd.

Iwamura, Jane Naomi, "Homage to Ancestors: Exploring the Horizons of Asian American Religious Identity," *Amerasia Journal* 22:1 (1996), 161–67.

Iwamura, Jane Naomi. "Re-Modeling Reporting on 'The Model Minority.'" USC Annenberg School Trans/Missions. June 26, 2012.

Iwamura, Jane Naomi. *Virtual Orientalism: Asian Religions and American Popular Culture.* New York: Oxford University Press, 2011.

Iwamura, Jane Naomi, Haeyoung Yoon, Leng Leroy Lim, David Kyuman Kim, Rita Nakashima Brock, and Rudy V. Busto. "Critical Reflections on Asian American Religious Identity." *Amerasia Journal* 22:1 (1996), 161–95.

Iwamura, Jane Naomi, Khyati Y. Joshi, Sharon Suh, and Janelle Wong. "Reflections on the Pew Forum on Religious and Public Life's *Asian Americans: A Mosaic of Faiths* Data and Report." *Amerasia Journal* 40:1 (2014), 1–16.

"Jane Imamura Remembered for Her Contributions to Buddhism." *The Rafu Shimpo,* February 2, 2012. https://tinyurl.com/vsnl3um.

Jin Chuan, Bhikshu. "A Christian Heart with a Buddhist Mind." *Dharmas,* January 19, 2012. https://tinyurl.com/utzfbad.

Jin Chuan, Bhikshu. "Connecting to My Family Roots." *Dharmas,* October 7, 2013. https://tinyurl.com/wub9uwe.

Jin Chuan, Bhikshu. "Heroes: Catholic and Buddhist Monks." *Dharmas,* October 31, 2011. https://tinyurl.com/sz2rll9.

Jin Chuan, Bhikshu. "How to Be a Good Son?" *Dharmas,* April 8, 2013. https://tinyurl.com/vnc33f7.

Jin Chuan, Bhikshu. "A Journey to Monkhood." *Dharmas,* October 20, 2011. https://tinyurl.com/tqp6axu.

Jin Chuan, Bhikshu. "Repaying the Kindness of My Parents?" *Dharmas,* November 13, 2012. https://tinyurl.com/up2bwvr.

Jin Chuan, Bhikshu. "What Is Success?" *Dharmas,* November 29, 2011. https://tinyurl.com/th9kryn.

Kalmanson, Leah. "Buddhism and bell hooks: Liberatory Aesthetics and the Radical Subjectivity of No-Self." *Hypatia* 27:4 (2012), 810–27.

Kandil, Caitlin Yoshiko. "Pilgrimage to an Ugly Past at Manzanar." [Orange County, CA] *Daily Pilot,* May 23, 2016. https://tinyurl.com/yagmcjvf.

Kashima, Tetsuden. "The Buddhist Churches of America: Challenges for Change in the Twenty-First Century." In *Shin Buddhism: Historical, Textual, and*

Interpretive Studies, edited by Richard K. Payne, 321–40. Berkeley, CA: Institute of Buddhist Studies and Numata Center for Buddhist Translation and Research, 2007.

Kawamoto, Jon. "Remembering the Remarkable Life of Jane Imamura." [Albany, CA] *Patch,* January 25, 2012. https://tinyurl.com/sm5cnaq.

Kerstetter, Todd M. *Inspiration and Innovation: Religion in the American West.* Hoboken, NJ: Wiley-Blackwell, 2015.

Koda, Tara K. "Aloha with Gassho: Buddhism in the Hawaiian Plantations." *Pacific World,* Third Series, no. 5 (Fall 2003): 237–54. https://tinyurl.com/t67f66p.

Kornfield, Jack, and Trudy Goodman. "Sandra Oh, Jack Kornfield, and Trudy Goodman on the Future of Buddhism." *Lion's Roar,* January 4, 2019. Originally published May 2016. https://tinyurl.com/vhfo8dz.

Lawton, Kim. "Tensions in American Buddhism." *Religion & Ethics Newsweekly,* July 6, 2001. https://tinyurl.com/rohlaut.

Le, C. N. "Reflections on a Multicultural Buddhist Retreat." Asian-Nation (website), July 15, 2009. https://tinyurl.com/u8lyklp.

Lee, Aaron. "TechnoBuddha Conference 2013: Striving for Happiness, Floating with Change." *Wheel of Dharma* 39:4 (April 2013), 4, 6. https://tinyurl.com/w6yy2f5.

Lee, Jonathan H. X. "Acting Out: Thai American Buddhists Encounters with White Privilege and White Supremacy." In *Southeast Asian Diaspora in the United States: Memories and Visions, Yesterday, Today, and Tomorrow,* 120–42. Newcastle upon Tyne, UK: Cambridge Scholars Publishing, 2014.

Lion's Roar Staff. "Forum: What Does Mindfulness Mean for Buddhism?" May 5, 2015. https://tinyurl.com/ybr7ra83.

Lion's Roar Staff. "Inside the First Issue of *Lion's Roar* Magazine." *Lion's Roar.* January 13, 2016. https://tinyurl.com/y8jblplk.

Liriel. "It's Not about Richard Gere." *Angry Asian Buddhist,* June 28, 2011. https://tinyurl.com/vawgung.

Littlefair, Sam. "Aaron Lee, the 'Angry Asian Buddhist,' Has Died, Age 34." *Lion's Roar,* October 25, 2017. https://tinyurl.com/y7arc7o6.

Liu, Kenji. "The Influence of Orientalism on U.S. Buddhism." Buddhist Peace Fellowship. June 7, 2013. https://tinyurl.com/me2gesw.

Loncke, Katie. "'We've Been Here All Along'—Love for Asian American Buddhists." Buddhist Peace Fellowship, December 7, 2016. https://tinyurl.com/y7r2nyzf.

Loundon, Sumi, ed. *Blue Jean Buddha: Voices of Young Buddhists.* Boston: Wisdom Publications, 2001.

Loundon, Sumi, ed. *The Buddha's Apprentices: More Voices of Young Buddhists.* Boston: Wisdom Publications, 2006.

Lu, Wanwan. "Interview with Aaron Lee." Unpublished video, 2014.

Lu, Wanwan, dir. *Youth Group.* Documentary film. 2015. https://cool939.wixsite.com/mva2015/youth-group.

Masatsugu, Michael K. "'Beyond This World of Transiency and Impermanence': Japanese Americans, Dharma Bums, and the Making of American Buddhism during the Early Cold War Years." *Pacific Historical Review* 77:3 (2008), 423–51.

Meissner, Ted. "Charles Prebish, Sarah Haynes, Justin Whitaker, Danny Fisher: Two Buddhisms Today." *The Secular Buddhist,* September 22, 2012. https://tinyurl.com/rm9966f.

Micu, Reuben. "Kogetsu-Do: Home of Over 100 Years Old Japanese Confection Recipes." *Fresno Foodways,* April 25, 2018. https://tinyurl.com/u5y9kfe.

Mitchell, Scott A. "'Christianity Is for Rubes; Buddhism Is for Actors': U.S. Media Representations of Buddhism in the Wake of the Tiger Woods Scandal." *Journal of Global Buddhism* 13 (2012): 61–79. https://tinyurl.com/wngys2o.

Mitchell, Scott A. "Locally Translocal American Shin Buddhism." *Pacific World,* Third Series, no. 12 (Fall 2010): 109–26. www.shin-ibs.edu/documents/pwj3-12/04Mitchell.pdf.

Nakai, Patti. "'Thank Buddha': Asian American Community Leaders." *Taste of Chicago Buddhism,* February 8, 2016.

Nattier, Jan. "Visible & Invisible: The Politics of Representation in Buddhist America." *Tricycle: The Buddhist Review,* Fall 1995, 42–49. https://tricycle.org/magazine/visible-invisible/.

Ng, Edwin. "The Autoethnographic Genre and Buddhist Studies: Reflections of a Postcolonial 'Western Buddhist' Convert." *Australian Religion Studies Review* 25:2 (2012), 163–84.

Ng, Edwin, and Zach Walsh. "Vulnerability, Response-Ability, and the Promise of Making Refuge." *Religions* 10:2 (2019), 9. doi:10.3390/rel10020080.

Nhat Hanh, Thich. "The Nobility of Suffering." In *Dharma, Color, and Culture: New Voices in Western Buddhism,* edited by Hilda Gutiérrez Baldoquin, 61–73. Berkeley, CA: Parallax Press, 2004.

Nhat Hanh, Thich, ed. *Plum Village Chanting and Recitation Book.* Berkeley, CA: Parallax Press, 2000.

Numrich, Paul David. *Old Wisdom in the New World: Americanization in Two Immigrant Theravada Buddhist Temples.* Knoxville, TN: University of Tennessee Press, 1996.

Numrich, Paul David. "Two Buddhisms Further Considered." *Contemporary Buddhism* 4:1 (2003), 55–78.

O'Connell, Zesho Susan. "10 Buddhist Women Every Person Should Know." *The Huffington Post,* March 30, 2012. https://tinyurl.com/wx9mgql.

Okihiro, Gary Y. "Religion and Resistance in America's Concentration Camps." *Phylon* 45:3 (1984), 220–33.

Paisley, Laura. "Students Meet the Many Faces of Buddhism in Los Angeles." *USC News,* July 14, 2014. https://tinyurl.com/urhjk2b.

Palo Alto Buddhist Temple. "Jodo Shinshu Center." n.d. https://tinyurl.com /wg9pmqs.

Perreira, Todd LeRoy. "The Gender of Practice: Some Findings among Thai Buddhist Women in Northern California." In *Emerging Voices: Experiences of Underrepresented Asian Americans,* edited by Huping Ling. New Brunswick, NJ: Rutgers University Press, 2008.

Petersen, Kristian. "Jane Iwamura, *Virtual Orientalism: Religion and Popular Culture in the U.S.*" New Books Network. August 22, 2013. https://tinyurl.com/ rx4oogv.

Pew Research Center. "Asian Americans: A Mosaic of Faiths." Washington, DC, July 19, 2012. https://tinyurl.com/rd7kun6.

Pew Research Center. "Millennials in Adulthood: Detached from Institutions, Networked with Friends." Washington, DC, March 7, 2014. https://tinyurl. com/pbpw3tv.

Pew Research Center. "The Rise of Asian Americans." Washington, DC, April 4, 2013. https://tinyurl.com/7dnpkpt.

Pew Research Center. "U.S. Religious Landscape Survey." Washington, DC, February 2008. https://tinyurl.com/rat3c67.

Pickert, Kate. "The Mindful Revolution: Finding Peace in a Stressed-Out, Digitally Dependent Culture May Just Be a Matter of Thinking Differently." *Time.* February 3, 2014. https://tinyurl.com/syw828f.

Pierce, Lori. "Buddha Loves Me This I Know: Nisei Buddhists in Christian America, 1889–1942." In *American Buddhism as a Way of Life,* edited by Gary Storhoff and John Whalen-Bridge, 167–82. Albany, NY: State University of New York Press, 2010.

Prebish, Charles S. *Luminous Passage: The Practice and Study of Buddhism in America.* Berkeley, CA: University of California Press, 1999.

Prebish, Charles S. "Two Buddhisms Reconsidered." *Buddhist Studies Review* 10:2 (1993), 187–206.

Quli, Natalie E. "Western Self, Asian Other: Modernity, Authenticity, and Nostalgia for 'Tradition' in Buddhist Studies." *Journal of Buddhist Ethics* 16 (2009): 1–38.

Rose, Marcia. "The Power of Metta: A Buddhist Story." The Mountain Hermitage. n.d. https://tinyurl.com/yxx5ooeq.

Seager, Richard Hughes. *Buddhism in America*. First Edition. New York: Columbia University Press, 1999.

Seager, Richard Hughes. *Buddhism in America*. Revised and Expanded Edition. New York: Columbia University Press, 2012.

Sharf, Robert H. "Introduction: Prolegomenon to the Study of Medieval Chinese Buddhist Literature." In *Coming to Terms with Chinese Buddhism: A Reading of the Treasure Store Treatise*, 1–27. Honolulu: University of Hawai'i Press, 2002.

Spencer, Anne C. "A Response to *The Oxford Handbook of Religious Conversion* from Two Perspectives." *Pastoral Psychology* 67:2 (2016), 219–26.

Suh, Sharon A. *Being Buddhist in a Christian World: Gender and Community in a Korean American Temple*. Seattle: University of Washington Press, 2004.

Tamekuni, Steven. "TechnoBuddha Conference 2012: Who Am I? The Search for Spiritual Self in the Digital Age." *Wheel of Dharma* 38:4 (April 2012), 5. https://tinyurl.com/tn44etn.

Tanaka, Kenneth K. "Epilogue: The Colors and Contours of American Buddhism." In *The Faces of Buddhism in America*, edited by Charles S. Prebish and Kenneth K. Tanaka, 287–98. Berkeley, CA: University of California Press, 1998.

Tanaka, Kenneth K. "Right Action, Buddhism, and Our Participation in the World." In *Dharma, Color, and Culture: New Voices in Western Buddhism*, edited by Hilda Gutiérrez Baldoquin, 169–78. Berkeley, CA: Parallax Press, 2004.

Tassja. "The Unbearable Whiteness of Being, Part III: A Brown Buddhist and a Handful of Mustard Seeds." *Irresistible Revolution*, June 21, 2011. https://tinyurl.com/yx8xzj79.

Tillakaratne, Mihiri Uthpala. *I Take Refuge*. Video. YouTube, November 26, 2011. https://youtu.be/EEw5BQq_ENM.

Tillakaratne, Mihiri Uthpala. "Multiculturalism, Ethnicity, Religious Identity and the 1.5 and Second Generation in Two Los Angeles-Area Sri Lankan Buddhist Temples." MA thesis, University of California Los Angeles, 2012.

Tran, Kim. "4 Signs You're Culturally Appropriating Buddhism—and Why It's Important Not to." *Everyday Feminism*, July 21, 2016. https://tinyurl.com/u2qr423.

Tricycle. "Losing Our Religion." *Tricycle: The Buddhist Review,* Summer 2007, 44–49. https://tinyurl.com/y7s45ape.

Tricycle. "Q&A with Lt. Jeanette Shin, U.S. Military's First Buddhist Chaplain." *Tricycle: The Buddhist Review,* October 4, 2011. https://tinyurl.com/t94jpcs.

Tricycle. "They Teach the Buddhist Faith." *Tricycle: The Buddhist Review,* Summer 1996. https://tinyurl.com/skes46q.

Tweed, Thomas A. "Night-Stand Buddhists and Other Creatures." In *American Buddhism: Methods and Findings in Recent Scholarship,* edited by Duncan Ryuken Williams and Christopher S. Queen, 71–90. Richmond, UK: Curzon Press, 1999.

Tworkov, Helen. "Many Is More." *Tricycle: The Buddhist Review,* Winter 1991. https://tricycle.org/magazine/many-more/.

Ukai, Nancy. "Jerome and Rohwer Revisited." *Pacific Citizen: The National Newspaper of the JACL,* May 18, 2018. www.pacificcitizen.org/jerome-and-rohwer-revisited/.

Unno, Mark. "The Original Buddhist Rebel." *Tricycle: The Buddhist Review,* Winter 2017. https://tinyurl.com/t42h352.

Unno, Mark. "The Voice of Sacred Texts in the Ocean of Compassion: The Case of Shin Buddhism in America." *Pacific World,* Third Series, no. 5 (Fall 2003): 293–307. https://tinyurl.com/wgn8834.

Usuki, Patricia Kanaya. "American Women in Jodo Shin Buddhism Today: Tradition and Transition." *Pacific World,* Third Series, no. 7 (Fall 2005): 159–75. https://tinyurl.com/w2npokw.

Varvaloucas, Emma. "Who Is the Angry Asian Buddhist? An Interview with arunlikhati." *Tricycle: The Buddhist Review,* May 21, 2012. https://tricycle.org/trikedaily/who-angry-asian-buddhist/.

Watson, Burton, trans. *The Complete Works of Chuang Tzu.* New York: Columbia University Press, 2013.

Weaver, Heather L. "Buddhist Student, Religious Liberty Prevail in Louisiana." American Civil Liberties Union, March 14, 2014. https://tinyurl.com/wsoq96y.

Williams, Duncan Ryuken. *American Sutra: A Story of Faith and Freedom in the Second World War.* Cambridge, MA: Harvard University Press, 2019.

Williams, Duncan Ryuken. "At Ease in Between: The Middle Position of a Scholar-Practitioner." *Journal of Global Buddhism* 9 (2008): 155–63. https://tinyurl.com/y8ap6eeg.

Williams, Duncan Ryuken. "Buddhist Protest of Inhumane Treatment of Migrant Children." Video. YouTube, August 11, 2019. www.youtube.com /watch?v=i3GbRteuoLM.

Williams, Duncan Ryuken. "Complex Loyalties: Issei Buddhist Ministers during the Wartime Incarceration." *Pacific World,* Third Series, no. 5 (Fall 2003): 255–74. https://tinyurl.com/snzsroa.

Williams, Duncan Ryuken. "Fort Sill and the Incarceration of Japanese 'Enemy Aliens' during World War II." 2019. https://tinyurl.com/uj88wr2.

Williams, Duncan Ryuken. "Masatoshi Nagatomi Remembered." *Tricycle: The Buddhist Review,* Fall 2001. https://tinyurl.com/van65ul.

Williams, Duncan Ryuken, and Tomoe Moriya, eds. *Issei Buddhism in the Americas.* Urbana, IL: University of Illinois Press, 2010.

Wilson, Jeff. "'All Beings Are Equally Embraced by Amida Buddha': Jodo Shinshu Buddhism and Same-Sex Marriage in the United States." *Journal of Global Buddhism* 13 (2012): 31–59. https://tinyurl.com/s3pwvcr.

Wilson, Mark. "Zendesk Unveils a Dynamic New Brand Inspired by Classic Danish Design." *Fast Company,* October 26, 2016. https://tinyurl.com/r7huc5s.

Winston, Diana. "Forum: Next-Gen Buddhism." *Lion's Roar,* December 1, 2008, Originally published in *Buddhadharma: The Practitioner's Quarterly.* www .lionsroar.com/forum-next-gen-buddhism/.

Wuthnow, Robert, and Wendy Cadge. "Buddhists and Buddhism in the United States: The Scope of Influence." *Journal for the Scientific Study of Religion* 43:3 (2004), 363–80.

Yang, Fenggang, and Rose Ebaugh. "Transformations in New Immigrant Religions and Their Global Implications." *American Sociological Review* 66:2 (April 2001), 269–88.

Yang, Jeff. "Angry vs. Angry and Why All of Us Lose." *Medium,* February 19, 2015. https://tinyurl.com/la8l2ss.

Yang, Larry. "Staying on Your Seat: The Practice of Right Concentration." In *Dharma, Color, and Culture: New Voices in Western Buddhism,* edited by Hilda Gutiérrez Baldoquin, 157–63. Berkeley, CA: Parallax Press, 2004.

Yoo, David K. "Enlightened Identities: Buddhism and Japanese Americans of California, 1924–1941." *The Western Historical Quarterly* 27:3 (Autumn 1996), 281–301.

Yoo, David K. *Growing Up Nisei: Race, Generation, and Culture among Japanese Americans of California, 1924–49.* Champaign, IL: University of Illinois Press, 2000.

yoshikami, emiko. "Review: Reading My History through 'American Sutra.'"
Buddhist Peace Fellowship, October 22, 2019. https://tinyurl.com/yc2s25wc.

Yu, Phil. "Archived Posts: May 2004." *Angry Asian Man,* May 2004. https://
tinyurl.com/s5r6t7o.

Yuasa, Joanne. "TechnoBuddha Conference 2011: The Journey." *Wheel of
Dharma* 37:4 (April 2011), 4, 6. https://tinyurl.com/s5emuut.

INDEX